W9-DIM-443

JOURNAL FOR THE STUDY OF THE NEW TESTAMENT
SUPPLEMENT SERIES

4

Editors
Ernst Bammel
Anthony Hanson
David Hill
Max Wilcox

Editorial Secretary
Bruce D Chilton

Department of Biblical Studies
The University of Sheffield
Sheffield S10 2TN
England

FOLLOWING JESUS

Discipleship in the Gospel of Mark

ERNEST BEST

Journal for the Study of the New Testament
Supplement Series, 4

Sheffield 1981

Copyright © 1981 JSOT Press

ISSN 0143-5108
ISBN 0 905774 28 0 (hardback)
ISBN 0 905774 29 9 (paperback)

Published by
JSOT Press
Department of Biblical Studies
The University of Sheffield
Sheffield S10 2TN
England

Artwork by Roger Evans
Sheffield University Printing Unit

Printed in Great Britain
by Redwood Burn Limited
Trowbridge & Esher
1981

CONTENTS

PREFACE

The present study began as lectures to, mainly, graduate students in the summer of 1969 in Union Theological Seminary, New York. Prepared somewhat hurriedly for that course it has been under continual revision and extension ever since. Other necessary tasks hindered its completion until now. Since books and articles on Mark from the standpoint of redaction criticism now flood the market the effort to read whatever was available as it appeared has itself delayed completion, though at the same time much of what I have read has led me to modify and rethink what I originally prepared. Some studies have not been available and others, I am sure, have simply been missed; I apologise to their writers that their views have not been taken into account. There comes a time however when a line has to be drawn and nothing more can be read nor more time be spent assessing what others have written. In particular I regret that the commentary of J. Gnilka appeared too late to be used.

My thanks are due to students and colleagues who have endured my lectures or ideas on Mark and discussed them, to my wife who has typed the manuscript and helped greatly with the proof reading and to my colleague, the Reverend J.K. Riches who also assisted with the proof reading.

ACKNOWLEDGEMENTS

For permission from their editors to re-use material previously appearing in the Scottish Journal of Theology, 23 (1970) 323-337 (C.U.P., 'Discipleship in Mark: Mark 8.22 - 10.52'), The Expository Times, 82 (1970/1) 83-89 ('The Camel and the Needle's Eye'), and the material about to appear in TU of the proceedings of the Oxford Conference of Biblical Studies, 1973 ('The Markan Redaction of the Transfiguration').

Chapter 1
INTRODUCTION

In this study it is assumed that Mark is independent of Matthew and Luke and was written in Rome after the beginning of the Jewish revolt of A.D. 66, and therefore also after the Neronic persecutions. It is not clear whether it was written just before or just after the fall of Jerusalem. The situation of the readers was thus one of persecution and the threat of impending further persecution in a possible apocalyptic atmosphere. This apocalyptic atmosphere must not be over-stressed /1/. It was certainly much greater than in any mainline church to-day but was not the dominating element. It is not difficult to find apocalyptic material in Mark: chapter 13, the expectation of the end, the teaching about the Kingdom of God, the title 'Son of man'. Much of this was traditional and Mark has used it without emphasising it. He has also much non-apocalyptic, if not anti-apocalyptic, material: the miracles are not related to the Kingdom of God in Mark /2/; the parables of growth imply a period before the coming of the Kingdom; 13.32 is a rebuke to those who know (a characteristic of apocalyptic communities) when the end is coming; when the twelve are sent out their message is not to tell about the end but to preach and exorcise; they preach about the cross and resurrection and they act to conquer existing evil and do not threaten apocalyptic evil; victory over Satan comes at the beginning of the gospel /3/ and is not envisaged, as it is in much apocalyptic writing, as a future contest: the greater proportion of the teaching of Jesus which Mark provides is irrelevant to the nearness of the end (e.g. 8.34ff, teaching which Mark stresses) /4/. The temptations to which the community is open are brought about mainly by factors other than the nearness of the end: in 4.14-20 the pressures of the 'world' entice; the community's evasion of the meaning of the cross is seen in the desire of some of the members for a position of importance within the community (9.33-7; 10.35-45); the rich man (10.17-22) is told to sell his goods, not because they will be of no use to him in the short period before the end or in the next world, but because the poor can be helped. It would be better to characterise the community as one which fails to live in the light of the cross rather than as one which lives too much in the light of the end; this is not a phenomenon peculiar to Mark's community but one which has plagued the church in every stage of its life.

So far as we know Mark was the first to put the traditions about Jesus into a connected narrative. Before he did so the material existed as individual discrete pericopae or else as small complexes consisting of a number of related pericopae (e.g. 2.1-3.5; 4.1-34; the passion narrative); these pericopae or complexes mostly lacked geographical or temporal data and consequently Mark was both free to provide such data and was indeed under a compulsion to create some such data if he was to weld the material together into a coherent account. To do this he must have had some organising principles but what these were can only be learned from the material itself as it is examined; clearly a straightforward biographical scheme was not his sole organising principle; others derived from the didactic, pastoral or polemical purposes which led him to write. What he wrote is a 'whole' and the once separate pericopae must now be understood and interpreted as part of that 'whole'.

If the order of the incidents is in large part Mark's, though it cannot have been entirely his for the baptism must precede the death, on the other hand he respected the material which he received and used the bulk of it (in particular what lay within the incidents) as he found it /5/. We must remember that it was well known to his readers since he was using the traditions of Jesus current in his own community. He did not create whole pericopae /6/ but in order to fit those he used into his account and to draw out the points he wished to make he reshaped and modified them internally. He may also have selected among available accounts those that were best suited to his purposes. Because of this it is important to separate tradition and redaction and it is erroneous to assume that all the material is equally important for our understanding of Mark; in a real sense much of it could not be manipulated; it continues to reflect its creation and use in the church before it reached him and his community.

Though Mark used the historical tradition about Jesus, or, perhaps we ought to say, the traditions about the historical Jesus, it was not his purpose simply to impart information about Jesus or to write his history. He used the historical material with a theological purpose in mind. Within Jewish tradition this was a regular practice as we see from Genesis and many other parts of the Pentateuch, from Joshua, Judges, 1,2 Samuel, 1,2 Kings, 1,2 Chronicles (the latter using the same historical material as 1,2 Samuel and 1,2 Kings but with a different theological interpretation), Daniel, 1,2 Maccabees. It is difficult, and outside our purpose, to assess the value of the traditions Mark used but there is no reason to doubt that he believed what he wrote had in broad outline actually happened /7/. He used the material that was at hand in order to drive home what he wanted to say and attained this purpose by careful arrangement and modification. Details of his method of working will appear as we examine the material.

If Mark's purpose was not primarily historical why did he use historical material to achieve it? Would it not have been simpler for him to write a sermon or homily and so have put his points across clearly and directly? The answer is not clear. He may have adopted his method: (i) to preserve the material about Jesus since the leaders of his community, probably including Peter, had died in the recent persecutions; (ii) to defend the historical reality of Jesus against dissolution into a gnostic saviour; (iii) to counter a false christology by showing the true nature of Jesus and of what God had accomplished through him; (iv) in simple imitation of the Old Testament historical books under a realisation that the 'history' of Jesus was not irrelevant to a true understanding of the Christian faith.

Mark termed what he wrote 'gospel' (1.1). Previously the gospel had been understood in terms of its content as a sermon or had been expressed in brief kerygmatic statements. With Mark the gospel is now expressed in historical form. The whole of what he writes is the 'good news'. As Mark now restates the 'good news' we see that in common with the earlier tradition it centres on the cross and resurrection with some side reference to the parousia. While much attention has been given in recent writing to Mark's Gospel as theologia crucis the book does not end with the cross but with the resurrection. To suggest that it 'ends' gives, perhaps, the wrong idea. The resurrection, no appearances are narrated, is so presented that it is also the beginning; from it new life opens out; when the book is read and its message lived the risen Jesus is present. This again will only become fully apparent as we work through some of its sections. The content of the gospel is defined much more in terms of the cross than of the parousia and the ability to be a Christian in terms of the presence of Christ than of the future hope of the end. Had Mark wished to emphasise the end he could have placed chapter 13 after the resurrection account as a post-resurrection address; instead in its present position it is subordinated to the cross and resurrection.

To say that Mark had a theological purpose in writing does not itself define that purpose. It was not primarily polemical in that he wrote to attack certain heretics or recognised heretical positions either within his own community or in some other part of the church, though of course whatever he does write may in itself be a correction of false views /8/. Nor was his purpose primarily informational in the sense of conveying information either about Jesus or the true faith of the church, though of course he will by the very nature of his writing give information about Jesus, most of it incidentally already known to his readers, and will instruct them in the nature of the Christian faith. His primary objective was pastoral: to build up his readers as Christians and show them what true discipleship is. In the course of carrying this out he naturally opposes false views and teaches what is true; as we proceed we shall see that for him a true understanding of discipleship depends on a true understanding of Jesus. True discipleship is also to be explained in terms of a relation to Jesus ('Follow me'), and this may be another reason he has chosen to do his pastoral counselling on the basis of the traditions about Jesus rather than through a letter or homily. Since good pastoral counselling never takes place in an intellectual vacuum he also imparts much information, not just simple historical information but also sound teaching in the faith.

If a writer wishes to talk about discipleship using men as examples, there are two obvious approaches. He may either set forward a series of examples of good discipleship with the implication that these examples should be followed (so Daniel 1-6; 2 Maccabees; 4 Maccabees) or he may instruct through the failures of his examples (so many of the stories about the patriarchs and David). Mark chose the latter course. Probably a number of factors led him to do so: (i) Jesus himself is the 'hero' of the story, and although Mark does not particularly stress the imitation of Christ, yet if imitation there was to be it would have to be of Jesus and not of lesser figures. (ii) The tradition as it was known to his readers already contained stories of the failure of disciples; these failures could not then be eliminated; this would be especially true if Peter before his death had been a leader in the community and had told it of his own failures /9/. (iii) The New Testament shows generally that success in discipleship depends not on the degree of robust faith or courage which the disciple can generate within himself but on his willingness to accept help from God; stories of the failure of disciples allow the need for such grace to be clearly seen. (iv) Many of Mark's readers may have already failed through public or private persecution or through other causes; the failure of the historical disciples followed by their eventual forgiveness and known success as missionaries (e.g. Peter) would then be a source of great encouragement.

Introduction

In any discussion of discipleship the central passage is 8.27-10.45 and our study will begin there and draw in other sections as necessary.

The purpose of this study then is to enquire what discipleship meant in Mark's eyes. Attention will not therefore be directed to questions of the type, 'Were the Twelve identical with the disciples /10/? Was Mark hostile towards the historical disciples /11/? What was the nature of the Messianic secret which was hidden from or revealed to them? What was the sociological nature of Mark's community' /12/? Instead we ask 'What has Mark to say to the Christians for whom he writes about the nature of their Christian lives?' Again this means that we are not searching to discover what Mark taught his community in relation to God, Jesus, his death, the Holy Spirit; these are proper areas of investigation and the results of such investigation will in part determine how Mark's Christians ought to express their discipleship; we intend, however, to concentrate our attention on the results for their own lives of what the Christians in Mark's community thought in those areas, and we are able to do this all the more easily because of the work that has already been carried out in the examination of Mark in respect of them. As we work through the material we shall in fact see that the Christians' understanding of their discipleship and their ability to follow as disciples emerge out of their understanding of the passion and resurrection of Jesus. This but illustrates a commonplace of systematic theology, that a christology or soteriology implies a doctrine of the Christian life and an ecclesiology.

We propose to direct attention to two main areas: (i) the disciple in relation to himself; how he must view himself and deal with himself and what is required from him in consecration, obedience and self-discipline (Part I); (ii) the disciple in relation to others: (a) to those who are not yet Christians (Part II); (b) to those who are his fellow disciples (Part III). We thus exclude the attitude of the disciple towards God and the detailed exegesis of the ethical rules set down for his obedience. In relation to the former we could point to passages where faith is demanded of the disciples as in the two sea narratives (4.35-41; 6.45-52); in the second of these, however, the concluding verse, which is redactional, places the emphasis on the failure of the disciples to understand and the first is probably part of a complex of miracle stories which Mark has taken over. Faith is necessary, but faith which is unrelated to the cross only misleads. The nature of discipleship becomes apparent only in the light of the cross, and not in the light of Jesus' mighty acts. So far as ethical rules go there are few in Mark's Gospel. Although he knows the love commandment, as 12.28-34 shows, he does not use it to detail conduct in relation to others but to define the relation of men to God. Moral rules are set out in 10.1-12; 12.13-17, but they are not stressed so much as rules as conditions of discipleship (10.1-12) and as part of a controversy between Jesus and Jewish leaders which serves to increase tension and so lead to the cross (12.13-17).

In conclusion we should make it clear that we are not writing about the historical Jesus and his disciples. Outside our perspective lie questions like 'Was Jesus a rabbi? How many disciples did he have? From what social class did they come? Did he weld them into a community before his death?' Instead we are faced with questions of the order, 'How are followers of the Christ to be called to discipleship? How are they to be faithful to their Lord? How are they to live together? How is their community to be expanded?' Our theme is not 'the disciples' but 'discipleship'.

Notes
1   This is the error of Kee and Perrin, The New Testament, pp.143-167.
2   Cf. Koch, pp.173-6.
3   Cf. Best, pp.3-60.
4   See discussion of these verses.
5   See Best, 'Mark's Preservation of the Tradition'.
6   Of course he created the summaries.
7   When he has doubts he gives us a clue to his doubts as in 11.13, 'For it was not the season for figs', a Markan insertion indicating it was the wrong time of the year to find figs.
8   Cf. Best, 'The Role of the Disciples in Mark'.
9   Cf. Best, 'Peter in the Gospel according to Mark'.
10   Cf. Best, 'Mark's Use of the Twelve'.
11   Cf. Best, 'The Role of the Disciples'.
12   This last question is the one Kee seeks to answer.

Part I
THE DISCIPLE AND THE CROSS

Chapter 2
THE WAY

It is now generally accepted that 8.27-10.45 forms the centre of Mark's instruction to his readers on the meaning for them of Christ and their own discipleship /1/, and for Mark the two are closely related: the understanding of discipleship emerges out of an understanding, not of the teaching of Jesus (though Mark instructs through the use of that teaching as understood in his own time), but of Christ and what he did. The failure in understanding of the disciples is emphasised throughout and the theme is highlighted by the two accounts of the healing of blind men which precede (8.22-26) and follow (10.46-52) this section /2/. The section itself is a well-constructed whole /3/ and is presented as a journey from the villages of Caesarea Philippi to Jerusalem /4/. It is undoubtedly true that Jesus did travel to Jerusalem before his death but whether that was his only visit and whether the journey concluded a week before he died are both uncertain. There are indications within the Markan material, quite apart from the Johannine, that he was at Jerusalem at times other than his last week. The journey Mark presents is consequently his own creation and the 'way' which Jesus goes is not just a literal journey to Jerusalem but is intended also to be understood spiritually.

Although verbs of motion are frequent throughout Mark there is here a steady movement towards a goal, Jerusalem, which is lacking elsewhere in the Gospel. This sense of movement is brought out especially in this section by Mark's use of the phrase ἐν τῇ ὁδῷ /5/. It is associated with each of the three passion predictions (8.27; 9.33f; 10.32) /6/. Mark also uses it at 10.17 at the commencement of the pericope of the rich man who rejects Jesus' call to follow and twice (10.46,52) /7/ in the story of Bartimaeus who does follow. It is generally accepted as part of Mark's redaction /8/. It is present also in the group of formal OT quotations (Exod. 23.20; Mal. 3.1; Isa. 40.3) with which Mark opens his Gospel /9/ and is the common theme connecting them; its use there is programmatic: Jesus is about to begin to go 'on the way' which is prepared by John the Baptizer and which ends in Jerusalem. His disciples are to follow him in this 'way'.

The conception of the Christian life as a pilgrimage is widespread but is generally found in the sense of a journey to a glorious consummation (e.g. to heaven). This is largely the emphasis in Hebrews: Jesus goes before his people opening a new and better way for them to the heavenly holy place (2.10; 3.7-4.16; 10.19f; 12.1f) /10/. In Acts Christianity is described as 'the way' (e.g. 9.2; 19.23; 22.4) /11/. Luke's great central section (9.51-18.14) is structured as a journey. One of Paul's favourite metaphors to describe Christian existence is 'walking' (περιπατεῖν,Gal. 5.16; Rom. 6.4; 13.13; 14.15; Phil. 3.17; 1 Th. 2.12). In the Fourth Gospel Jesus is described as 'the way' (14.6) /12/. In early Christianity we have 'the two ways' (Barnabas 18-20; Did. 1-5; see also 1 QS 3.13-4.26; 1 Clem. 35.5; Did. 6.1). Both the word and the conception can be traced back into Judaism and the OT - the conception to the pilgrimage of Abraham to the Promised Land and the journey of Israel through the wilderness, and the word to such phrases as 'the way of the Lord', 'the way of righteousness' /13/. In some of the Qumran material (e.g. 1 QS 8.13-16; 9.16-21; 10.20f; cf. Jub. 23.20f) it is developed to describe the life of the community /14/. The precise interpretation which Mark gives to this is necessarily different from that of pre-Christian material since he sees the 'way' fulfilled by Jesus but also sees Jesus as calling men to go on the 'way' /15/.

Mark first uses ἡ ὁδός in 1.2,3 /16/: John prepares the way; the end of his way was death at Herod's hands. It is surprising to find John's death narrated in so much detail by Mark when he rarely takes attention off the central figure, Jesus. Here, then, in the Baptizer is the first clue to 'the way': it leads to death /17/.

Notes

1   From 8.27 onwards the crowd appears much less often: ὄχλος and πλῆθος occur 24 times prior to 8.27, 6 times in 8.27-10.45 and 10 times from 10.46 onwards. This can serve only as an inexact criterion since Mark's indefinite plural would also need to be taken into account; unfortunately, however, its precise reference is often difficult to determine.

2   The precise divisions of the Gospel are a matter of dispute. We take these two pericopae to be transitional and for that reason do not treat them as part of 8.27-10.45 but separately. For discussion of them see Ch. 12 (a),(b).

3   'Mark. 8,27-10,52 stellt eine wohldurchdachte Komposition

dar, in der erzählende und belehrende Stücke in bewusste und genaue Beziehung zueinander gesetzt sind', K. Weiss, 'Ekklesiologie, Tradition und Geschichte in der Jüngerunterweisung Mark. 8,27-10,42'.

4   Schreiber, pp.190f, points out that prior to 8.27 Mark does not depict Jesus as on a journey.

5   Cf. W. Michaelis, TDNT, V, pp.42ff; S.V.McCasland, 'The Way'; J.A.Fitzmyer, 'Jewish Christianity in Acts'; E. Repo, Der 'Weg' als Selbstbezeichnung des Urchristentums. Trocmé writes of Mark picturing 'Jesus as continually on the move, (p.201). Cf. W.H. Kelber, The Kingdom in Mark, pp.67ff.

6   On each occasion it is omitted by Matthew and Luke. This is surprising in the case of Luke because of his 'travel narrative' (9.51ff) and his use of ὁδός in Acts. Repo (as n.5), pp.15ff, suggests that in Acts he uses it under the influence of the tradition.

7   In 10.17,52 it is again omitted by Matthew and Luke; in 10.46 it is retained, but there Mark had used the phrase παρὰ τὴν ὁδόν.

8   Cf. Schreiber, pp.190ff; Bultmann, p.257; Horstmann, p.9; Hahn, p.224; Michaelis, TDNT V, pp.66-68; Minette de Tillesse, pp.306f. Schreiber, however, goes too far in seeing almost every reference in Mark to ὁδός as redactional; in 4.4,14f it appears naturally in the context of the story; it is possible, but unlikely, that in 2.23 we should generalise it to mean 'the way of discipleship' and view this pericope as a story about discipleship. In 6.8 this is probably its meaning. 8.3 could be a natural creation but may carry the overtone that Christ feeds his disciples (with the Eucharist?) when they are weary and toiling in their discipleship. 11.8, though it continues the entry into Jerusalem, is not an unexpected use of the word; 12.14 is sufficiently similar to OT usage to cause no suspicion. Thus it is principally in 8.27-10.52 that the word is used redactionally.

9   Elsewhere Mark's quotations of Scripture appear to be integrated better into the narrative and are found on the lips of speakers. On his use of the quotations in 1.2f see A. Suhl, pp.132-137; Marxsen, pp.17ff. If the quotation in Mark consisted originally only of Isa. 40.3 and v.2 is a gloss, this does not affect the issue since the word is still present. Whoever added v.2 (if it is a gloss) surely saw deeply into Mark's purpose! This confirms the originality of the verse (pace J.A.T. Robinson, 'Elijah, John and Jesus').

10   E. Käsemann aptly terms his study of Hebrews, Das wandernde Gottesvolk.

11   If the usage of Acts, which probably predates Acts (cf.

Repo, as n.5, pp.15ff), was known to Mark then he may be deliberately expounding the notion of 'the Way', i.e. the nature of Christianity.

12 In 2 Pet. 2.15 we find ὁδός associated with ἐξακολουθεῖν ; in Mark discipleship is linked both to ὁδός and to ἀκολουθεῖν.

13 'The conviction that Israel's special vocation was to walk in the "Way of the Lord" has determined not only the shape of Old Testament liturgical practice, but also the structure of Old Testament "ethics". The imitation of God, for Israel, took quite concrete form in the situations and relationships which the course of life threw up. There Israel must reproduce the "ways" which God had adopted towards his people in the course of revelatory history. The "way" of Israel was to be an extended mime of the Lord's relations with Israel as they had been revealed in the sacred history.' So E.J.Tinsley, The Imitation of God in Christ, p.56. While this may be true of the OT the element of imitation does not enter so largely into Mark.

14 Cf. McCasland (as n.5); Repo (as n.5), passim.

15 Mark may see it as a divinely ordained way, cf. 14.21a.

16 The association of at least Isa. 40.3 with John may well be pre-Markan; cf. R.Trevijano, Comienao del Evangelio, pp.21ff.

17 Cf. Best, pp.119f.

Chapter 3
MARK 8.27-9.1

It is generally agreed that we have here three units, viz., 8.27-30; 8.31-33; 8.34-9.1. Were they already united in the pre-Markan tradition (though not of course necessarily originally) or did Mark bring them together? We shall see that each of these units has itself been extensively edited by Mark; this would imply that even if they previously existed as a unit in the tradition Mark has certainly remoulded that unit. Justification for this and for the probable conclusion that Mark was the first to associate the three pericopae can emerge only as we study each in detail /1/, and to this we now turn.

Note
1   For analyses which with varying views of his creative activity consider that Mark united the three pericopae cf. Reploh, pp.89ff; Bultmann, pp.257-59; Hahn, pp.223-28; Ambrozic, p.232; U.B. Müller, 'Die christologische Absicht des Markusevangeliums und die Verklärungsgeschichte', E. Haenchen, 'Die Komposition von Mk VIII 27-IX 1 und Par'. Even a conservative scholar like V. Taylor can write, 'This section (8.34-9.1) consists of excerpts from a collection of sayings and is inserted at this point for topical reasons' (p.380). Pesch, II, pp.1ff, takes the first two pericopae to have been already united in the pre-Markan passion narrative and to have undergone no Markan redaction. His form of the pre-Markan passion narrative emphasises the three passion predictions so much by the omission of most of the remaining material as to make it unacceptable.

(a) Mark 8.27-30
Bultmann /1/ has described this unit as a 'faith-legend' and placed its historical origin in the post-resurrection period as a creation of the church to meet confessional needs. Whatever its historical origin, and this we do not need to determine, it will have been used within the primitive community for confessional or, possibly, catechetical purposes /2/.
     There are clear signs of Mark's hand in v.27. He regularly begins his pericopae with καί plus a verb of motion, of which

the most usual is ἔρχεσθαι or, as here, one of its compounds. The use of a singular verb with a plural subject (Jesus and the disciples) is also a normal Markan feature /3/; strictly the reference to the disciples in v.27a is unnecessary, that in v.27b being sufficient. ἐξέρχεσθαι /4/ itself is a Markan favourite. We assume then that all of v.27a, with the possible exception of the geographical reference, is Markan. What then of the reference to Caesarea Philippi? We cannot conclude it is non-Markan because the remainder of v.27a is non-Markan, for v.27b might have begun, 'In the villages of Caesarea Philippi he asked his disciples...', omitting ἐν τῇ ὁδῷ which, as we have seen /5/, is Markan. The geographical datum is both imprecise ('in the villages of...') and peculiar /6/. It is difficult to see how a story used for confessional or catechetical purposes should have preserved its geographical situation when so much of this information disappeared from other pericopae, and, even more if it is a church creation, how it ever obtained a geographical location. Horstmann /7/ thinks it was in the tradition because Mark does not normally introduce new geographical data, but if Mark wished to describe a journey then he had to supply some topographical information /8/. It is moreover a somewhat odd site if it is original, for if Jesus ever did ask his disciples about Jewish opinion concerning himself he would surely not have done so outside Jewish territory but within it when the disciples were in contact with Jewish opinion. Mark therefore must have supplied the name; why did he supply this name and not some other? It is impossible to answer this, but we note: (i) It was easily recognisable as a non-Jewish name and therefore indicated that Jesus was in Gentile territory; it is thus in keeping with Mark's emphasis on the gospel as a gospel for Gentiles. (ii) It was a well-known city. (iii) It was sufficiently far away from Jerusalem for him to represent Jesus as now beginning to move from the farthest part of his activity back to Jerusalem and his death /9/. (iv) Lohmeyer /10/ has suggested that since the Jews expected the place of Messianic revelation to be Jerusalem a place name is given here from outside Jewish territory in order to stress the universality of the gospel; but, as we shall see, Mark probably does not consider the confession of 8.29 to be an adequate confession for his community. Lohmeyer also suggested that the choice of the place may have been dictated by the presence of Christian churches in these villages; this depends on his assumption of a Galilean redaction of the Gospel, which is unacceptable /11/. We conclude that the reference to Caesarea Philippi is Markan and that therefore all of v.27a comes from Mark /12/.

Removing ἐν τῇ ὁδῷ from v.27b as Markan we assume that prior to Mark the pericope began, 'Jesus asked his disciples...'. The question and answer of vv.27b-28 have a fuller parallel in 6.14-16 and are partly unintelligible without that parallel (6.14-16 makes clear how the confusion with John the Baptizer could have arisen by suggesting his possible resurrection). However 6.14-16 is less essential to the succeeding story than is 8.27b-28; Mark therefore probably introduced it there in order to build up the death of John as a minor passion, parallel to that of Jesus /13/. He is thus able to use it in abbreviated form in the place it occupied in the tradition. Clearly it goes back to the earliest days of the church if not to Jesus himself; only in a Jewish Christian community was it necessary to distinguish Jesus from John and in such a community the confession of Jesus as Messiah was most relevant. The nature of the alternatives to Messiah suggest a very primitive dating in a situation in which there was possibly conflict with the supporters of John.

If then Mark took over this pericope from the tradition, did he himself regard its climax (the confession of Jesus as Christ) as an important and valid confession for his own community? Mark will certainly have allowed that it is a true confession; Jesus is the Messiah; hence the following command to silence (v.30). But for him it is probably an inadequate confession since when Jesus begins to speak (v.31) he uses the term 'Son of man' (cf. the similar change in 14.61f); all the important statements made by Jesus about himself in Mark use this term, and all the important statements made about him by others use the term 'Son of God' (1.11; 3.11; 9.7; 15.39). Obviously the term 'Christ' would have become confessionally less important once the Church was no longer solely Jewish but mainly Gentile, and in Mark it has lost its original characteristic flavour relating to a figure who appears at the End; indeed it sometimes requires to be interpreted through other terms (14.61) /14/. The incomplete nature of this confession is also seen in the preceding pericope (8.22-26) /15/. In this story Jesus at his first attempt to restore sight to a blind man only partially restores it, implying that it is possible to have a real yet imperfect sight. 'Jesus is the Christ' falls into this category for Mark's community, where instead Jesus is confessed as Son of God and Son of man. True confession will be linked to a true understanding of discipleship; yet what we have is enough to serve as a base from which to begin instruction in discipleship.

Verse 30 is completely in line with Mark's conception of a Messianic secret /16/, and the actual wording bears clear evidence of his hand in the use of καί and ἐπιτιμᾶν (cf. 1.25;

3.12; 4.29; 9.25; 10.13,48) followed by ἵνα (cf. 3.9,12; 5.43; 6.12; 7.36; 9.9,18; 10.48; 13.34) rather than by the infinitive in accordance with classical usage /17/. The verb is a key-word in the present context, re-appearing in vv.32f. We attribute the whole of the verse to Mark. What is the significance of the command to silence for Mark's readers? It may be that the terms of the confession are so inadequate that they ought not to be used at all; this is hardly likely since Mark goes on from the confession, though correcting it to 'Son of man', to explore the nature of discipleship /18/. More probably, since the confession could carry the wrong overtones to those outside the community in Rome where the church had already suffered persecution and could suffer again if it was thought to be a revolutionary movement as the title might imply, Christians would need to be wary in its use with outsiders. Verse 31, of course, removes any implication that Jesus was a revolutionary /19/.

We do not need to explore the full meaning of the confession but we should note that it is followed by (i) a clarification of the role of Jesus, and (ii) a discussion of the nature of discipleship. Discipleship is thus closely linked to the confession of Jesus and, as vv.31-33 will show, to a correct understanding of him in that confession.

Notes
1   Pp.257-59.
2   Schweizer, p.166.
3   Cf. 10.46b; on both occasions Matthew omits the reference to the disciples and Luke rewrites the material.
4   45-38-44-30.
5   See pp.15-18 above.
6   Swete notes that the phrase 'in the villages of...' occurs frequently in Joshua and 1,2 Chronicles.
7   Pp.9f. Cf. E. Dinkler, 'Peter's Confession'.
8   It has often been pointed out that most of Mark's references to Galilee are in editorial passages so that it is clear that he is not averse to supplying geographical data.
9   Cf. H.J.Ebeling, Das Messiasgeheimnis, p.213.
10   Ad loc.
11   The most recent examination of Lohmeyer's theory is that of W.D.Davies, The Gospel and the Land, pp.221 and Appendix IV, 'Galilee - Land of Salvation', by G. Stemberger in the same volume.
12   Cf. Schmidt, pp.215ff.

13   Cf. Best, pp.75f, 119.
14   Cf. Horstmann, pp.18-20.
15   Cf. Ch. 14(a). We must disagree with Horstmann's conclusion (pp.16ff) that the confession of Jesus as the Christ is for Mark a 'vollgültiges Bekenntnis', but to dispute this would take us far beyond the discussion of discipleship. There appears to be a modification of this view later (cf. p.28). On the inadequacy of Peter's confession, cf. Best, pp.165f; Schweizer, ad 8.27-33; N. Perrin, What is Redaction Criticism, pp.53ff; A Modern Pilgrimage in New Testament Christology, p.114; Q. Quesnell, p.133.
16   Taylor (p.37) attempts to defend its historicity (cf. recently, R. Pesch, 'Das Messiasbekenntnis des Petrus [Mk. 8.27-30]'): 'The prohibition is more credibly explained (than by Wrede's theory) as a counsel of prudence in view of the political repercussions of such a confession' (that Jesus is Messiah). Even if this is true, it is not its significance for Mark; he has indeed reformulated it in his own language. Most recent commentators take it straightforwardly as a creation of Mark, e.g. Schweizer, Minette de Tillesse (pp.248ff). Since Wrede's original enunciation of his theory many variants have been evolved. There is a comprehensive survey in Minette de Tillesse. See also H. Räisänen, Das 'Messiasgeheimnis'.
17   περὶ αὐτοῦ is unusual in the commands to silence but that provides no reason for taking the verse as historical; it flows naturally out of the conversation (cf. Horstmann, pp.10f).
18   Cf. Horstmann, p.17.
19   Perhaps within the Markan community the commands for silence addressed to demons and those who are healed function as an instruction not to talk too much about healings that come through Christ's power in the community or about his original mighty works lest this give the wrong impression of the purpose of the community to outsiders.

(b) Mark 8.31-33
Here again our first task must be to distinguish between redaction and tradition. In v.31 the seam καὶ|ἤρξατο διδάσκειν is Markan, for ἄρχεσθαι is used here in Mark's habitual manner as an auxiliary verb and does not mean 'begin' /1/ and διδάσκειν is also a Markan favourite, appearing regularly in redactional seams /2/ and normally introducing fresh material /3/.
   The body of v.31 is a logion which appears with variants at 9.31 and 10.33f; of these 9.31 is the simplest. At one stage, not

necessarily the earliest, the tradition will have read, 'The Son of man will be betrayed (rejected) and killed and after three days rise'. Parallel to this is another form, 'The Son of man must suffer many things and be rejected' (9.12; Lk. 17.25). It is unnecessary for our purposes to determine whether these two forms themselves go back to a common earlier form /4/, for the form of 8.31 is certainly pre-Markan. Signs of primitive tradition are 'be killed' rather than 'be crucified', 'after three days' rather than 'on the third day' and 'to rise' (ἀνύστημι) rather than 'be raised' (ἐγείρειν) /5/. Mark may have received one of the three variants of our form and evolved the other two from it, or he may have received the three forms and seen that they could have varied application, or he may have received two forms and evolved the third /6/. We shall argue that 8.31 was already integrated into the pericope in which we now find it and therefore cannot have been created by Mark, but the use of the form elsewhere implies Mark knew it also as an isolated logion. As an isolated logion it would probably have been used credally /7/. That it should also have had a narrative context as in our passage where it is not used credally is not impossible; it is a methodological error to assume that a logion could have had only one setting in the community.

Proceeding further, v.32a is Markan. λαλεῖν τὸν λόγον is an early church phrase meaning 'preach the gospel', found also at 2.2; 4.33 /8/; the imperfect is characteristic of Mark; the phrase is dropped by Matthew (Luke omits all of vv.32f). παρρησίᾳ can mean either 'publicly, openly, clearly' or 'confidently, boldly' /9/. We prefer the former range of meanings, for: (i) the latter would suit the situation of enemies rather than disciples, and (ii) it emphasises the feelings of Jesus, which Mark does not otherwise do /10/; (iii) Mark's stress on the failure of the disciples to understand requires a clear and open rather than a bold declaration of Jesus' sufferings. Thus the clause means 'he preached the gospel clearly'; the gospel is the necessity of Jesus' suffering and death and his resurrection; this needs to be proclaimed again and again to Mark's own community.

Verses 32b and 33 must be taken together. Verse 33 is introduced clumsily /11/. Jesus, whenever he sees the disciples, is made to appear to rebuke Peter (v.33) /12/; the basic saying of v.33b, which will have belonged to the tradition, is in the singular. In view of Mark's interest in the disciples we may attribute their introduction to him /13/; he indicates thereby that the rebuke to Peter concerns them all, i.e. this is not a personal attack on the apostle Peter but on Peter as a sample disciple who in the ultimate analysis represents Mark's community /14/. If Mark has introduced the reference to the disciples this implies that the reference to Peter lay in the tradition and that v.33 existed with a simpler introduction ('And he turned and rebuked...' or even more simply 'And he rebuked...'). But a simplified v.33 could not have existed by itself without some statement of the reason for the rebuke to Peter. This means that something like v.32b was a necessary preliminary. It might be argued that the vividness of the writing in v.32b,33a (προσλαβόμενος, ἐπιστραφείς, ἰδών) betrays Mark's hand throughout or represents Mark's report from an eye-witness (Peter?). It is true that Mark does write graphically, but: (i) many preachers retell the stories of Jesus much more vividly than they appear in the Gospels; this does not mean they were eye-witnesses; (ii) the actual 'vivid' touches lie mostly in agreed redactional material; (iii) if Mark did use traditional material he may still have retold it in his own way (hence the twofold use of ἐπιτιμᾶν); (iv) all the evidence shows that Mark did not create incidents but utilised existing material /15/.

If then Mark received tradition in which Peter rebuked Jesus and was in turn rebuked, there still remains the question of what produced Peter's rebuke. We have either to invent a new reason or to assume a reason similar to that which is basic to v.31, viz. Jesus' way was the way of suffering (Peter would hardly have objected to Jesus being raised!). The precise form of v.31 may, of course, have come from Mark.

Thus we have a pre-Markan unit of tradition incorporating vv.31,32b,33 which has been worked over by Mark, and which was not earlier associated with vv.27b-29 /16/. By his use of vv.27b-29 in association with vv.31,32b,33 Mark has connected a confession of Christ, which now appears for him inadequate and to need supplementation with a 'Son of man' suffering statement, to a statement of the difficulty of disciples in understanding the true nature of their Saviour; in vv.34ff he connects this again to a true understanding of the meaning of their own existence as disciples /17/.

Notes
1   Cf. Taylor, pp.48,63f; J.C. Doudna, pp.51-53,111-117; Pryke, pp.79-87. It might be argued that in 8.31 the meaning 'begin' is appropriate since this is the first time Mark depicts Jesus as teaching explicitly about his death (so Grundmann), but at 10.32, in the introduction to the third prediction, we find ἄρχεσθαι where the meaning 'begin' is impossible; it is then

easier to take the verb as an auxiliary in our passage. In any case it comes from Mark, for if it means 'begin' it shows him as consciously introducing the first of the predictions at this point.
2   Cf. E. Schweizer, 'Anmerkungen zur Theologie des Markus'.
3   1.21f; 2.13; 4.1f; 6.2,6,34; 9.31; 10.1; 12.35; cf. Horstmann, pp.13f.
4   Lohmeyer (p.165) maintains the priority of the form 9.12 and has been generally followed. G. Strecker, 'The Passion and Resurrection Predictions in Mark's Gospel', has argued for 8.31; cf. Horstmann, pp.21-26. Schweizer (ad 9.31) argues that 9.31 is the earliest. See also Tödt, pp.161ff.
5   See Best, 'Mark's Preservation of the Tradition'.
6   See discussions below of 9.31; 10.33f. We reject the view that Mark composed all three predictions, though he may have modified whatever tradition he did receive, e.g. by the addition of πολλά (a favourite term) in 8.31.
7   Probably in the form of 9.31 as containing less detail.
8   Cf. Best, p.70.
9   An adverbial dative as regularly with this word.
10 Cf. Lohmeyer, ad loc.
11 Cf. E. Dinkler, 'Peter's Confession'.
12 Cf. Horstmann, p. 12.
13 Horstmann (pp.26f) argues that ὀπίσω μου (v.33) is also redactional and equates its meaning with the same phrase in 1.17 and 8.34, from the latter of which it is assumed to have been drawn. However ὀπίσω μου is not a phrase complete in itself but requires a verb. In 1.17 δεῦτε acts as the verb; in 8.34 we have ἐλθεῖν; but in 8.33 it is ὑπάγειν whose fundamental meaning in Mark is 'away from' (cf. C. H. Turner, JTS 29 (1928) 287). Thus we can accept neither Horstmann's view that the phrase is redactional nor the understanding of it as a call to Peter to return to discipleship. Moreover the theme of discipleship does not enter until v.34; what has caused Peter to rebuke Jesus (v.32) is not his fear at the prospect of suffering (so Horstmann, p.27) but his failure to understand the need for suffering on the part of Jesus. The phrase in v.33 must be given the general sense: 'Away from me so as to be out of my sight' (cf. Best, pp.28ff).
14 The name 'Peter' is not improbable in a gospel appearing in Rome. Without making any claim to the originality of the incident it would be natural to use him as an example there.
15. Cf. Best, 'Mark's Preservation of the Material'. Müller, 'Die christologische Absicht', argues that 8.33 was composed by Mark in order to refute the christological heretics at Rome who do not adequately understand the crucifixion; indeed Müller

holds that all of 8.31-33 is Markan. Mark is supposed to set up Peter to represent the position of the heretics. Even if we assume that there were christological heretics of this type at Rome (as distinct from those who failed to understand the cross in relation to their lives), Müller provides no verbal or stylistic evidence to identify Mark's hand in v.33b nor does he offer any general evidence that it was Mark's habit to compose material of this type. He does not indicate why Mark picked on Peter as Jesus' opponent. The argument from theology alone, which Müller makes here, unsupported by other evidence, is always difficult to accept. It is much simpler to assume that Mark used tradition, and that therefore the reference to Peter belonged to the tradition. (Müller does not attempt to argue that Mark was attacking an actual Petrine or 'Twelve' party in Rome or elsewhere, but only that Peter 'represents' the heretics at Rome.) Quesnell, p.147, links the choice of Peter as Jesus' opponent with the 'denial theme' of 8.34, for it is Peter who is later said to deny Jesus. This, again, seems more than a little far-fetched. To deny oneself and to deny Jesus are two different conceptions. Our internal analysis of 8.27-33 agrees largely with that of H. Räisänen, Das 'Messiasgeheimnis' im Markusevangelium, pp.95ff, except that he views 8.27-30 and 8.31-33 as united in the pre-Markan tradition.

16 Cf. U. Luz, 'Das Geheimnismotiv und die markinische Christologie', at n.60; cf. R. Pesch, 'Das Messiasbekenntnis des Petrus'. Dinkler (as n.11), and Hahn, pp.223-8, incorrectly taking v.32b as redactional, suppose that Mark introduced v.31, and they are then compelled to connect v.33 with v.29. But at what stage in the tradition would a confession of Jesus as the Christ have been followed by a rebuke delivered at the confession? It could not have been in the Palestinian community because it accepted Jesus as the Messiah; nor would it be likely to have appeared at any later stage because even if 'Jesus is the Messiah' was not a suitable expression of the faith in a Gentile environment it was not regarded as incorrect (all the evidence implies that Mark was the first to draw out its inadequacy - which is not its incorrectness). We are thus forced to see its origin in the life of Jesus. Even if vv.27b-29 can be taken so far back, is it likely that a confessional 'faith-legend' was preserved intact until Mark's time linked to a denial of its correctness? The only possible Sitz im Leben for a true 'confession' is one of approval (cf. Horstmann, pp.11-16).

17 Horstmann (pp.26ff) argues that Mark has introduced v.31 only for its forward reference to discipleship. We believe it has both a backward reference (to the inadequate confession of

v.29) and a forward. There were available to Mark two possible logia to use here, either one in the form of 8.31 or one in the form of 9.12 (Lk. 17.25 shows it also existed as a detached logion). The latter, which lacked (i) any detail suggesting a limited application to Jesus' death, and (ii) any reference to the resurrection, would have been more appropriate if it had been his purpose here to look forward to v.34 and discipleship. Instead he chose the former because he still wished to focus attention on Jesus' death; discipleship enters fully only at 8.34.

(c) Mark 8.34-9.1

This passage consists of a set of logia which though they may have been spoken on different occasions were at least in part a unit prior to their incorporation in the Gospel /1/. Was this unit previously related to 8.31-33, or at least to whatever formed the pre-Markan core of that passage? If 8.31-33 was assembled by Mark there cannot have been any earlier connection. But was there a connection between 8.34-9.1 and any of the elements of 8.31-33? There would appear to be grounds only for suggesting a link between 8.31 and 8.34 since 8.34 refers to a cross, the mode of Jesus' death. If 8.31 however was a detached logion it did not have any connection with other parts of the tradition. Our initial question thus arises only if the core of 8.31-33 existed as a pre-Markan unit; since we have held this to be so /2/ we must attempt to answer it.

The introduction to the logion of 8.34 is largely Markan; the logion itself is certainly, at least in its major part, pre-Markan since it has independent parallels in Lk. 14.27; Mt.10.39. In the introduction προσκαλεῖσθαι is a Markan word /3/; it is found in Markan seams at 3.13,23; 6.7; 7.14; 8.1; 10.42 and probably also at 12.43 /4/. If Mark has provided this verb he must have modified the original introduction to the logion which could well have begun either without a defined reference, 'He said (to them)', or with one, e.g. 'He said to the crowd (the disciples, the crowd with the disciples)'. The manner in which the disciples are introduced ('with the disciples') makes it very probable that Mark has introduced them /5/. We have therefore only to consider whether the crowd was mentioned in the original introduction or not. It is certainly surprising to find the crowd present in non-Jewish Caesarea Philippi.

How is ὄχλος used in Mark's Gospel /6/? It appears only once in a saying of Jesus (8.2) but comes regularly in narrative material. In a minority of cases the presence of the crowd is necessary to the story and is therefore not redactional (2.4;

5.27,30,31; 8.6 bis; 9.17; 12.41; possibly also 3.32; 4.36; 7.33) but in many instances it does appear in redactional passages. Sometimes the crowd is said to gather to Jesus (3.20; 5.21,24; 3.7f) /7/ and on a number of occasions he teaches it (2.13; 3.32; 4.1 bis; 6.34; 7.14; 8.34; 10.1; 12.37); by contrast he is never said to teach his enemies /8/. The crowd and the disciples are often mentioned together (8.34; 10.46), usually in contrast, often with special teaching being given to the disciples (3.9; 4.1 [cf. 4.10-12]; 4.36; 6.45; 7.17; 8.1,2; 10.1 [cf. 10.10-12]); once the crowd appears to be the recipient of Jesus' teaching (6.34) in a way which suggests they are the equivalent of the church /9/. Sometimes the crowd and the authorities who plot against Jesus are contrasted (11.18,32; 12.12; 14.2) /10/ but sometimes the crowd is itself hostile and supports the authorities (14.43; 15.8,11,15; these passages are probably all from the tradition and therefore not redactional) /11/. While we cannot draw rigid conclusions from these passages a more or less consistent picture does appear if we think of the 'crowd' as the unevangelised mass /12/, still existing in Rome in Mark's day, from which the church (the disciples) gained recruits by teaching in the same way as Jesus called Levi from the crowd to be his disciple; the crowd lies outside the church and therefore cannot receive the full teaching which is given to the disciples in secret, though it does receive much of the essential teaching as here in 8.34; because of the goodness of the disciples it often supports them against the authorities who would persecute, but it itself can and often does persecute /13/. This suggests that Mark knows what he is about in his use of ὄχλος /14/.

If we now turn to 8.34 we can see that the teaching given in it is of the type suitable for both disciples and crowd since it concerns the essential nature of discipleship and is as relevant at the beginning of discipleship as at its end (cf. 3.32) /15/. It is possible that the reference to the crowd was already present in the introduction to 8.34 and if so Mark deliberately and consciously retained the reference; but in the light of Mark's usage it is inherently more probable that it was not and that in the pre-Markan tradition the catena of sayings in 8.34ff began, 'Jesus said...' /16/. We conclude that the reference to the crowd in 8.34 is deliberate /17/ and that almost all of 8.34a is Markan /18/. If the reference to the crowd was in any way original then since Jesus taught Jews alone /19/ he will have spoken the succeeding sayings in a Jewish area and there cannot therefore have been any original connection between them and 8.27-29 which is supposed to have taken place in a non-Jewish area. But the connection could have been pre-Markan without being original; in that case Mark with his interest in Gentiles may have wished to stress that they were taught the essence of discipleship by Jesus.

Will there not have been a pre-Markan connection between 8.31 and 8.34 in its simplified form since both deal with suffering? Schweizer /20/ points out that in Jn 12.24-26 we find connected together a reference to suffering, a saying parallel to Mk 8.35 and a call to follow (cf. Mk 8.34). There is no dependence of John on Mark at this point because the terms in which John describes suffering are entirely different from those of Mk 8.31. Therefore the connection of the three concepts existed independently of Mk 8.27-9.1. In view of the terminological differences we cannot conclude that the ideas were necessarily related in the pre-Markan tradition but only that they are a natural collocation in Christian thought. When we come to examine 9.31ff and 10.33ff we shall see that Mark has deliberately created the connection of at least two of the elements, viz. suffering of Christ, suffering of his disciples; he may well have done so here also. Is there not, however, an intrinsic connection between the cross of the disciple (8.34) and the death of Jesus (8.31) on a cross which would have drawn these two sayings together at an early pre-Markan stage of the tradition? We have seen that the pre-Markan connection of v.31 was with vv.32b,33; the thought does not then move directly from the suffering of Jesus to that of his disciples; the emphasis throughout 8.31-33 lies on Jesus' suffering as part of God's plan. Further if the logion of 8.34 followed directly at this point it is difficult to see why Mark should have inserted a long introduction to it in v.34a; the latter reads much more like the way in which he joins together existing units of the tradition which had not previously been combined. Moreover if v.34b followed directly on v.33 there is a sudden jarring change of meaning in the phrase ὀπίσω μου; this is not nearly so noticeable when v.34a intervenes. Thus we assume that Mark has added v.34 to vv.31-33. This conclusion will be reinforced once we have shown that 8.34-38 was a pre-Markan unit.

If we argue that 8.34-38 was a pre-Markan unit this does not mean that we do not recognise that its various logia at one stage existed separately; 8.34 has parallels in Lk. 14.27 and Mt. 10.38; 8.35 has parallels in Lk. 17.33 and Mt. 10.39; 8.38 has parallels in Lk. 12.9 and Mt. 10.33. Jn 12.24-26 is also, but more remotely, a parallel to vv.31,34,35. Since Mark frequently uses γάρ it has been argued that he employed it here to join the separate logia together /21/. There are however strong grounds for viewing their union as pre-Markan: (i) vv.34 and 35 were independently joined in the tradition (Mt. 10.38,39) and v.38 has its parallel adjacent thereto in the same Matthean section (10.33) /22/; (ii) Mark uses γάρ to emphasise the connection in already existing sequences of sayings /23/; (iii) there is no evidence that Mark compiled long sequences of logia; the evidence indicates instead that he drew such sequences from the tradition when the initial saying or sayings fitted his argument, even though the remainder did not (cf. 4.21-25; 9.42-9; 11.22-25) /24/; in our sequence v.38 has little to do with the theme of suffering and vv.36,37 are 'secular proverbs' /25/ suggesting a 'merit'-ethic; (iv) vv.36,37 are joined to v.35 by the catch-word ψυχή; the use of catch-words is characteristic of oral rather than written material; Mark himself does not appear to use them; (v) the sudden change of introductory formula from γάρ to καὶ ἔλεγεν αὐτοῖς suggests that 9.1 stood in a different category from 8.34-38 in Mark's mind, i.e. he consciously added 9.1 to what was an earlier unit. We thus conclude that vv.34-38 were a pre-Markan unit /26/.

It is generally agreed that Mark added 9.1 to this unit for he employs a characteristic introductory phrase καὶ ἔλεγεν αὐτοῖς (cf. 2.27; 4.2,11,21,24; 6.10; 7.9; 8.21; cf. 3.23; 6.4; 7.14; 9.31; 11.17) /27/; this phrase always joins what follows to what precedes /28/.

We must now return to v.34 and beginning with it examine individually the verses of the passage.

In 8.34 Mark appears to put the disciples and the crowd on the same level /29/ in that the same appeal is made to each, whereas elsewhere he regularly distinguishes between these two groups in that Jesus withdraws from the crowd to give his disciples secret instruction (4.10ff; 6.31; 7.17; 10.10) or teaches them apart from the crowd 'in a house' /30/ or 'in a boat' /31/. Moreover it is to the disciples that instruction is given on the meaning of the cross and resurrection (e.g. 9.9; 10.45) while it is to the crowd and possible disciples in it that the call is made to some form of activity (1.16-20; 2.14; 10.17-22). This seems to be the reverse of the modern evangelist's practice: to preach Christ crucified and then explain to converts the nature of discipleship and the activities involved therein. Does this mean that it was the custom in Mark's community to challenge the uncommitted with the hard call to dedicated service and leave the difficult matter of the cross until they had accepted the call to committal? This would probably be to misunderstand Mark. In his Gospel Mark is not writing for the outside world but for those who claim to be Christian but the depth of whose committal he doubts; he therefore wishes to draw out for them what was involved in their initial response to Christ - activity for Christ in the light of an understanding of his cross and resurrection. But probably preachers in Mark's church when addressing the outsider did include something like 8.34b, unlike their modern contemporaries who tend to speak of the joy of being a Christian, of the wonder of being saved from sin, or of a gracious deliverance from the wrath to come. Justification for Mark's inclusion of the crowd and the disciples together in 8.34a may also lie in the belief that there is essentially no difference in the meaning of Christianity for the new Christian and the experienced convert of long-standing: for each it is as simple and as difficult as taking the cross and denying the self. One last question remains in this area: after the prediction of 8.31 we have crowd and disciples faced together with the challenge of 8.34b while after 9.31 and 10.32f we still have an explanation of discipleship but no reference to the crowd? The reason appears to be, and this will become more apparent as we work through the passages which follow the second and third predictions, that in those passages it is life within the community which is stressed, i.e. the way in which one member should treat another (Mark is writing to the community about itself) and not the general essentials of personal discipleship. It is only after the latter have been expounded that the more direct application to the community can be taken up.

There are parallels to v.34b in Mt. 10.38 and Lk. 14.27 as well as the normal synoptic parallels (Mt. 16.24; Lk. 9.23). Mk 8.34b is put positively whereas Mt. 10.38 and Lk. 14.27 are put negatively. Both these appear to be older than the Markan form; it is unnecessary for our purposes to determine which of the two is the older /32/.

Within v.34b there is a significant change of tense from the aorist infinitive ἐλθεῖν and the aorist imperatives ἀπαρνησάσθω, ἀράτω, to the final present imperative ἀκολουθείτω. This suggests an initial act, or set of actions, 'come, deny, take up', followed by a process, 'keep on following' /33/. Matthew has left the tense system unchanged (16.24) though he makes it refer only to disciples who, strictly speaking, would be past the initial stage. Luke who has a vague 'all', probably referring to disciples, qualifies the second (and probably the first also) aorist with καθ᾽ἡμέραν, thus removing any idea of initial action and so making it suitable for disciples. When we examine the accounts of the calls which Jesus makes to disciples in Mark we find an initial aorist or aorists followed in most cases by a present imperative, or its equivalent, setting out what lies ahead (cf. 1.16-18,19f; 2.14; 10.21). The aorist denotes an act which at the moment of discipleship is complete. But can this be so in the case of the taking up of the cross and the denying of self in 8.34? These are processes which begin in the response to the call but continue all through discipleship; this is why it is not surprising to find them addressed to disciples as well as to the crowd. The aorists in 8.34b cannot therefore be punctiliar but denote processes which begin with the decision to follow Jesus and continue right through discipleship. Grammatically this can be paralleled in passages like Rom. 13.14 where the aorist ἐνδύσασθε, addressed to existing Christians who surely must already have put on the Lord Jesus, is followed by a present ποιεῖσθε (cf. Eph. 4.22f). We also find sequences of tenses where aorist and present vary for no easily discoverable reason of grammar or content (cf. 1 Pet. 2.17; Mt. 4.11; 6.25-34; 13.44; 2 Tim. 4.5; the separate sections of the social code in 1 Pet. 2.13,18; 3.1 are introduced with different tenses of ὑποτάσσειν; cf. the use of γράφειν in 1 Jn 2.12-14) /34/.

Within 8.34b two phrases, ὀπίσω μου ἐλθεῖν and ἀκολουθείτω μοι are almost identical in meaning and probably derive from the same Semitic background /35/. The basic conception is 'movement after' (e.g. אחרי הלך), and this appears in a number of contexts. It is frequently used of those who go after strange gods (e.g. Deut. 4.3; Judg. 2.12; Jer. 2.5; Ezek. 20.16) and occasionally (and therefore probably a deliberate formation from the former) of going after God (Deut. 13.5; 1 Kings 14.8; 18.21; 2 Kings 23.3; Hos. 11.10; cf. 1 Sam. 12.14; Num. 14.24; 32.11f; Deut. 1.36; Jos. 14.8,9,14; 1 Kings 11.6) /36/, but it is generally agreed that this usage has not produced that of the Gospels. Nor does the Gospel usage derive from the images of the ark (Num. 10.33ff; Josh. 3.3ff) or of the pillars of cloud and fire (Exod. 13.21f) going before the people; the ark and the pillars are impersonal but in the Gospels there is implicit a measure of personal allegiance to the one who is followed. More important in the OT background is the following of prophets by their 'servants' or pupils, especially Elisha's following of Elijah (1 Kings 19.19-21; cf. 2 Kings 2.3-12). Whether this had any direct influence on the formation or moulding of the 'call' narratives in the Gospels must be left until later /37/. It is doubtful if it directly affected Jesus in his choice and instruction of disciples. It had little effect on the concept of the Rabbi and his pupils /38/. The latter itself has been taken by many scholars as the main influence on Jesus /39/. Recently Hengel /40/ has pointed to other possible influences: in the OT the following of a charismatic or prophetic leader in Holy War (e.g. Judg. 3.28; 4.14; 1 Sam. 11.7; Josephus, Ant. 6.77, renders the last of these with ἀκολουθεῖν; the LXX has ἐκπορεύεσθαι ὀπίσω; see also 1 Macc. 2.27, ἐξέρχεσθαι ὀπίσω) and in the period more or less contemporary with Jesus the following of an apocalyptic prophet or zealot leader (ἀκολουθεῖν is used sometimes but ἔπεσθαι appears more often, e.g. Josephus, Ant. 20.97,167,188. In the Rabbinic writings we find similar references to Moses as followed by the people, Mek. Ex. 14,15). Berger /41/ has pointed to texts about Moses in the Samaritan tradition which say the same. All this implies that it would come naturally for a leader in the Palestine of Jesus' time to use the concept 'follow' for those he wished to associate with himself in some God-given activity. There are difficulties in depicting Jesus as a Rabbi (e.g. the eschatological strain in his teaching which implies that the End was linked to his own activity, his failure to train his alleged 'scholars' to take his place in a succession of Rabbis) but with this wider background it is not necessary to regard him as a Rabbi in order to explain his call to men to 'follow' him; conversely there is sufficient in his Jewish background to make it certain that we owe the introduction of the idea to him.

Given that the idea of following Jesus goes back to the beginning and was natural in the Palestinian environment, yet Mark is writing in a Hellenistic environment; what is there in that environment to encourage acceptance of the idea? Certainly Mark does not set out Jesus as a Rabbi teaching the Law to his pupils nor does he show him in terms of the apparently parallel Hellenistic image, the philosopher and his pupils. In neither case does the attachment to the person arise in the way it does in Mark; the Rabbi attached the loyalty of his pupils to the Law; the philosopher attached the loyalty of his pupils to the truth. We come nearer a personal relationship between teacher and pupil in the Pythagoreans /42/ and in the followers of the theioi andres /43/ of whom the most famous was Apollonius of Tyana /44/. The idea might thus not be entirely unfamiliar to Mark's Gentile readers but the way in which following is linked to the death of the one who is followed would be new.

In v.34b there are four elements: (a) the call to discipleship /45/, and the references to (b) self-denial, (c) cross-bearing, (d) following. Are any of these Markan? All four re-appear in Mt. 16.24; Lk. 9.32, but in the form derived from the double tradition (Mt. 10.38; Lk. 14.27) we have only three; (c) and (d) can be easily recognised; (a) re-appears, but in a negative form, 'not worthy to be my disciple' (Mt. 10.38) and 'he cannot be my disciple' (Lk. 14.27), and at the close instead of at the beginning. The two forms of (c) and (d) in this tradition are clearly translation variants of the Markan form /46/; the forms of (a) have a much less clear relationship to Mark. Both Mt. 10.38 and Lk. 14.27 are linked to a logion about the disciple's attitude to his relatives: neither form of (a) in them is due therefore to Matthew or Luke; the form in Luke with its less personal manner of commitment is probably the earlier; it is also the form which is nearer to Mark's (a) since 'to go after someone' means 'to be his disciple'. We can therefore safely assume that at an earlier period the saying consisted of three elements (a),(c),(d), of which (a) and (d) were somewhat similar.

The actual form of (a) in Mark cannot be said to reveal his hand. Elsewhere it appears in Mark at 4.23; 7.16 (if this is the correct text) and 9.35. The last of these is a pre-Markan logion; the first and second (if it is part of the text) could be a Markan reformulation of 4.9, but if so this may have been to bring 4.9 into a more widely recognised shape (cf. Rev. 13.9). The εἴ τις is very frequent in the NT; it comes occasionally in pre-written tradition (2 Th. 3.10; 1 Tim. 3.1; 1 Cor. 16.22) and regularly in statements about discipleship (Rom. 8.9; 1 Cor. 7.12,13; 11.16,34; 2 Cor. 5.17; 1 Tim. 5.8; Jas. 1.5,23,26; 1 Pet. 4.11; 2 Jn 10; Rev. 20.15). It is unlikely therefore that the form of (a) in 8.34 is due to Mark.

The earlier form of the logion as we have seen did not contain (b). Reploh /47/ argues that Mark added it. ἀπαρνεῖσθαι is not a Markan word; where it appears in 14.30,31,72 it probably comes from the tradition, and is retained by Matthew and Luke; Luke uses it independently in 12.9. As our discussion of v.35 will show (b) is closely related to it in meaning; v.34 and v.35 belonged together in the tradition prior to Mark, /48/ and indeed probably from a fairly early stage /49/; (b) could have been added at any point after they came together. We see no reason then to attribute it to Mark /50/. We conclude that the logion v.34b in its present form was pre-Markan. Possible confirmation lies in the fact that Matthew and Luke took it over with only one variation, Luke's addition of 'daily'. This would suggest that they knew it in that form in the oral tradition (which of course did not disappear once Mark had used it) whereas it is frequently argued that they knew v.35 without 'and of the gospel' and so omitted this when they used v.35.

The double emphasis in clauses (a) and (d) on movement behind and after Jesus corresponds with Mark's addition at various points of the phrase 'on the way'; discipleship is move-ment. On each occasion when Jesus calls disciples he himself is described as 'in motion' (1.16,19; 2.14; 10.17) and calls them to move behind him. We may associate with this the stress in the sending out of the Twelve (6.7-13) on what they should take for, and how they should behave on, their journey. Finally Mark is particularly rich in verbs of motion /51/.Jesus is 'on the move': he summons disciples to come after him. Neither the rabbi nor the contemporary philosopher sought to attach pupils to himself in this way. The pupil might change his rabbi or his philosopher in his search to understand the Law or truth, but for Mark there is no alternative to following Jesus.

What then does it mean to follow Jesus? To live like him, to take him as a model, to imitate him? To join in with him as he proclaims the nearness of the Kingdom, to exorcise and heal as he does, to be 'with him' (3.14f)? It is generally agreed that 'imitation' played little or no part in the teaching of the historical Jesus /52/. The disciples, rather, were involved in a movement instituted by Jesus in relation to the coming of the Kingdom of God. Has Mark's understanding of 'following' changed discipleship into a concept of imitation, and if so in what way? 'Following' is ambiguous here; it could refer to the whole concept of discipleship in Mark or to his use of the word ἀκολουθεῖν: the former can only be dealt with slowly as we work through all the relevant sections of the Gospel; the latter we can deal with immediately, more particularly since the verb comes in 8.34.

The verb is not exclusively Markan; it is found in the non-Markan sections of Matthew and Luke with reference to discipleship (Mt. 8.19 = Lk. 9.57; Mt. 8.21f = Lk. 9.59f; Mt. 10.38; Lk. 9.61; Mt. 19.28; 8.23) as is ὀπίσω with a verb of motion (Mt. 10.38 = Lk. 14.27). In Mark it is used in relation to discipleship both in the pre-Markan tradition (1.18; 2.14, first occurrence; 9.38; 10.21) and in redactional material (2.14, second occurrence; 2.15; 6.1; 10.28; 10.32; 10.52; 15.41) /53/. It is a verb that appears naturally in narrative material and so we sometimes have it without discipleship overtones of any kind (11.9; 14.13; in 14.54 the use of ἀπὸ μακρόθεν with it may be intended to impart some idea of 'discipleship'). It is used twice in relation to crowds following Jesus (3.7; 5.24) and both occur in redactional passages. In 5.24 /54/ the reference to the crowd is essential in view of the content of the following story and ἀκολουθεῖν is a natural word to use when movement in the company of other people is being described. There is then no special significance to be attached to it in 5.24. Mk 3.7 is much more difficult. The whole of 3.7-12 is probably redactional /55/. Textual grounds for the omission of ἠκολούθησεν are not strong

/56/. The punctuation which places a colon after it and associates only Galilee with it is preferable /57/. Mark thus depicts the crowd as following Jesus. But we note: (i) this is one of the only two places where he used πλῆθος for the crowd; (ii) it is only the crowd from Galilee which is said to follow Jesus; the rest of the crowd only comes to him. It may be that Mark with his special emphasis on Galilee of the Gentiles here foreshadows the association of the Gentiles with Jesus and by using an unusual (for him) word for the crowd differentiates them from the uncommitted mass or it may simply be that while Mark normally associates 'following' with discipleship he has used the verb in a natural way here and no significance should be attached to it. Like ἀκολουθεῖν, ὀπίσω with a verb of motion also comes from the tradition and is associated in 1.17,20 as here with discipleship; it is not so associated in 8.33 /58/; 1.7; 13.10. Mark has not himself used it redactionally of discipleship.

Thus the word ἀκολουθεῖν lay in the tradition prior to Mark and was used in relation to discipleship; Mark understood its significance and extended its use; but his use of the word in itself has little to teach us about discipleship apart from what may be implied by its background in Judaism and Hellenism and what can be garnered from its context in particular passages. We must therefore now look at the two concepts to which it is related in 8.34, viz. self-denial and cross-bearing.

The denial of the self, as we have seen, is lacking in Mt. 10.38 and Lk. 14.27, but was added at some point prior to Mark /59/, and was intended to develop the understanding of discipleship. The saying about cross-bearing runs the danger of being taken too literally and therefore of being irrelevant to most of the life of the disciple; the addition of self-denial serves to widen it /60/. Self-denial as it is used in our verse must not be confused, as it regularly is, with the denial of things to the self, i.e. with asceticism or self-discipline. It is not the denial of something to the self but the denial of the self itself /61/. It is the opposite of self-affirmation, of putting value on one's being, one's life, one's position before man or God, of claiming rights and privileges peculiar to one's special position in life or even of those normally believed to belong to the human being as such (e.g. justice, freedom) /62/. Self-denial thus obviously involves the willingness not to affirm any right to life when faced by the persecutor, though it cannot be confined to this since by itself it does not contain any idea of literal death. Although Jesus denied himself /63/, no attention is drawn to this in Mark's Gospel and we cannot therefore see self-denial as the attempt to lay down Jesus as the pattern to be followed. Since the element of imitation was originally absent from the tradition /64/ and only gradually entered it, this reinforces our earlier conclusion that the clause about self-denial was probably added at a relatively early stage in the growth of the tradition and certainly prior to Mark.

Coordinate (they are not to be taken as temporally successive acts) with self-denial as a condition of discipleship is another: the command to take up the cross. We are not concerned with the origin of this saying /65/ but with its meaning in the present context in which it carries an explicit reference to the death of Jesus; this is implied by the prediction of v.31 and, of course, all Mark's readers know how Jesus died. But in how far is the phrase to be taken literally, and only literally? Luke by his addition 'daily' quite obviously intends the phrase to be understood metaphorically. For Jesus the cross was certainly a literal cross; Mark's community was either being persecuted, or had just emerged from a period of persecution /66/; v.35 speaks of the loss of life; the verb in our phrase is in the aorist indicating a single action rather than continued activity; consequently some writers take the saying about cross-bearing in Mark to be an explicit and necessary reference to the potential martyrdom that awaits the disciple /67/. Since the condemned criminal was expected to carry the crossbar for his cross to the place of execution, and since crucifixion was then so common a punishment, the vividness of the imagery would be directly appreciated by Mark's readers. Yet such a literal interpretation of the phrase immediately requires to be qualified and with so many qualifications that it soon begins to lose its literal value. (i) Even though Mark and his community may be enduring, have endured, or be expecting to endure a period of persecution he cannot expect that everyone will die literally on a cross; those who perished in the Neronic persecutions were not crucified; in Mark John the Baptizer's death prefigures that of Jesus, and he was beheaded; Mark's readers will know, if the Gospel was written in Rome and tradition is correct, that Paul was not crucified but beheaded. The phrase is therefore at least partly metaphorical, indicating death but not its exact manner. (ii) The introduction by Mark of 'the crowd' in v.34a shows that he is not just presenting a new demand to be made on already existing disciples who now find themselves in a situation of persecution but is presenting a task also to those who are not yet Christian, i.e. the saying may not be as distinctly tied to a particular situation in Rome (or Galilee) as those who argue for literal crucifixion suggest. (iii)

If the tense change /68/ is important then the present imperative ἀκολουθείτω implies a period of discipleship after taking up the cross, and not just a quick walk in the footsteps of Jesus to the place of execution (which could have been an earlier meaning). If the aorist tense is not to be taken as punctilear then we cannot argue from it to a single act of martyrdom. (iv) Mk 9.1, which Mark has added to the sequence of logia, envisages the survival of some of the community to the parousia; he cannot therefore be expecting them all to be martyred, let alone be crucified. (v) On the whole the NT does not say much about martyrdom (Stephen, James, John [?], the martyrs of Revelation) but a great deal about persecution which might end in martyrdom but did not necessarily do so. (vi) The addition of the clause about self-denial takes away the literal meaning from 'cross-bearing'.

Cross-bearing then implies the willingness to make any sacrifice, even life itself, for Christ. Self-denial is the inner attitude; cross-bearing is the outward activity which should accompany the inner attitude. Both imply a definite action on the part of the disciple, a resolve to adopt a particular course of action. Crosses are never thrust on men; they are not a part of a situation in which the disciple is inevitably involved (e.g. a painful back, the loss of a loved relative), but are deliberately accepted as new factors in an already existing situation.

Because cross-bearing takes up a precise event in the life of Jesus the element of 'imitation' would appear to enter into it much more than in the case of self-denial. That the disciple's cross-bearing need not be literal as Jesus' was does not affect this since Jesus' cross-bearing is symbolic of all his loving activity. There is thus here the beginnings of an imitatio Christi theology, though it cannot be said to dominate the thought of Mark /69/. The concept of 'following' from now on gradually carries more and more of the significance of imitation.

Reverting briefly to the aorists of v.34b, while they can be thought of as beginning for the member of the crowd at the moment he becomes a disciple this cannot be so for the existing disciple; he has already been denying himself and bearing his cross; this is not something new for him. There is an interesting parallel in thought here to the aorists in Rom. 13.14 and Eph. 4.22-24. In content, if not in expression, there is a similarity between putting off the old man and self-denial since the latter equally speaks of the death of past life: the 'old self' is denied as the 'old man' is put off. Perhaps there is also a parallel to cross-bearing in the putting to death (νεκρώσατε, aor. imperat.) of the evil desires and passions (Col. 3.5) since 'cross' symbolises 'death'.

Verse 35 is found in varying forms in varying contexts /70/. In the form before us the balance of the two halves of the verse is lost by the addition in the second of ἕνεκεν ἐμοῦ καὶ /71/ τοῦ εὐαγγελίου. Since the variant forms in Lk. 17.33 and Jn 12.25 lack this addition we can conclude that the original form did not have it. The Matthean and Lukan synoptic parallels (Mt. 16.25; Lk. 9.24) lack καὶ τοῦ εὐαγγελίου; it is also lacking in Mt. 10.39 which does however have ἕνεκεν ἐμοῦ. The latter is probably an earlier addition than the former. Matthew and Luke probably knew the saying without the reference to the gospel and recognising it as an addition in Mark omitted it. But did Mark add it? Its use of εὐαγγέλιον accords with his usual practice, for he invariably uses it absolutely /72/ whereas Matthew normally qualifies it (e.g. with 'of the kingdom') and Luke prefers to use a verbal form which Mark never does. We may thus attribute it to Mark. Why did he add it? It is often argued that he uses it to equate the gospel with Christ /73/; τοῦ εὐαγγελίου is then epexegetical. While it is probably true that for Mark the gospel is Christ there seems no reason for him to say so at this point. Marxsen /74/ argues that Mark added it in order to emphasise that Christ is present when the gospel is proclaimed in Mark's day, and, not only in Jesus' own life-time but ever since, the disciple must lose his life if he is to gain it. Again this is true but it is difficult to see how so much can be read into the words at this point; to do so is to divert attention from the main drive of v.35 /75/. 'Gospel' is a much more objective term than 'my' (= Christ); the latter implies a personal loyalty to Christ, the former to the way in which God sets out salvation /76/. Schnackenburg /77/ points out that though Mark's usage of 'gospel' is probably based on Paul's he differs from him in that he more regularly associates κηρύσσειν with εὐαγγέλιον (cf. 1.14; 13.10; 14.9; in Paul only at 1 Th. 2.9; Gal. 2.2; (?) Col. 1.23). The gospel is thus that which the preacher communicates verbally, and perhaps, as Schnackenburg also suggests, the community by their sufferings. It is not then for Mark a term which is directly equivalent to Christ. Its addition /78/ is probably indicative of the less personal way in which being a Christian gradually came to be regarded in the early church /79/. Mark likes to drive home points in a twofold way /80/; here adhesion to Christ and to God's plan stresses the motive for action in the logion. The expression, 'the gospel', drawn from the mission-terminology of the church, is beginning to replace the personal commitment of 'for my sake'.

The whole addition 'for my sake and the gospel's' clearly

shows that for Mark discipleship cannot be simply equated with imitation of Jesus. If it were the phrase would have been 'as I do', i.e. 'whoever will lose himself as I do (did), will save himself'. This is not to say that imitation is not a part of discipleship; it appears, as we have just seen, in cross-bearing (v.34) but the total relationship of the disciple to the Lord is too complex to be resolved into imitation alone. It involves also action, not necessarily imitative, on the part of the disciple, called out by personal commitment to Christ and loyalty to the mission of the church. The original logion, lacking both parts of the addition, will have stated the depth of commitment necessary to Jesus' eschatological cause. This cause centred on Jesus and was to be triggered off by his activity. When the End did not come with Jesus then the addition 'for my sake' made personal loyalty to the crucified, and now risen, Christ the centre of the faith; it was no longer joint activity with him on his mission. The addition 'and the gospel's' restores the concept of mission but in a new way, for Jesus himself was never on this mission.

The use of γάρ in v.35 shows that v.35 is closely bound to v.34 and explains or expounds it /81/. We have already seen that 'cross-bearing' (v.34) is interpreted with varying degrees of literalness; the same is true of our logion. The key word ψυχή is capable of a number of meanings ranging from the physical life to the real or essential person /82/. Because of the threat of persecution to Mark's community the word has often been restricted in our text to 'physical life': whoever wishes to save himself from martyrdom will lose his life /83/. This interpretation is difficult because it requires ψυχή to change its meaning between the two halves of v.35a and the two halves of v.35b. The man who saves his physical life loses something other than this, viz. his real being (v.35a); the man who loses his physical life, saves something other, viz. his real being (v.35b). Consistency in the meaning of ψυχή throughout seems required by the use of the pronouns for it in the second half of each contrast, and it can have this consistency only if it is given the deepest possible meaning throughout, viz. the real or essential person. This links it closely to 'self-denial' which it expounds. The man who denies himself is the same as the man who loses (destroys) himself for the sake of Christ and the gospel; he saves himself. The man who refuses to deny himself but rather affirms himself is the same as the man who wishes to save his whole being (to preserve it for himself); he loses (or destroys) himself /84/. ψυχή indeed might be replaced here by the reflexive personal pronoun, for which it is often used in biblical

Greek /85/.

The same concept of ψυχή must be carried on into vv.36f /86/; no one could be said to gain the whole world by martyrdom (v.36); no earthly treasure or position can make up for the loss of real life (v.37). These last two sayings are not as profound as those of vv.34,35 /87/. On the one hand a more Greek conception of 'soul' begins to enter, for both can be understood with ψυχή meaning 'immortal soul', i.e. nothing earthly is to be compared with the saving of the soul; however this meaning is not essential if ψυχή is understood as the actual but essential life of a man, which can be denied (v.34) or lost (v.35) even while physical life continues /88/. On the other hand the commercial element of weighing one advantage against another may be present in a contrast of earthly and heavenly; the rich young ruler acted in this manner deciding that the enjoyment of present possessions was better than a possible future eternal life /89/; in the interpretation of the parable of the sower those who are put off by tribulation and persecution are like those who give up 'life' in order to preserve their earthly lives (v.36) /90/. Yet neither ψυχή as immortal soul nor this commercial flavour should be over-stressed in these verses; v.35, in the light of which they must be understood, ultimately excludes them. In the context of v.35 the 'secular proverbs' of vv.36f have been de-secularised; they no longer emphasise the ultimate value of salvation but rather the abandonment of the world to follow Christ.

In v.38 /91/ there are two variant readings of which the second (καί for μετά) need not detain us since whatever decision is made the aspects of the verse which concern us are not affected /92/. The first, the omission of λόγους, played an important role in T.W. Manson's theory of a corporate Son of man ('...ashamed of me and mine' [the disciples]). The evidence for omission is slender /93/; if it was originally lacking and the need was felt for an addition we should expect that different additions would have appeared in different textual groupings; its omission could easily have arisen through haplography over -ους /94/; its presence fits the context and is not un-Markan; we therefore accept it. It is not however found in the Q parallel (Mt. 10.33; Lk. 12.9) /95/; this is generally accepted as earlier, with the Lukan form more primitive than the Matthean /96/. If this is so the original logion experienced considerable development. Into its second half has been inserted a reference to the parousia, using the imagery of Dan. 7.13f; this is probably pre-Markan. αὐτοῦ attached to 'Father' implies the identification of the Son of man with the Son of God and, since Mark identifies the two elsewhere by implication and stresses Jesus' sonship, this may have been his addition; but it could have appeared at any time after Jesus and the Son of man were identified /97/. At the same time in the Markan form the presence of Jesus is stressed less as 'witness' (Lk. 12.8f) and more as 'judge' /98/. In both halves of the verse we have the replacement of (ἀπ)αρνεῖσθαι with ἐπαισχύνεσθαι. The former more correctly balances ὁμολογεῖν in primitive theology /99/. The implication however still remains of confession in a public situation /100/ (2 Tim. 1.8,12,16; cf. Phil. 1.20; 1 Pet. 4.16) though it does not necessarily imply that this is one of active persecution (Rom. 1.16), and certainly not one of appearance before a tribunal or court /101/, for if it was the latter we would have had an addition of something like 'before governors and kings' as in Mk. 13.9. The two words may well be translation variants, and in any case the use of ἐπαισχύνεσθαι almost certainly predates Mark /102/. In the first half of v.38 ἐν τῇ γενεᾷ ταύτῃ τῇ μοιχαλίδι καὶ ἁμαρτωλῷ has been added; it is traditional in form but not necessarily Markan /103/. It implies that the 'confession' or 'being ashamed' takes place in public, not in church, and confirms that the situation is 'missionary' rather than 'juridical'. At issue then is not the recital of a creed at baptism or the Eucharist but the acknowledgment of discipleship in a situation which may be fraught with physical danger but will certainly lead to persecution and trial of a lesser but more subtle order.

Finally we come to καὶ τοὺς ἐμοὺς λόγους which is again an addition; it serves to up-date the logion to the post-resurrection situation where loyalty is given both to Christ and to the gospel (cf. 'for my sake and the gospel's', v.35), and where Christ could not be literally followed. Is the addition Markan? If he had made it, would he not have used the singular λόγος? For him this is equivalent to 'the gospel' (cf. 1.45; 2.2; 4.33; 8.32) and if at v.35 he added 'gospel' (cf. Rom. 1.16) would he not have added 'word' and not 'words' here? He uses the plural twice: 13.31 probably comes from the tradition but 10.24 is redactional /104/. Both 10.24 and 8.38 lie within 8.27-10.46 one of whose main themes is discipleship and within which there are many sayings ('words') of Jesus to which attention is directed; it is to these very logia of Jesus which express discipleship against the background of the cross that Mark's community are paying too little attention. Thus the choice of the plural at this point is probably his /105/ and dictated by his desire to drive home the demands that must be fulfilled by the true disciple, demands which are expressed not so much by the statement of the gospel itself as by the words of Jesus which have come to him in the tradition and which he uses in this section. Verse 38 thus forms a strong warning to his community.

The Q form of v.38 has a companion (Lk. 12.8 = Mt. 10.32) expressing the reverse, 'whoever confesses me...', a promise rather than a threat. This is not found allied to v.38 in Mark. Without it v.38 coheres better with vv.34,35; the point of the latter would be blunted by any suggestion that faithful discipleship would bring reward at the parousia or the judgement, for it would create the temptation to lose oneself now in order to find oneself then. Possibly Mark himself dropped the 'promise' /106/ but more probably it had already disappeared before his time, for Mark feels himself called on in some way to balance the threat which lies in 8.38 and uses 9.1 to do this; it is by no means as good a logion for this purpose, which again suggests he probably did not know the original logion in its position alongside 8.38.

Mark, as we have seen already, added 9.1 /107/ to the logia sequence 8.34-38 in such a way that it relates backwards, but he appears to have made little internal alteration. ἑστηκότων /108/ is hardly relevant to Mark's community; 'kingdom of God' belongs to an early stage of the tradition /109/. Horstmann suggests that Mark added both ἐν δυνάμει in 9.1 /110/ and ἐν τῇ δόξῃ in 8.38 /111/. The two form a word-pair (cf. 13.26), and help to link 8.38 to 9.1: they both stress the same christological claim in elevating Jesus towards the position of God. Whether these two phrases are Markan is more difficult to determine for neither contains a specifically Markan word /112/; it may be that their presence in the sayings was one of the factors that led Mark to associate the sayings /113/. More importantly in this connection is the easy transition from the parousia (8.38) to the complete inauguration /114/ of the kingdom (9.1). If Jesus as Son of man has come as judge, then the kingdom will have been established /115/. By implication this means that those disciples who see the kingdom come, and of course also those who have died in the faith, will be in the kingdom. In this way 9.1 compensates for the omission of the parallel to 8.38 which we find in Lk. 12.8, but there is much less emphasis in it on what happens to faithful disciples when the kingdom comes; the emphasis lies instead on the certainty of the realisation of the kingdom, about which Mark's readers under continual external pressure may have required re-assurance: some of them before dying will experience the kingdom /116/.

Bultmann /117/, followed by Horstmann /118/, has argued that 9.1 was connected in the pre-Markan tradition to 9.11-13.

The grounds offered are slight and amount ultimately to no more than that 'first' in 9.11 links to the temporal datum of 9.1. This does not make the temporal datum of v.1 any easier to understand since vv.11-13 argue that what is to happen 'first' has already happened. If it is necessary to attach vv.11-13 to anything from the pre-Markan tradition in this context, then 8.38 is a better candidate; both use ἔρχεσθαι; 'first' could refer to the coming of the Son of man; it is more logical to compare the coming of the Son of man with the coming of Elijah than with the coming of the kingdom. But, in fact, in so far as the 'first' is relevant vv.11-13 might as easily have belonged originally after any apocalyptic prophecy, e.g. 13.4 or 13.22. But we cannot deny that 9.11-13 could have belonged with 9.1 and that 9.2-8 may also have belonged with 8.27b-29; a double sandwich would not be un-Markan (cf. 3.20-35) and he could have interlaced the two sets of tradition.

Horstmann /119/ also argues that 9.1 was added to 8.38 in order to bring out the Christological significance of the kingdom. It is certainly true that Christ, gospel and kingdom are all related in Mark and that the relationship of the first and third appears here; but this is really a by-product of, and not the reason for, the addition of 8.38 to 9.1; if it was the reason it was one which Mark really failed to make clear. The sequence of logia in 8.34-8 is concerned primarily with discipleship and received this slant through Mark's redactional work; it is much easier to assume that in adding 9.1 he continued this; though, as always in Mark, the nature of discipleship is founded on the meaning of Christ, and so a Christology is implicit in the connection of 8.38 and 9.1.

The latter consequently functions for the Christian of Mark's community as a promise of the certainty of the coming of the kingdom. Without it the sequence of discipleship logia in 8.34-8 would end with a threat; no good pastor would leave this as the final impression; Mark does not do it elsewhere; hence 9.1 is necessary.

Notes

1   See below.
2   See discussion of 8.31-33 in preceding section.
3   6-9-4-0. Mark uses it normally (seven times) as here as an aorist participle followed by a verb of speech (3.23; 7.14; 8.1,34; 10.42; 12.43; 15.44). See further, p.130 n.8 and p.180
4   Matthew retains it in his parallels to 6.7; 7.14; 8.1; 10.42; he has no parallel to 3.13; 12.43; 15.44. He uses it independently

at 18.2,32, of which the second is certainly not redactional. Luke never preserves it, but uses it independently at 7.19; 15.26; 16.5; 18.16, of which only 7.19 and 18.16 may be redactional.

5   Cf. Grundmann, Schmidt, p.221, Horstmann, pp.34f. In a similar way Mark added 'with the Twelve' at 4.10, though on this occasion he drew it from a separate piece of tradition; cf. Best, 'The Twelve'. See·also W. Nützel, pp.107f.

6   Cf. B. Citron, 'The Multitude in the Synoptic Gospels'; A.W. Mosley, 'Jesus' Audiences'; E. Trocmé, 'Pour un Jésus public'; Tagawa, pp.57-73; P.S. Minear, 'Audience Criticism and Markan Ecclesiology'; C.H. Turner, JTS 26 (1925) 227,237f; Ambrozic, pp.65f; J.A. Baird, Audience Criticism and the Historical Jesus; Best, 'The Role of the Disciples'; U. Hedinger, 'Jesus und die Volksmenge'.

7   3.7f offer the only two occurrences of πλῆθος in Mark.

8   Cf. Ambrozic, p.58.

9   See pp.210f.

10   λαός; this word also appears at 7.6 in an OT citation. When Mark uses this word just as when he uses ὄχλος he is not intending to signify the crowd as Israel; he has in mind the uncommitted masses of his own time. His use of λαός is thus not designed to stress the deliberate rejection of its Messiah by the historical Israel.

11   A few passages like 9.14,15,25 are difficult to classify.

12   Lohmeyer incorrectly suggests that the distinction between disciples and crowd represents that between ecclesiastical officials and laity; rather it is that between the uncommitted (who can become hostile) and the committed (who may be only partially committed and need to be further instructed). Minear (as n.6) goes too far when he makes the crowd 'a continuing audience of committed believers'. It is rather the source from which such believers come, otherwise it is difficult to preserve a distinction between 'crowd' and 'disciples'.

13   Mark's use of πολλοί (2.2; 6.2,33; 10.48; 11.8) is in line with his use of ὄχλος.

14   If we compare the total use of the singular (20-37-25-22) with the plural (29-1-16-0) we see that Mark and John appear to present the crowd as a unity, i.e. as a theological rather than a population group. The use by Matthew and Luke of the plural accords with later Greek usage, meaning 'the masses' (cf. N. Turner, p.26; Bauer, s.v.).

15   For 'the crowd' in 3.31-5 see Best, 'Mark III. 20,21, 31-35'.

16   The crowd is, of course, out of place at Caesarea Philippi in Gentile territory.

17   Matthew (16.24) omits the reference to the crowd; Luke

(9.23) changes the whole phrase to a reference to 'all' which in his context must mean 'the disciples'. R.P. Meye, pp.120-25, does not believe that 8.34 is a 'call' to discipleship. Instead the verse 'lays down two conditions for following Jesus' (p.122; Meye's emphasis). It is difficult to distinguish 'conditions' from 'call', especially when the crowd is introduced. Meye does not seem able to account for the presence of the crowd and has not sufficiently examined the manner of its appearance in the Gospel. It is true that there is a difference between 8.34 and 1.17; 2.14 in respect of the call in that in the latter two verses no conditions are laid down but a condition is implicit in 1.18 and is explicit in 10.17-22. There is thus no reason for concluding that because 8.34b gives 'conditions' that it is not also a 'call'.

18   The conjecture of A. Pallis, Notes on St. Mark and St. Matthew, pp.27f, that we ought to read τὸν Πέτρον for τὸν ὄχλον is only a conjecture and in the light of Mark's use of ὄχλον does not require serious discussion.

19   Cf. J. Jeremias, Jesus' Promise to the Nations.

20   Ad loc.

21   Cf. Haenchen, pp.297f. and 'Die Komposition von Mk VIII 27-IX 1', p.97; Kuhn, p.48; R. Schnackenburg, 'Mk 9.33-50'.

22   8.34,35,38 were probably united from a very early stage in the tradition; cf. Best, 'An Early Sayings Collection'.

23   Cf. Best, 'Mark's Preservation of the Tradition', n.26 for discussion and fuller references.

24   Best (as n.23), pp.28ff.

25   Cf. Bultmann, p.97.

26   Cf. Horstmann, p.34; Trocmé, p.31; Pesch, II, p.57. Reploh, pp.125ff, believes that Mark added vv.36f and v.38 to the already existing unity of vv.34f. It is difficult to produce evidence other than the use of γάρ to support this. The arguments we have given above confirm the pre-Markan linking of v.38 with vv.34f. Reploh's reason (pp.136f) for the union of v.38 with vv.36f (the minatory nature of v.38) would apply as easily at an earlier stage of the tradition as at the time of Mark.

27   Cf. W. Marxsen, 'Redaktionsgeschichtliche Erklärung der sogenannten Parabeltheorie des Markus'; Pryke, pp.76f; Kuhn, p.74, n.130 and further references there. H. Räisänen, Die Parabeltheorie im Markusevangelium, pp.93ff, denies that the phrase is redactional in Mark; but if it was already present in the pre-Markan material he could easily have omitted it to produce a more clearly unified passage. Lane, p.312, says, without offering any evidence, that it indicates 'the conclusion to a larger discourse of which only the most salient point has

been preserved'.
28 Ambrozic, p.231: Zerwick, p.67. For a discussion and rejection of the traditional view which links 9.1 to the Transfiguration see Best, 'The Markan Redaction of the Transfiguration'.
29 Lane, p.306, agrees with this but takes the crowd to represent the church in Rome.
30 Cf. Part III, ch. 28 below.
31 Cf. Part III, ch. 29 below.
32 On the logion about cross-bearing see especially E. Dinkler, 'Jesu Wort vom Kreuztragen' and 'Zur Geschichte des Kreuzsymbols'; J.G. Griffiths, 'The Disciple's Cross'. We do not, of course, need to determine the origin of the phrase 'bearing the cross'; it is undoubtedly pre-Markan.
33 N. Turner (p.76) comments on the parallel in Lk. 9.23: 'the self-denying is a decision, once and for all (om. the harmonising vl. καθ' ἡμέραν), but the following (emphasis his) is a continuous discipline'. A few commentators (e.g. Klostermann) take the present imperative to represent a Semitic jussive, 'and so he is to be my follower', cf. Schulz, pp.83f. While this may be the tradition lying behind the imperative it is unlikely that Mark or his readers would have taken it in that way.
34 F. Stagg, 'The Abused Aorist', argues that the aorist tense is basically a-temporal rather than punctilear.
35 Cf. H.D. Betz, Nachfolge und Nachahmung Jesu Christi im Neuen Testament; Schulz, pp.63ff; M. Hengel, Nachfolge und Charisma; Th. Aerts, 'Suivre Jesus'; K.H. Rengstorf, TDNT IV, pp.390ff; G. Kittel, TDNT I, pp.210ff; Tinsley, The Imitation of God in Christ.
36 In the Samaritan writing Memar Marqah (ed. J. Macdonald) we also find references to following God, I.2 (p.9); IV.12 (p.183).
37 See Part II, ch. 19.
38 So Hengel (as n.35), p.19.
39 Above all by Schulz, pp.19ff.
40 Pp.19ff (see n.35).
41 K. Berger, p.434. See Memar Marqah (ed. J. Macdonald) IV.2 (p.140); IV.5 (p.154); IV.7 (p.160).
42 Hengel (as n.35), p.28, instances Empedocles; cf. Diels-Kranz, Fragment der Vorsokratiker, I, pp.354f, frag. B.112.
43 On the concept see most recently, C.H. Holladay, Theios Aner in Hellenistic Judaism.
44 Evidence of a group accompanying Apollonius may be seen in Philostratus, Apollonius of Tyana, 1.16; 4.20,37,47; 5.43. On the Hellenistic background see Hengel (as n.35), pp.27ff;

Rengstorf, TDNT IV, pp.421ff.

45 The variant ἀκολουθεῖν (p⁴⁵ D W θ fam1 28 it) for ἐλθεῖν (ℵ A B fam13 syr) probably represents assimilation to Mt. 10.38.

46 Black, pp.195f.

47 Pp. 125f; cf. E. Schweizer, Lordship and Discipleship, p.17. Schulz, pp.82ff, takes the Q form which lacks (b) to be the earlier.

48 See above.

49 Cf. Best, 'An Early Sayings collection'.

50 G. Schwarz,'"... ἀπαρνησάσθω ἑαυτὸν ...'?" sets this clause on the lips of Jesus with the meaning 'Let him become a non-Jew'. Whether this is the original meaning or not it cannot be the meaning in Mark.

51 If we count the occurrences of ἄγειν, βαίνειν, ἔρχεσθαι, πορεύεσθαι, and their compounds as given in R. Morgenthaler, Statistik des Neutestamentlichen Wortschatzes.

Matthew has 425	out of a total word count of	18278
Mark	307	11229
Luke	363	19404
John	360	15420

Some of the compounds (e.g. συνάγειν 24-5-6-7) are not strictly verbs of motion and if we correct for this the relative frequency of Mark's usage is even more noticeable.

52 See the very detailed examination in Schulz, pp.15-197, with which Betz (as n.35) and Hengel (as n.35) agree.

53 For the discussion of 2.14 see pp.175ff, for 2.15 see pp.175f, for 10.28 see pp.112f, for 10.32 see p.120, for 10.52 see p.139. Both occurrences in 2.14 may well be redactional.

54 5.24 is a Markan seam.

55 L.E. Keck, 'Mark 3.7-12 and Mark's Christology', has argued for a core of tradition which Mark has enlarged. He attributes to this core from vv.7,8 the words, 'And Jesus departed with his disciples to the sea and a great crowd (πλῆθος) followed him', and to this he adds vv.9,10. This has been severely and rightly criticised by T.A. Burkill, 'Mark 3.7-12'; Egger, pp.92ff and 'Die Verborgenheit Jesu im Mk 3,7-12'; T. Snoy, 'Les Miracles'. It would be difficult to find a Sitz im Leben for the tradition which Keck isolates.

56 D fam13 28 it syrˢ bo. There are also variations in its position and form.

57 So Nestle, Kilpatrick, UBS. Cf. Metzger, ad loc.

58 See above p.26 n.13.

59 See above, p.35.

60 Cf. Reploh, pp.125f. Self-denial is thus not just a readiness

to die (so Schulz, pp.86-88).

61 ἑαυτόν is the direct object of the verb.

62 Mark uses the same verb to describe Peter's denial of Jesus (14.30,31,72) but this does not help us to interpret the present passage. It is better to relate Peter's denial of Jesus to the confession and denial of him by his believers in the church or in public (cf. Lk. 12.8f).

63 The idea may be present in Phil. 2.6-8 if we understand this of a denial by Jesus of the exercise of the privileges of deity.

64 See the literature listed in nn.35 and 52.

65 See the literature listed in n.32.

66 We assume Mark was written in Rome after the Neronic persecutions. If it was written in Galilee after the flight to Pella conditions were equally serious and persecution might be directed at the Christians by the Romans who would crucify. The pressure of persecution on the community is seen especially in chap. 13.

67 E.g. Haenchen, pp.296ff and 'Die Komposition von Mk VIII 27-IX 1 und Par.', pp.92f.

68 Above, pp.32-33.

69 It emerges more clearly in Ignatius, Rom. 6.3 (cf. Schulz, p.267, n.56).

70 Kee, pp.140ff, classifies the sayings of this verse with many of the other discipleship sayings as 'sentences of holy law' (cf. E. Käsemann, 'Sätze Heiligen Rechtes im Neuen Testament'). Many of the sayings Kee adduces do not function in the same way as those instanced by Käsemann; on such sentences see K. Berger, 'Zu den sogenannten Sätzen Heiligen Rechts'; C.J. Roetzel, Judgement in the Community, pp.148ff. For an alternative explanation of the ὃς ἄν form see Best, 'An Early Sayings Collection'.

71 ἐμοῦ καί is lacking in P45 D 28·700 itPl syrS arm. It may have been added under the influence of 10.29. But Mark likes double expressions; both Mt. 16.25 and Lk. 9.24 read it, and this suggests it lay in their copies of Mark for, while Matthew might have taken it from his other parallel in 10.39, Luke could not have taken it from his other parallel in 17.33. It should therefore be read.

72 On the use of εὐαγγέλιον in Mark see especially Marxsen, pp.79-85 and the literature quoted there. He holds that Mark introduced the word into the gospel tradition from Paul. See also G. Strecker, 'Literarische Überlegungen'; Martin, pp.24-28; R. Schnackenburg, 'Das Evangelium'.

73 At least from Wellhausen, ad loc., onwards.

74 P.85.

75 See the more detailed criticisms of Marxsen's view in Roloff, pp.215ff and Reploh, pp.133f.

76 Cf. Roloff, pp.217f.

77 See n.72; cf. W. Feneberg, Der Markusprolog, pp.146-9.

78 As we shall see shortly we have the somewhat parallel additions in 8.38 of 'my words' and in 9.7 of 'Hear him'.

79 See also Trocmé, p.159, n.1.

80 F. Neirynck, 'Duplicate Expressions in the Gospel of Mark'.

81 Whether Mark supplied the γάρ or not is uncertain. On his use of γάρ see C.H. Turner, JTS 26 (1925) 145-56; C.H. Bird, 'Some γάρ Clauses in St. Mark's Gospel'; M. Thrall, Greek Particles in the New Testament, pp.41ff; Pryke, pp.126ff.

82 On ψυχή see most recently G. Dautzenberg, pp.13-48; G. Bertram et alii, TDNT, IX, pp.608ff; R. Jewett, Paul's Anthropological Terms, pp.334ff.

83 Haenchen, p.298, supports this view with the argument that there were persecutions where the Christian was asked 'Are you a Christian?' and, if he answered 'Yes', was executed. Persecution for the name of Christ comes from a later period; the earliest possible allusion is 1 Pet. 4.14, and even here it probably does not have this reference, cf. Best, 1 Peter, (London, 1971), pp.37f.

84 σῴζειν and ἀπόλλυναι are regularly found in contrast in relation to the two classes into which men fall, the redeemed and the unredeemed (1 Cor. 1.18; 2 Cor. 2.15; cf. Jn 3.16f; 2 Th. 2.10; Jas 4.12; Jude 5). The contrast in our verse approximates much more to this than to a situation of persecution.

85 This interpretation of ψυχή which does not restrict it to martyrdom is confirmed by the setting of the variant in Mt. 10.39 in the context of broken family relationships (10.35) and of the preference for a member of the family rather than Christ (10.37). The Lukan setting (17.33) is eschatological and does not refer to persecution. In English the phrase 'save the soul' has often been wrongly interpreted of conversion; a person is said at that point to save his soul. The text is opposed to such an understanding: the person who sets out to save his eternal soul (and this is not what ψυχή means here) will actually lose it, for his act will be essentially an affirmation of his soul or being as important, and so he will lose his real being.

86 Note again the linking γάρ.

87 Bultmann, p.97, characterises them as 'secular proverbs'.

88 Luke substitutes the reflexive pronoun showing that he understands it in this way. On the Palestinian background to the saying, see Daube, pp.352ff.

89 Dautzenberg, p.75, argues that v.37 was originally

associated with 10.17-22 or 10.28-31. Our analysis of 10.17-31 (see pp.110ff) leaves little room for it; they must have been separated at a very early stage, if they were ever connected. Reploh, pp.135f, severely criticises the retention of a reference to riches in its present context.

90   Dautzenberg, pp.74f (cf. Lane, p.309; Pesch, II, p.63), traces vv.36f to Ps. 49.8f. Even if this was an original influence it is unlikely to have been picked up by Mark's readers for there is little resemblance in Mark to the LXX.

91   There is a detailed discussion of this verse and the underlying tradition in C.K. Barrett, 'I am not ashamed of the Gospel'.

92   The evidence for καί is not strong (P[45] W syr[s] cop[fay] arm); it probably arose through harmonisation of Mark and Luke.

93   P[45] vid W it[k] cop[sa] Tert.

94   Cf. Metzger's note and Barrett (as n.91), pp.32f.

95   Cf. also 2 Tim. 2.12; Rev. 3.5.

96   So A.J.B. Higgins, Jesus and the Son of Man, pp.57-60; Tödt, pp.40-48,55-60; M.D. Hooker, The Son of Man in Mark, pp.116-22; Hahn, pp.28-31.

97   Hahn, pp.307ff, argues that 'the Son' belongs to a different Christology from that under which Lk. 12.8 and Mk. 8.38 were shaped.

98   Cf. Horstmann, pp.46f.

99   Jn 1.20; 1 Jn 2.22f. It also carries more firmly the idea of confessing and denying in a public situation like a trial (Peter's denial took place in public and not in a 'church' context); if the second halves of the logia of Lk. 12.8,9 refer to heavenly trials then the first halves may refer to earthly (cf. Horstmann, pp.43f).

100   ἐπαισχύνεσθαι may be part of the missionary vocabulary of the Hellenistic churches (Rom. 1.16; 2 Tim. 1.8; etc.); cf. Fuller, p.138, n.75.

101   Best, 1 Peter, pp.37f and at 4.16. Horstmann, pp.43f, similarly argues that whereas Lk. 12.9 is structured in terms of the heavenly court Mark is interested in the earthly situation of the disciples; therefore the heavenly court imagery no longer dominates the logion.

102   It is found widely in this kind of connection: Rom. 1.16; 2 Tim. 1.8b; Ign., Smyrn. 10.2; Hermas, Sim. viii.6.4; ix. 14.6; 21.3. Pesch, II, p.64, points out that it is a more suitable verb to use with 'my words' than (ἀπ)αρνεῖσθαι which generally has a personal object.

103 Horstmann, pp.44f, regards this addition as Markan because of its use of OT type allusions and refers to Suhl, pp.81f. But this use of OT language is by no means exclusively Markan and the phrase could have been added at any period prior to him.

104 See pp.110f

105 Cf. Tödt, p.45, n.2; Reploh, pp.131,137; Horstmann, pp.43f. Hortsmann's further point that καί is epexegetical here as in 'and of the gospel' (v.35) is incorrect here as there. Also the use of the plural λόγους makes a difference in the interpretation of the two phrases.

106 Pace Hooker (as n.96), p.117, the positive side is not found in v.34. She is more probably correct when she says (p.118) in respect of its absence, 'following Jesus is therefore its own reward'. There seems no particular reason why, as Reploh suggests (p.137), the negative or threat form should be used alone because of the danger of martyrdom; the reward or promise form could equally well brace the martyr to endure.

107 For the history of the interpretation of this verse see M. Künze, Das Naherwartungslogion Markus 9,1 par.

108 The textual variants at this point indicate the difficulty interpreters have found with the verse. Did Jesus really believe the kingdom would come in the life-time of some of his disciples? Codex Vaticanus undoubtedly gives the correct reading.

109 γεύεσθαι θανάτου is not necessarily Semitic; it could be Hellenistic (cf. J. Behm, TDNT, I, pp.675-7); the verb is frequently used metaphorically of 'experiencing'. We see no reason for assuming that the phrase is Markan (so Ambrozic, pp.207f).

110 P.65.

111 Pp.47f.

112 ἔρχεσθαι is ocasionally used with 'kingdom' in the tradition, e.g. Mt. 6.10; Lk. 17.20; 22.18 and the first and third of these are probably very early. There is no need then to see a Markan addition here (cf. Ambrozic, pp.205f).

113 Perrin goes much too far in attributing 9.1 to Mark. He speaks of its 'distinctively Markan characteristics: the concept of "seeing" the parousia, and the use of "power" and "glory" in this connection', Rediscovering the Teaching of Jesus, p.199 (cf. pp.16-20, 199-201). But it is not the parousia which is seen here but the kingdom, and 'seeing the kingdom' is not a Markan phrase; 'seeing the parousia' (cf. 13.26; 14.62) is derived from Dan. 7.13f and is therefore not Markan; while glory (8-3-13-15) in association with the parousia also comes from Dan. 7.13f and 'power' is closely related to it. Almost every word of our verse belongs to the apocalyptic tradition of the primitive commun-

ity; there is nothing which betrays Mark's hand as its creator (cf. Ambrozic, pp.207f).

114 Whatever ἐληλυθυῖαν originally referred to it cannot refer in Mark to something which lies in the past of the ἑστηκότων; cf. Taylor's discussion and his references, ad loc.).

115 Whether, as Vielhauer, 'Gottesreich und Menschensohn in der Verkündigung Jesu', maintains, there was no original connection in thought between 'Son of man' (8.38) and 'kingdom of God' (9.1) is not important for us because they were associated in the primitive tradition. See the critical discussion in Tödt, pp.329-47.

116 The attempt to refer ἑστηκότων to Peter, James and John with the transfiguration in mind is too ingenious to be satisfying.

117 P.121. This view had been held earlier by A. Loisy, Marc, p.262 and C.G. Montefiore, The Synoptic Gospels, I, p.215.

118 Pp.57f.

119 Pp.97ff.

There are a large number of problems relating to the origin of the transfiguration account, e.g. its relation to the Feast of Tabernacles, its possible origin in a resurrection appearance. These have mostly been discussed in isolation from the place of the account in Mark; our concern is with the latter. We assume that Mark did not create the story though he may have revised it considerably /1/. Unlike other incidents reported in the Gospels we possess an independent account of the transfiguration in the N.T. at 2 Pet. 1.16-18 /2/ and there may be evidence to suggest that Matthew and Luke were aware of a non-Markan account which they used in addition to Mark's /3/.

Turning now to Mark's handling of the incident we reject the arguments of Schmithals /4/ that Mark received the pericope as a resurrection account and moved it to its present position /5/. The grounds also for viewing the 'six days' (9.2) as symbolic are insufficient /6/. This unusual temporal note must then refer to some other event /7/. There is no reason why we should not look for this event in the immediate context. If Mark had moved the incident from a position in which the 'six days' was relevant to one where it was not he would have been under no compulsion to retain the reference. Within the immediate context there are three possibilities, 8.27-30, 8.31-33, 8.34-9.1. Of these the last /8/ is a sequence of logia and a temporal datum would not follow it appropriately; the time reference implies a preceding incident. For a similar reason the transfiguration will not have been attached to 9.1, which, as we have seen /9/, Mark added to 8.34-38. In both 8.27-30 and 8.31-33 Peter is isolated for special attention, as he is in the transfiguration itself. If the latter followed 8.31-33 then it provided confirmation that the one who had to suffer was God's chosen son; but it would appear to fit better after 8.27-30 and serve as God's confirmation of Peter's confession. If this was the earlier position of the pericope Mark has altered it, probably by adding 8.31-33 /10/ and certainly 8.34-9.1. We shall return to the significance of their insertion.

If we move now to internal evidence of editing we accept the 'six days' in v.2 as pre-Markan. Since Peter is a part of the story we have to conclude that he alone, or all three disciples, was already mentioned in the introduction; it is possible that Mark replaced an earlier reference to Peter or to the disciples generally with the names of Peter, James and John for they are found linked together elsewhere in the Gospel (5.37; 14.33; cf. 1.16-20; 13.3) /11/. The 'high mountain' recurs as a 'holy mountain' in 2 Pet. 1.18 and is almost certainly pre-Markan; the symbolism of the 'mountain' was in general use to identify places of revelation. None of the words in v.2 is distinctively Markan apart from κατ' ἰδίαν μόνους; here we can detect his hand for: (1) he loves double expressions /12/; (ii) he uses κατ' ἰδίαν frequently in redactional passages (4.34; 6.31,32; 7.33; 9.28; 13.3); (iii) he regularly depicts Jesus isolating the disciples, or a group of them, for special teaching (4.10,34; 7.17,24; 8.10, etc.) and we have here such a separation of three disciples from the remainder and from the crowd (8.34) and they are given special instruction (9.7) and revelation. We conclude then that the pre-Markan tradition began 'After six days Jesus (taking Peter, James and John?) led the disciples (Peter?) up to a high mountain. And he was transfigured...'

Within the pericope we find a Markan motif in the fear of the disciples (v.6b) /13/. It does not link up easily with Peter's words in v.5, καλόν ἐστιν... /14/. ἔκφοβοι γὰρ ἐγένοντο is a typical short Markan explanatory clause utilising γάρ /15/; as he tends to insert these into existing material v.6a may be from the tradition. On the other hand we find almost exactly the same words used at 14.40; both there and here they are omitted by Matthew and Luke. Moreover the ignorance of the disciples is also a Markan theme /16/. Probably therefore the whole of v.6 is Markan /17/ though Mark probably has re-written an earlier and vaguer reference to the disciples or Peter as puzzled. The stupidity of Peter belonged to the tradition /18/ and there was perhaps also always something which implied the difference between Jesus on the one hand and Moses and Elijah on the other /19/.

In v.7 the first clause of the words of the divine voice is pre-Markan since it is also found in the independent tradition of 2 Pet. 1.17, but since the second clause ἀκούετε αὐτοῦ is not there it may be Markan. It is similar to other additions we have already traced to Mark, viz. 'and of the gospel' in 8.35 and 'and my words' in 8.38, and possibly also 'the word' in 9.10. The present phrase has similar import: the words of Jesus are to be obeyed /20/. The change in the words of the divine voice at the baptism from the second person to the third person has permitted the addition of our phrase. Its presence also accords with Mark's emphasis on 'hearing' (cf. 4.3a, ἀκούετε, which is missing in Matthew and Luke; 4.9 is a detached logion which he inserts there and at 4.23; cf. 7.16, if it is the correct reading), and corresponds to the continual failure of the disciples to understand, another Markan theme. Lastly it accords with the addition of the teaching Mark has inserted in 8.34-9.1; as we have seen he broke the direct connection between the transfiguration and Peter's confession; the disciples, and Mark's community, are thus to listen to the teaching of 8.34-9.1 with its demand for faithful discipleship.

Is the clause inspired by Deut. 18.15? If it is we should expect Mark to be influenced here by a Moses typology. Yet in v.4 we have the peculiar phrase 'Elijah with Moses' /21/. There are similar phrases at 4.10 and 8.34, in both of which Mark has edited the tradition. Since in 9.11-13 Mark takes up the figure of Elijah but makes no further use of Moses it is probable that he has brought forward Elijah's name from an original 'Moses and Elijah', which we find in v.5, to give it the position of stress in v.4 /22/. Verse 5 proves both names belonged to the tradition /23/. Whatever evidence there is for a Moses background to the transfiguration is much stronger in Matthew and Luke than in Mark /24/. There is no clear Moses typology elsewhere in Mark. The chance coincidence of two common words with two words of Deut. 18.15 cannot be held to overthrow this conclusion in respect of the transfiguration. Mark has perhaps unconsciously picked up Biblical language from Deut. 18.15.

But why do Moses and Elijah appear in the story at all? Many suggestions have been made to account for their presence /25/. Clearly there is a contrast between Jesus on the one hand and Moses and Elijah on the other; they come from heaven, he is on earth. Here as in the Apocalypse of Peter they are heavenly inhabitants setting the scene for the divine voice, though of course they may originally have played a different role.

If we now look back along the path we have come we can see that the position Mark has given to the transfiguration and the additions he has made to the account cohere to emphasise the same theme. In the tradition its purpose was christological - to confirm the confession made by Peter of Jesus' true identity. If man, that is Peter, has confessed Jesus as Messiah, God confesses Jesus as his son. Unlike the baptism the words are here addressed directly to the disciples and the second clause of 1.11, 'in you I am well-pleased' no longer appears /26/; this results in attention being concentrated on the title and the words that follow, 'hear him'. Material has been inserted between 8.30 (or 8.33) and the transfiguration and this material has to do with discipleship (8.34-9.1). Within the incident Mark has reinforced the attention given to the disciples, perhaps by adding the reference to Peter, James and John (9.2), certainly by introducing the fear of the disciples and emphasising their lack of understanding (9.6), and either by adding the words 'hear him' (v.7) or by stressing them through the omission of the second clause of the baptismal formula. These additions relate much more to discipleship than to christology. Mark has not neglected the original christological setting of the pericope in the tradition but has added another dimension - discipleship - and this in keeping with his whole train of thought in 8.27-10.45 /27/. He acts as a good pastor, not just content to supply his congregation with a more adequate christology but using this at the same time to exhort his readers to a truer discipleship. Christ, who was transfigured, has to be heard and obeyed; hearing and obedience do not lie in grandiose statements about his glory but in the acceptance of his call to deny self, take up the cross and go on his way (8.34ff.). Thus the transfiguration is given a new perspective. Fear and lack of understanding were a possible reaction before the mighty deeds of God in Christ, and these mighty deeds were not confined to Palestine in Jesus' time but took place in Mark's own community as in all the early communities; but the reaction of the true disciples is to be an obedience firmly governed by the cross. At the same time with the clause 'hear him' Mark indicates that the sayings of the earthly Jesus are also the sayings of the exalted Lord /28/ having behind them all the authority of revelation. God tells men to obey his son. This could not have been said at the baptism because at that stage Jesus' teaching had not been given.

Finally, inasmuch as Jesus is set out as the one whose words are to be obeyed, he is given a unique position vis-à-vis the disciples, one which is alien to the concept of discipleship as 'imitation'. Obedience entails the acceptance of what is in 8.34-9.1 and much more besides; this may include imitation but it cannot be exhausted by imitation. The emphasis here on obedience serves, then, to bring out a new facet of discipleship: to 'follow' means to 'obey'.

Notes

1   Some of these problems have been touched on in my paper 'The Markan Redaction of the Transfiguration' where fuller literary references will also be found. I am grateful to the editor of SE for permission to reproduce some of the material appearing there. To the literature referred to in it, add, H. Weihnacht, Die Menschwerdung des Sohnes Gottes im Markusevangelium, pp.53-60; Nützel; R.H. Stein, 'Is the Trans-

figuration (Mark 9:2-8) a Misplaced Resurrection-Account?'; Kelber, The Kingdom in Mark, pp.76ff.
2 See Best (as n.1); contrast Nützel, pp.3f.
3 See the contrasting conclusions of T. Schramm, Der Markus-Stoff bei Lukas, pp.136-9 and F. Neirynck, 'Minor Agreements Matthew-Luke in the Transfiguration Story'.
4 W. Schmithals, 'Der Markusschluss, die Verklärungs-geschichte und die Aussendung die Zwölf'.
5 See Best (as n.1) for detailed discussion.
6 Best (as n.1). Nützel, pp.228ff, gives insufficient support for his argument that Mark introduced the reference to the six days. Even if it is true that Mark created the chronology of the passion it does not follow that he introduced the six days at 9.2.
7 Two further explanations of the 'six days' need only be examined briefly. (a) T.J. Weeden, pp.118-124, argues that Mark pre-dated the transfiguration from an earlier position after the resurrection in order to attack the position of Peter, James and John. Originally it contained a theios aner tradition and validated their position. Its transference made it 'nothing more than an event in the public ministry of Jesus which these disciples were forbidden to pass on until the Son of Man was translated' (p.123). Thus 9.9 is not part of the secrecy motif but Mark's explanation why the Transfiguration was mistakenly taken to be a resurrection appearance; the disciples are forbidden to talk about it until after the resurrection. Apart from general criticisms of Weeden's position (infra, Part III, ch.31) his argument is inadequate here: he offers no stylistic evidence to indicate that it was Mark and not the early church which altered the position of the pericope; it is almost impossible to believe that Mark's readers could have picked up the interpretation he offers of 9.9; he practically assumes, without careful discussion, that the transfiguration was originally a resurrection appearance. (b) F.R. McCurley, '"And after Six Days"', explains 'after six days' as part of a Semitic literary device, of which there are some examples in the OT and many more in Ugaritic literature and in which after six days a climax comes on the seventh day. Particularly relevant to the transfiguration account is Exod. 24.16, where the cloud covers Mt Sinai for six days and on the seventh God speaks out of it. Originally the transfiguration described how the risen Jesus was overshadowed by a cloud for six days; on the seventh he re-appeared transfigured to the eyes of his disciples. Mark, however, connects the story to 8.27-9.1 so that it becomes the climax to Peter's confession: God announces that Jesus is his son. The evidence McCurley provides that the Semitic formula

was still alive in NT times is inadequate; even if it was the device would hardly have been appreciated by a Gentile readership in Rome. Why does not Mark make it clearer by an explicit reference to the seventh day as in Exod. 24.16? It is much more probable that, if the story originated as McCurley supposes, Mark was unaware of the seventh day significance when he transferred the story. McCurley's central point - the christological significance of the story - is easily seen to be true without his elaborate literary scheme, though Mark, as we shall see, has stressed the discipleship theme equally.

8   Lane, p.317, is one of the few who support this view.

9   Cf. p.31.

10   Pesch, II p.69, believes 9.2-13 followed 8.33 in the pre-Markan passion narrative.

11   Nützel, pp.91f, takes the names of the Three to be pre-Markan.

12   Cf. Neirynck.

13   Cf. 10.32; 9.32; 16.8b; 6.50; 4.41. On the 'fear' of the disciples see Tagawa, pp.99ff.

14   See C. Masson, 'La Transfiguration de Jésus'.

15   For Mark's use of γάρ see p.51 n.81.

16   E.g. 4.10-13; 6.52; 7.18; 8.17,21. Cf. Tagawa, pp.174ff, Minette de Tillesse, pp.174ff.

17   So Horstmann, pp.81-3; Nützel, pp.122ff. Nützel allows that the theme of the fear of the disciples may have been pre-Markan but not their ignorance.

18   See Best, 'Peter'.

19   Reploh, pp.112f, argues that the motif of fear is pre-Markan because it is essential to the story, for v.7 exists as an answer to it. But v.7 need only be an answer to the misunderstanding of Peter, which was more probably part of the tradition. Even if the 'fear' of the disciples was in the tradition Mark has re-written and intensified it as his characteristic wording shows.

20   In Biblical language 'to hear' is almost the same as 'to obey'.

21   Matthew and Luke replace it with the simpler and chronologically more correct, Moses and Elijah.

22   So Horstmann, pp.85-8; A. Feuillet, 'Les perspectives propres'.

23   For fuller discussion, see Best, as n.1. Nützel's attempt, pp.105f, 216ff to argue that Mark introduced Moses' name lacks supporting evidence from the rest of the Gospel which would indicate Mark's interest in Moses.

24   Best, as n.1.

25   Best, as n.1; cf. Nützel, pp.113ff.

26   It is found in Mt. 17.5 and 2 Pet. 1.17; it appears in some texts of Lk. 9.35 but is probably not original. Matthew wholly, and Luke partially, appear to have conformed what they found in Mark to their baptismal accounts.

27   Cf. Suhl, pp.108f.

28   Cf. Horstmann, p.96. The question whether it is the risen Jesus or the Jesus of the parousia whom Mark envisages as appearing in the transfiguration is probably an unreal question since Mark did not make the neat distinctions which we tend to make; see Best, as n.1.

Chapter 5
MARK 9.9-13

This is normally regarded as one section, but it may consist of two, vv.9f and vv.11-13; it is also not immediately clear whether vv.9f go more closely with vv.2-8 or with vv.11-13 /1/; and while vv.11-13 embodies a unit of pre-Markan tradition the whole of vv.9f may be Markan. We examine the latter first.

There are a number of clear Markan features in these verses /2/: (i) διαστέλλεσθαι is used redactionally by Mark in three other passages (5.43; 7.36; 8.15) in relation to secrecy /3/; (ii) πρὸς ἑαυτούς though appearing in the other evangelists is much more frequent in Mark /4/; (iii) συζητεῖν is a favourite word of Mark /5/; (iv) the somewhat clumsy and non-classical use of the genitive absolute at the beginning of v.9 is probably Markan, but is not necessarily so since the usage appears frequently in Hellenistic Greek /6/; (v) the absolute use of ὁ λόγος /7/ accords with Mark's use of 'my words' in 8.38 and 'the gospel' in 8.34; (vi) the command to silence is also a Markan motif. Yet the actual logion '...the Son of man rises from the dead' is probably not Markan; ἀνίστημι is used here of resurrection instead of the normal N.T. word ἐγείρειν; Mark uses both; it is difficult to determine his preference in relation to Jesus' resurrection for when each appears it does so in pre-Markan formulations (ἀνίστημι in 8.31; 9.31; 10.34; ἐγείρειν in 14.28; 16.6): if he was writing freely we should on the whole expect him to choose the word normally used by contemporary Christians. ἐκ νεκρῶν is unique in Mark in relation to the resurrection of Jesus but does occur frequently in other parts of the N.T. (Lk. 24.46; Jn. 20.9; Acts 17.3; Rom. 4.24; 6.4; etc.); if the logion is read in the light of 8.31 it seems an unnecessary addition /8/. We thus have a Markan framework for a traditional logion. The transfiguration account may have ended, 'And they (i.e. Peter, James and John; or possibly Peter alone) told nothing (to the other disciples) until after the resurrection from the dead of the Son of man'; Mark would then have adapted this to his secrecy motif.

Whatever the redaction two Markan themes appear together /9/: (i) the command to silence (v.9); (ii) the failure of the disciples to understand Jesus (v.10). This is the only place in which a temporal limitation is set to the period of silence. We cannot be sure that this limitation is Markan; it may have lain in the ending of the transfiguration story as Mark received it. Mark's community would draw from it the knowledge that the risen Lord and the exalted Lord who dwells in the heavenly regions with Moses and Elijah are one and the same.

The presence of Peter, James and John in the transfiguration account creates a division between them and the other disciples; this division appears again in the succeeding story where they rejoin the other disciples who in the meantime have failed to heal a sick boy /10/. Peter, James and John have access to knowledge from which the others are excluded. They had the same access at the healing of Jairus's daughter (5.43), and the knowledge on both occasions relates to resurrection. But if the three have this access, so have all Mark's readers; there can be no suggestion of an inner elite among them; if ever such existed it is now abolished.

It is generally agreed that vv.11-13 contain a unit of tradition which Mark has modified by at least the addition of the two Scriptural allusions in vv.12b, 13b. Verse 12b hangs so clumsily in the structure of the pericope that it has been regarded as a gloss from Mt. 17.12b /11/, but since it is introduced by Mark's favourite γέγραπται it is much more likely to have been added by him /12/. The insertion of the two scriptural allusions serves to qualify the assertion of the scribes that Elijah (a) comes before the End and (b) restores all things (though ἀποκαθιστάνει appears on Jesus' lips in Mark in the tradition it was probably part of the objection of the scribes; the original pericope reflected controversy with Jews about Jesus as Messiah). In Mark's Gospel, apart from 12.28-34, the scribes are always presented as critical of Jesus /13/; his teaching is contrasted with theirs (1.22); he controverts their teaching (2.16; 7.5), twice as here by quoting Scripture (11.27; 12.35). Mark then answers the scribal objection of v.11 by saying that Elijah has come as John the Baptizer but that he has not restored all things, for if he had the Son of man would not have suffered (v.12). The suffering of John and of Jesus go together; John's is a minor passion (1.14; 6.14-29) foreshadowing what was to happen to Jesus; what was to happen was itself foretold in scripture (v.13) /14/. In part then the scribes are correct - in relating John (Elijah) and the Messiah - and in part wrong - because they fail to understand the significance of suffering for John and the Messiah, and, by implication, for the disciples of the Messiah, Mark's community.

What we have in vv.11-13 is then another reminder that the way of Jesus the beloved son of God (9.7) is one of suffering; on this occasion this idea has been tied to the transfiguration through the common use of 'Elijah'. In the transfiguration Peter's question suggested that a permanent position of 'glory' had already been reached (the three 'tents'); this cannot yet be, for the suffering of Jesus is still to come, and by implication suffering for the disciples must continue; there is no escape into an immediate state of glory. Equally if the 'tents' refer to the idea of God dwelling with his people (Lev. 23.42f) and Peter (or Mark's church) is viewed as thinking this has already come to pass, then this is not so; much has yet to be suffered before God is fully and completely with his people; the church is still a suffering and not a triumphant body. Triumph and exaltation lie in the future; yet something of what they mean ('restoration', ἀποκαθιστάνει) is seen in the transfiguration.

At this point and from another angle we can see again the central importance for Mark of 8.34-9.1. If, as we have argued, 8.27-30 or 8.27-33 had been united with 9.2-8(13?) in the preceding tradition Mark has created one of his 'sandwiches' by introducing 8.31-9.1 or 8.34-9.1 as its 'filling' with the intention that the latter passage should be seen in the light of both 8.27-30 and 9.2-8: discipleship is 'under the cross' and the sayings of Jesus which teach its nature have the authority of sayings of the exalted Lord /15/.

Notes

1 Cf. Wellhausen, ad loc.
2 Cf. Nützel, pp.158f.
3 1-4-0-0.
4 0-7-2-2. We find it at Mark 1.27; 9.10; 10.26; 11.31; 12.7; 14.4; 16.3. See C.H. Turner, JTS 29 (1928) 280f.
5 0-6-2-0.
6 Cf. N. Turner, pp.322f.
7 It does not refer here to the gospel as in 2.1; 4.14ff.; 4.33; 8.32, but means 'the saying' as in 10.22; 14.39.
8 Indeed its presence in 9.10 has misled some commentators (e.g. Grundmann) into thinking that 9.9f refers to the general resurrection rather than to the resurrection of Christ.
9 Cf. Horstmann, pp.128f.
10 Reploh, p.112, overlooks this in arguing that in vv.9f Mark has in mind all the disciples and not the three alone.
11 So Bultmann, p.125. Others have attempted to re-arrange the order of the clauses in vv.12f (e.g. F.C. Grant, The Earliest Gospel, p.101, following Torrey) or regarded it as a post-Markan but pre-Matthean gloss (e.g. Strecker, 'The Passion and Resurrection Predictions in Mark's Gospel', n.32). It contains a

pre-Markan formula either derived from those of 8.31 etc. or, more probably, developed independently in the primitive community (cf. Lk. 17.25; cf. Tödt, pp.169,196). If 9.12b has been formed out of 8.31 (cf. Suhl, pp.123-32) then it is certainly not part of the tradition received by Mark. On the variant readings caused by the difficulties of the expression, see O. Linton, 'Evidences for a Second-Century Revised Edition of St. Mark's Gospel'.

12   Cf. Nützel, pp.256ff; Hahn, p.369. Hahn does not however think v.13b comes from Mark; but v.13 pre-supposes v.12b (cf. Reploh, p.117); they are linked by the use in both of ἐπί meaning 'with reference to'. Doudna, pp.31f picks this out as a Markan peculiarity saying it is without parallel in Attic Greek and the papyri. Mark uses γέγραπται to introduce formal references to Scripture (cf. 1.2; 7.6; 11.17; 14.21,27).

13   Cf. Cook, pp.77ff.

14   It is not clear to what passage or passages Mark alludes.

15   R. Lafontaine et P.M. Beernaert, 'Essai sur la structure du Marc 8.27-9.13', discover a closely balanced structure in this passage:

$$A. 8.27-28$$
$$B. 8.29-30$$
$$C. 8.31-33$$
$$D. 8.34-9.1$$
$$C^1.9.2-6$$
$$B^1.9.7-10$$
$$A^1.9.11-13$$

Undoubtedly balancing parallels exist between some of these sections in language, content, etc.; this is natural since Mark has put them together to develop a double theme: who Jesus is; what the nature of the Christian life is. But there are parallels which fail, e.g. 'elders and high priests and scribes' in 8.31 is not balanced by 'scribes' in 9.11; there is no parallel to 'one of the prophets' (8.28) in 9.11-13; Moses appears in 9.2-6 but not in 8.31-33. To obtain the supposed structure normal units have to be broken up (8.27-30; 9.2-8). D is the centre of the passage and of it vv.36f are the centre; but are vv.36f the centre of the thought? Verses 34,35 give much more of the essential content of discipleship. Finally it does not appear that this structural analysis adds anything to our understanding of the passage; much the same conclusions are reached as to Mark's message in the passage when we dispense with the use of the structural analysis.

Chapter 6
MARK 9.14-29

In this section it is extremely difficult to disentangle the redaction from the tradition /1/. Some scholars assume that two distinct incidents have been amalgamated /2/; others assume that either the inability of the disciples to heal /3/ or the discussion with the father /4/ was the basic incident and that this gradually gathered accretions. Schenk /5/ finds a basic exorcism by Jesus to which have been added the references to the failure of the disciples and the faith of the father. There are those who see in the vivid imagery of the pericope a guarantee of the originality of the whole /6/. Opinions also vary in relation to the stages at which the basic story, whatever it be, received the various additions which have given it its present form.

Verses 28f are Markan. Healing stories and exorcisms normally end with a reference to the amazement or praise of the spectators (cf. Lk. 9.43) /7/; instead of that we have here an ending which is full of Markan motifs, stylistic characteristics and vocabulary: retiral to a house /8/; κατ'ἰδίαν /9/; εἰσελθόντος...εἰς, where repetition of the preposition is Markan /10/; ἐπερωτᾶν /11/. The introduction, vv.14f, while not entirely Markan, has probably been re-written by him /12/. Caesarea Philippi (8.27) is the immediate context; this is an improbable area for scribes or for a crowd aware of Jesus' healing ability. Kertelge /13/ takes vv.16-19 also to be Markan, but provides no real evidence; it is true that the description of the illness in these verses may have been drawn from vv.20-27 but that does not prove that Mark transferred it (and equally the description may have been transferred from vv.16-19 to vv.20-27). The failure of the disciples in these verses, while it is in harmony with the Markan theme of their blindness and misunderstanding, is not quite the same; it is a failure to act rather than a failure to appreciate who Jesus is and what he demands from them in suffering. If Mark had written these verses he would have made them cohere more closely with his theme. Moreover there are no other sections, except the summaries, in which Mark can be said to have written so large a portion of material. If we set aside the description of the illness, which by its very nature can hardly be proved to be Markan or non-Markan since the words in it are of rare

66

occurrence and since some description of the illness is necessary to the story, there still remain some Markanisms, but no very distinctive ones (and any passage which Mark incorporates will necessarily contain some signs of his hand); there are also non-Markanisms. Mark prefers δύνασθαι (33 times) to ἰσχύειν (4 times); the latter never appears in redactional passages (2.17; 5.4; 9.18; 14.37) while the former does (1.45; 6.5; 7.24; 9.28) and it is used of the inability to heal in the strikingly similar passage 6.5 (cf. 1.40; 3.23; 9.28). References to the 'generation' are a feature of Q rather than of Mark; Mark regularly rebukes disciples and scribes but rarely the crowd (which would correspond to the 'generation'). Both these non-Markanisms come at a vital point in the story and it therefore looks as if the inability to heal is pre-Markan. In the present form of the story the rebuke 'faithless generation' is pointless /14/; it is the disciples who have failed and should be upbraided /15/ but this is neither an appropriate manner of address for them nor is it the way in which Mark normally shows them as rebuked by Jesus. Probably therefore in an earlier form of the story it was some other group which was described as failing; the survival in v.14 of 'the scribes' /16/ who play no further part in the story /17/ taken together with the known fact that the Rabbis practised exorcism suggests that they formed that group. But did Mark make this alteration or had it already taken place before him? It is difficult to determine; whichever be true, Mark has emphasised the disciples in re-writing the introduction (v.14) and in providing a new conclusion (vv.28f). Thus Mark has directed his readers' attention to the disciples and their failure, but not so much to stress that failure in and of itself but to show how exorcisms are to be carried out, viz. by prayer (v.29). In 3.15; 6.7 the Twelve are given a commission to exorcise (6.15 shows it included healing in general). This is now followed up (9.14-29) with instruction in how they are to exercise this ministry /18/. It is also relevant to Mark's community for the NT indicates that Christians were active in healing the sick (1 Cor. 12.9,28; Rom. 15.19; 2 Cor. 12.12; Jas 5.14f; Acts 3.1ff; 9.36ff; 16.18; etc.).

We turn now to the other section of the pericope, viz. the discussion between Jesus and the father about faith; this has been regarded as secondary by those who take the first part as original. It is missing in Matthew and Luke; if they had access to another strand of the tradition which did not contain it, this would account for their agreement in omission, and also imply that it was not part of the earliest tradition /19/. Some of the vocabulary may be Markan but it is equally the vocabulary of the early church /20/. These verses may then have been a separate fragment which Mark added here, or they may have been added at an earlier stage. If Mark added them, it is difficult to see his reason, for they do not cohere with the stress on the disciples which he elsewhere introduces into the pericope. Vv.14-19 and vv.28f point to the failure of the disciples as 'healers' whereas in vv.22b,23 the failure, if there is one, is on the part of the father as suppliant for healing /21/. The very mention of faith is surprising since elsewhere the exorcisms in the Gospels are depicted as struggles between Jesus and the demonic world; faith does appear in other types of healing (2.5; 5.34; 10.52). The exorcism is thus being submerged here by other material; it is difficult to see Mark doing this in view of his interest in exorcism. We note also that in the final lesson to the disciples (vv.28f) they are not told to have more faith but to pray. We conclude then that vv.22b,23 are pre-Markan, occasioned perhaps by the use in v.19 of ἄπιστος, which (v.19) we saw was itself pre-Markan. The remainder of vv.20-27 describe the nature of the illness and the cure, repeating in part the description from vv.16-19. While Mark may have partly re-written these verses he has not done so to the extent of introducing his exorcism motif (the recognition of Jesus' true nature by the demons - 1.24;3.11f; 5.7) so we can accept it as largely pre-Markan.

Many commentators consider that the present situation of the pericope is related to the transfiguration /22/. If the pericope, as is most probable, had no important position in an earlier collection /23/, then its present position is due to Mark, but he does not relate it to the transfiguration. For: (i) vv.9-13 intervene between the transfiguration and this incident /24/; (ii) even if we read the singular ἐλθὼν ... εἶδεν /25/ instead of the plural in v.14 there is no mention of the 'mountain', i.e. no attempt to link the incidents, as Luke (9.37) may be attempting to do by introducing the 'mountain'; (iii) there is no suggestion that Jesus arrives in v.14 with 'shining' or 'transfigured' face as Moses did (Exod. 34.29f /26/; this passage is not necessarily important for the transfiguration itself /27/). Mark has given the pericope its present position because for him its meaning is the instruction of the disciples /28/, one of the two major themes of 8.27-10.45 /29/. Possibly its position within this larger complex was governed by the need to have a temporary separation between Jesus and at least some of the disciples so that their inadequacy might be shown up, and the trans-figuration was the only incident which offered the opportunity.

If then this pericope is oriented towards the instruction of the disciples in exorcism, and probably in all healing activity /30/ since exorcism as such is not expressly emphasised, this instruction does not take the form 'Exorcise as Jesus did (does)', i.e. it is not a passage teaching imitation of Christ. In order to exorcise the disciples are taught to pray /31/, but in Mark's Gospel, unlike Luke's, Jesus is not continually depicted as a man of prayer, and neither in the present passage nor elsewhere does he exorcise by prayer but by authority. The pericope is thus made to fit the post-Easter situation of believers; if they are to perform mighty deeds they must learn dependence on God through prayer. It is not enough to receive a commission to exorcise (3.15; 6.7); the commission cannot be carried out in the believer's own strength.

If Jesus is not set out here as the pattern for disciples /32/, still less is the father in his attitude of 'faith' /33/. For they are summoned to prayer and not to faith, which is not to say that faith and prayer are unrelated (cf. 11.22-5), and he is a member of the 'crowd' /34/ and not of the church. His simultaneous possession of faith and his need of it represent the attitude of those who would become disciples, who wish to experience in themselves the saving power of Christ /35/; indeed the father's faith in v.24 is linked so lightly to the need for the healing of his child that its understanding as 'saving faith' stands out.

Notes
1   This pericope has been discussed in detail most recently by Kertelge, pp.174-9; Roloff, pp.143-152; W. Schenk, 'Tradition und Redaktion in der Epiliptiker-Perikope, Mk 9.14-29'; P.J. Achtemeier, 'Miracles and the Historical Jesus in Mark 9:14-29'; all of these survey earlier writing on the pericope. See also Reploh, pp.211-221; Tagawa, pp.105-7; H.J. Held, 'Matthew as Interpreter of the Miracle Stories'.
2   E.g. Bultmann, pp.211f. Haenchen, p.318, n.1, and Achtemeier (as n.1), believe their union to be pre-Markan. Taylor supposes that two stories about the same original incident have been combined. On the grounds that it must have been carried through at a written stage of the material Koch, pp.114ff, believes Mark must have combined the two accounts.
3   E.g. Roloff, pp.143-152.
4   E.g. Kertelge, pp.174-179, following J. Sundwall, pp.58ff.
5   See n.1. That much has happened to the story in the course of transmission can be accepted, but all of it can hardly be attributed to Mark as Schenk urges, for nowhere else does Mark

so radically transform an incident. There is much more non-Markan material than Schenk allows. Schenke, pp.314ff, sees vv.19,23f as Markan additions.

6   E.g. Taylor, ad loc., Schmidt, p.227.

7   If Luke and Matthew, who have a number of agreements against Mark, had access not only to Mark but to another strand of tradition this may have been its conclusion and there would probably have been a parallel conclusion in the tradition Mark used. Achtemeier (see n.1 above), argues against the view that Matthew and Luke used a separate account as well as that in Mark.

8   See Part III, ch.28.

9   See p.56.

10   E.g. 1.16,21,42; 2.1; 3.1.

11   8-25-17-2. For fuller details of Markanisms cf. Schenk (as n.1), p.78; Minette de Tillesse, pp.237ff; Reploh, pp.212-6, Koch, pp.120f.

12   Cf. Schenk (as n.1), pp.81-3; Achtemeier (see n.1 above). Nützel, pp.160f, sees an allusion in v.15a to Ex. 34.29-35, but the connection is too slight. Koch, pp.119f, takes 9.14-16 as Markan. Curiously Schenke, pp.314ff, assumes the greater part of 9.14-16, 28-9 to be pre-Markan.

13   Pp.176f.

14   See Lohmeyer, ad loc. Nineham writes here of Jesus 'as an incarnate deity whose human form and earthly existence are only temporary and who already has one foot in the next world' (p.243). This may be true of an earlier stage of the tradition but it does not represent Mark's christology and conflicts with the attention he gives to the instruction of the disciples.

15   Trocmé, pp.112f, suggests that our story indicates the existence of a group of Christians among whom healing was rare. 9.28f would rather imply that their methods were inadequate.

16   In view of Mark's implied geographical siting of the incident it is surprising that they are present at all. Cook, p.65, n.26, takes their presence as Markan because of their un-suitability to the context.

17   The variant which refers to them in v.16 should be rejected; it is not well supported.

18   Cf. Meye, p.112; Schenke, pp.343-5.

19   Cf. Roloff, p.147, especially n.144. Held (as n.1), pp.189ff, believes that Mark himself added the conversation with the father in order to show Jesus as instructing his disciples about the source of miracle working power; if so Mark has done it most clumsily since here he writes about faith and in vv.28f

about prayer, and here it is a question of the faith of the recipient of healing whereas in vv.28f it is the prayer of the healers.

20 E.g: δυνατός, δύνασθαι, πιστεύειν.

21 The father's faith apparently takes the place of that of the sick person; cf. 2.1-12; 5.21-23, 35-43; 7.24-30.

22 'It seems, in fact, not improbable that, here as elsewhere, the arrangement of the episodes is due to Mk., who attached this story to that of the Transfiguration because it presupposed, in the form in which it came to him, an absence of Jesus from the disciples, such as the Transfiguration setting provided for it. On this view the dramatic contrast, immortalized by the art of Raphael, between the ideal beauty of the holy vision granted to the three disciples upon the mountain, and the piteous spectacle below of the epileptic boy and the disputing crowd, is due in the first instance to our evangelist' (A.E.J. Rawlinson, St Mark, p.123); cf. Nineham, Schniewind, Bundy, G. Dehn, Der Gottessohn, pp.179ff, and most recently G. Bornkamm, 'Πνεῦμα ἄλαλον', pp.21-36 (cf. Koch, pp.114ff); he instances: (i) the sudden manifestation of Jesus in v.15 which accords with the previous epiphany of the transfiguration (but see n.27); (ii) epilepsy is the 'divine sickness' (but Mark nowhere identifies the illness as epilepsy and, since he composed vv.28f, must be regarded as viewing it as demonic possession); (iii) in his epiphany Jesus contends with Satan (but the 'demonic' element of the exorcism is not stressed and in any case Bornkamm makes the association with Satan through 'epilepsy'); (iv) the dispute of 9.14-16 picks up that of 9.10; and (v) the 'hear him' of 9.7 balances the normal silencing of demons (these last two points are rather vague). Bornkamm is strongly criticised by Schenke, pp.341ff.

23 It may either have existed as an isolated pericope or as one of a series of healing pericopae.

24 Bornkamm, (as n.22), p.23, considers that because 9.9-13 is Markan therefore Mark has joined 9.14-29 to the trans-figuration. If Mark wished this union he could have made it much clearer in the intervening verses.

25 A C D θ minusc. plurimi it vg sy[s] [pe] bo. Achtemeier (see n.1) suggests that the singular may represent the original introduction to the story; if so it would not have followed the transfiguration.

26 So Schniewind. Many commentators allude to Exod. 34.29f without concluding that Jesus' face shone like Moses's, e.g. Grundmann.

27 The astonishment of the crowd is a Markan motif but it

appears usually at the end of an incident and not at the beginning as here. In v.15 it probably relates not to Jesus' physical appearance but to his sudden manifestation (cf. Roloff, p.146; Taylor). Bornkamm (as n.22), pp.26f, stresses this manifestation as an epiphany and thereby relates our incident to the transfiguration; but the appearance belonged to the pre-Markan tradition and Mark in his re-writing of this section has not stressed it; if in the pre-Markan material Jesus had been presented as 'divine man' then it would have been appropriate.

28 This has been generally recognised since Held (as n.1), pp.187f. Bornkamm (as n.22), p.22, considers it appropriate because it deals with 'faith' (cf. vv.9,18,23f,28f).

29 There is no link to the other major theme, christology; the insertion of a confession in the exorcism (cf. 1.24; 3.11f; 5.8) could easily have been used to show Jesus as son of God, the title given to him in the transfiguration. Some commentators (e.g. Taylor) have difficulty in seeing why Mark has located the incident at this point because, while they doubt the reality of the connection to the transfiguration, they do not recognise the importance of the theme of discipleship in 8.27-10.45.

30 The pericope has features both of a healing and of an exorcism; normal in a healing but unusual in an exorcism are the reference to the need for faith and the absence of a confession on the part of the demon; the description of the demon's area of control, 'a dumb and deaf spirit', reads more like that of a physical illness in healing which Jesus restores human faculties which have been lost (e.g. 7.31-37; 8.22-26; 2.1-12). In particular τοῦτο τὸ γένος should not be understood restrictively as if it were only some special kind of demons which required exorcism with prayer.

31 The variant reading which adds 'and fasting' in v.29 is certainly to be rejected. The evidence supporting it, though widespread, represents the conforming of the text to later current church practice.

32 Lohmeyer's attempt to depict Jesus as the 'true believer' and thus as an example to the disciples goes far beyond the possibilities in the story.

33 Contrast Kertelge, pp.177f, Schweizer, Schniewind, etc.

34 See pp.28f.

35 There is a distinction between the faith which moves mountains and the faith which is the believing response to God's acts.

Chapter 7
MARK 9.30-32

The section 8.27-10.45 is divided by the three predictions of the passion; each introduces the same theme but is thereafter developed differently. Thus after the second prediction (9.31) we find the theme of discipleship expressed in relation to problems that did not appear in 8.34-9.29.

The kernel of the short section, 9.30-32, is the passion prediction of v.31. We have already suggested that Mark found this as an isolated logion and did not formulate it from either 8.31 or 10.33f /1/. He has fitted it into his structure by giving it a position in Jesus' journey (v.30) and relating it to two of his motifs, viz. the ignorance of the disciples (v.32) and their private instruction /2/. The journey of Jesus to fulfil his prediction is taken a stage further with Jesus returning back into Galilee from Caesarea Philippi /3/; the two verbs of motion, ἐξέλθοντες, παραπορεύοντο, emphasise the fact of the journey as does διά with Galilee: Jesus no longer stays in Galilee as he did in the earlier chapters of Mark; he is on his way through it to the cross. At 9.33 he reaches Capernaum and by 10.1 is in Judea itself. But though Jesus is back in Galilee it is not to seek the crowds; he wants to escape attention (v.30b) /4/ so that (γάρ, v.31) he may instruct his disciples more about himself and themselves. As ever they fail to understand what the cross means and are frightened: the combination of these two ideas implies that their failure to understand is only partial: they understand enough to be afraid to ask to understand more. This is how Mark sees his readers: aware of the depths of the demands Jesus is making on them but unwilling to find out what those depths really are because they realise what the consequences of understanding might be for themselves.

In the section which follows, 9.33-10.30, Mark uses a number of units from the tradition; some of these may have been joined together previously but there was no intrinsic or extrinsic connection between any of them and 9.31: nothing in what follows refers to being handed over, being killed or rising again, whereas in the previous section 8.34 with its reference to the cross points back easily to 8.31. Yet 9.33-10.30 is taken up entirely with teaching about the nature of discipleship to disciples, or those who might become disciples; 10.1-12 is the sole passage which may not deal with discipleship /5/. Thus

73

once again discipleship is viewed from the perspective of the cross; if Jesus died and rose what does this require from a disciple? It would be wrong to assert that the basic insight which connects discipleship and the cross was Mark's but the particular exposition which follows is. It is now necessary to examine the individual pericopae.

Notes

1 See Ch.4(b).

2 The vocabulary of vv.30-32, apart from the logion, is also Markan: παραπορεύεσθαι (1-4-0-0); ἐπερωτᾶν (8-25-17-2); καὶ ἔλεγεν αυτοῖς (cf. Kuhn, pp.130f); we note also the use of the imperfect of διδάσκειν and of ὅτι recitativum (cf. C.H. Turner, JTS 28 (1926/7) 9-18); Galilee normally appears in editorial sections (cf. Lohmeyer, Galiläa und Jerusalem, p.26, n.2). ῥῆμα (5-2-19-12) is the only non-Markan word. On the Markan redaction see Reploh, pp.104-7; W.G. Thompson, Matthew's Advice to a Divided Community: Mt. 17.22-18.35, pp.40-2.

3 The precise reference of κἀκεῖθεν ἐξέλθοντες is not clear; does it refer back only to the preceding pericope or to the transfiguration or right back to the last geographical reference at 8.27? Probably it is no more than a device to make Jesus appear to be moving again on his journey. The similar phrase at 6.1 (cf. 10.1) is equally indeterminate.

4 This Markan motif re-appears in John (7.10) as do many Markan ideas.

5 But see pp.100f where its suitability to the theme of discipleship is indicated.

Chapter 8
MARK 9.33-50

There are good reasons for supposing that most of this section came to Mark in the tradition as a unit /1/: (i) It is held together, not by any logical development of thought but by catch-words /2/; their use is typical of oral speech rather than of written material. Kuhn /3/ points out that Mark himself uses catch-words to unite material, e.g. τελώνιον–τελῶναι in 2.14 and 2.15-17; the other examples he offers are of similar brief passages, none of them nearly as complex as 9.33-50; some of them can be challenged in respect of alleged Markan redaction /4/; in others, as in that quoted, content rather than verbal catch-word suggested the union. Kuhn also acknowledges that catch-words were in use in the pre-Markan material; σπείρειν and cognates were the link in the original collection of parables in chap.4 (vv.3-9,26-29,31-32) /5/. (ii) There are good grounds for seeing in vv.38,39,42,45,48 an Aramaic substratum which existed as a unit /6/. (iii) If Mark did bring together the sayings in this sequence it is difficult to see his purpose; vv.49,50a, while they relate to discipleship, have clearly no relevance to the dispute about greatness in v.34, though of course the final clause of v.50 is relevant; equally it is difficult to see why Mark should have introduced vv.42-47. There is consequently no satisfactory redactional justification for the view that Mark brought the various elements together /7/. It is much more probable that we have here an instance of Mark's tendency to use a sequence of sayings, whose beginning related to his subject even if its end did not. (εἰρηνεύετε ἐν ἀλλήλοις may have been a concluding addition by Mark to attempt to remove this anomaly, or if it was already present it may have given him additional reason to use the whole existing complex of sayings /8/). While arguing in this way we must also allow for some Markan redaction. It is probable that he has supplied vv.33f and possible that he has inserted an incident (vv.38-40) as distinct from logia and made other slight modifications /9/. We must now examine his redaction /10/.

The sequence has a twofold introduction, viz. vv.33f and v.35a. In v.33 Jesus goes into a house and begins a discussion with his disciples (αὐτοὺς v.34, refers back to 'disciples' in v.31); in v.35 he sits down, summons the Twelve and begins to teach. Are the disciples identical with the Twelve or are they a

Following Jesus: Discipleship in Mark

larger or smaller group? The difficulty created by these two
sets of people makes it reasonably certain that Mark did not
compose both vv.33f and v.35a, though he may have worked
over both if they have an origin in the tradition; he has either
written only one or taken both from the tradition. There are
clear signs of his hand in vv.33f /11/: the reference to
Capernaum is part of the artificial geography of the journey to
Jerusalem /12/, the house motif is Markan, 'on the way'
develops his journey motif. If v.33 is Markan then that part of
v.34 which refers back to it will be also, i.e. the references to
the silence of the disciples and to their discussion. V.35a has at
least one non-Markan feature, the use of φωνεῖν where Mark
prefers προσκαλεῖσθαι. If we were to omit v.35 there is no easy
movement from the question in v.34, 'Who is greatest?', to the
reception of the child in vv.36f. Jesus is not saying in vv.36f
that a child is as important as a disciple and therefore that
greatness is unimportant, i.e. the disciple should behave as a
child /13/. If Mk 10.15 came here (and many commentators
think it would be more suitable than at 9.37) then this could be
the sense; unfortunately for this argument it does not. So we
conclude that vv.33f are Markan whereas v.35a is from the
tradition /14/.

Mark probably introduced vv.33f to heighten the dramatic
irony: it is 'on the way' to the passion that the disciples are
made to ask 'Who is the greatest?'. Certainly Mark knew of a
controversy about greatness for he uses it at 10.35ff. Making
use of that knowledge he relates the controversy, there as here,
to the cross, and here also, of course, to the child incident. In
Matthew the disciples come straightforwardly to Jesus and put
the question about greatness; this is necessary because the link
to the passion has been broken by the insertion of 17.24-27. In
Luke the disciples discuss the question among themselves but
Jesus knows what is going on in their minds and provides an
answer. Thus both Matthew and Luke have entirely re-written
the Markan introduction.

Setting aside temporarily the dispute about greatness let us
look at the logion of v.35. It appears elsewhere in variant forms
(Mt. 20.26f; 23.11; Mk 10.43f; Lk. 9.48c; 22.26; cf also Mk 10.31;
Mt. 20.16; Lk. 13.30) and is therefore not a Markan creation.
Has then Mark introduced it here /15/?. He could have received
it as a detached logion; he regularly joins material with καί and
the motif of separating a group to receive special instruction is
his. On the other hand he received v.35a in the tradition and it
must have introduced some saying, or set of sayings. It is
easier, therefore, to conclude that Mark did not add in the

logion at this point but took up in v.35 a section of tradition in which the Twelve were instructed and which began with the logion of v.35 /16/.

Was the reference to greatness implicit in this logion and did Mark make it explicit by introducing vv.33f ending in the question about greatness or was it explicit in whatever introduction preceded it in the tradition? The former seems more probable for it is difficult to see how a reference ('and Jesus spoke about greatness'?) could have been present in v.35a which Mark would not have retained and the movement from 'greatness' to the thought of vv.36f is by no means clear /17/. The theme was not then explicit in the tradition /18/.

Looking back over the way we have come we can see that Mark created a deliberate connection between the passion prediction and the desire for greatness among the disciples (the Twelve). Their fear and lack of understanding leads directly to their discussion concerning the greatest among them and to Jesus' answer. If earlier we moved from the passion of Jesus (8.31) to the possible suffering of disciples and their self-denial (8.34) now we move to their need for service - for 'servant of all' interprets the logion about who is first and who is last. Matthew qualifies both the question 'Who is greatest?' and its answer with the addition 'in the Kingdom of heaven' (18.1,4) and consequently the dispute can be understood to relate to the status of the disciples in the future New Age; in this way its sting is partially removed. In Mark, however, it relates to the present age and therefore must be viewed as applying to his community: the cross faces the believer with a challenge to his self-importance as much as it warns him about martyrdom.

Has Mark been led to relate 'greatness' to the cross through a power struggle within his own community which has involved the 'officers'? This may be so if the Twelve (v.35) is understood to indicate the 'officers' (officials, leaders, ministers, or whatever they were called if there were names at all for their position) as distinct from the community as a whole. Assuming for the moment that the Twelve do represent 'officers' there is no suggestion that one of them, or one particular official in Mark's community, is demanding primacy; the lesson is for all the Twelve, or all the 'officials'. There is no suggestion either of any contrast between the Twelve and the rest of the disciples as if Mark was attempting either to teach 'officers' that they must not arrogate 'greatness' to themselves over against the community or to attack the status of the historical Twelve as upheld by some members of his community. The power struggle is within the group, whether the 'officers' of

Mark's day or the historical Twelve /19/. If however we do not assume a distinction between the Twelve, as representing the 'officers' of Mark's community, and the community as a whole but regard the Twelve as representatives of the whole community then the teaching is more general. Grundmann /20/ points out that 'rank' featured prominently in the Qumran community and that there were Rabbinic disputes about greatness, but it would be wrong to imagine that our passage was compiled with Qumran leaders or Rabbinic scholars in mind. The real background is human nature in general, of which those were particular examples. In any active organisation, and the church was such in Mark's day, there are many who desire to be 'first'; Mark's teaching deals with this general human sin /21/.

The sequence of thought from v.35 to vv.36f would appear to be: the true follower of Jesus is servant of all; 'all' includes children, the least likely to receive attention /22/; attention given to them is the same as attention given to Christ, and so the same as given to God. Before we justify this interpretation we need to examine these verses for signs of Markan redaction. There is nothing which really betrays his hand in v.37 but in v.36 we have the very rare word ἐναγκαλίζεσθαι which appears also at 10.16 /23/. This has led Reploh /24/ to conjecture that Mark composed the whole of v.36, the impulse to do so coming from 10.13-16. In confirmation he points also to the sudden appearance of the child, unprepared for in v.35, and the clumsiness of ἓν τῶν τοιούτων παιδίων in v.37 /25/. If, however, we remove v.36 the relation of v.35 to v.37 is even more difficult and the phrase is left hanging without reference; we are forced to assume that v.37 began ὃς ἂν παιδίον δέξηται.. It would seem more probable that Mark, who likes vivid concrete detail /26/, has inserted καὶ ἐναγκαλισάμενος αὐτό into v.36 from 10.16 /27/. It is most unlikely that he composed both v.36 and v.37 /28/ for there is nothing to connect v.35 to v.38 whereas v.37 is linked to what follows by catchwords. Reploh /29/ ultimately takes the position that v.35b, and therefore all of vv.33-37, derives from Mark. Unfortunately for such a view there is no real evidence in the Gospel that Mark either composed extensive sections, other than summaries, or created actual incidents. Perhaps then Mark added vv.35b-37 from the tradition; we have seen that v.35a suggests the beginning of new material and since it is introduced so formally this material will hardly have consisted of v.35b alone. The tradition (i) may have contained vv.35b-37 and perhaps something in continuation which has been lost or

(ii) may have jumped from v.35b to some later point in vv.38-50 or (iii) what originally followed v.35b may have been completely dropped by Mark. The retention of the formal opening suggests that the third alternative is improbable. There is no easy transition from v.35b to any point of vv.38-50, and this renders the second alternative unlikely. It is therefore easier to conclude, as we have done, that almost all of vv.36f was already attached to v.35b in Mark's source; the use of the catchwords confirms this.

What is the significance of the child in vv.36f? He has been understood as an example of the needy or of the humble, as representing the weakest members of the Christian community or Christian missionaries, and in many other ways /30/. Differences of interpretation arise from the different places from which commentators begin their discussions and not all of them make any serious attempt to distinguish between the meaning of the saying of v.37 for Mark and its original meaning outside its present context. As a detached logion it is dominated by the shaliach principle and understood most easily in terms of the disciple /31/ or missionary who is sent by Christ as Christ was sent by God; if the missionary is received, Christ is received; and if Christ is received, God is received (cf Mt. 10.40; Lk. 10.16; Jn 12.44; 13.20). It is difficult to maintain this view in the present context for it completely divorces vv.35b from vv.36f and the 'physical' term ἐναγκαλίζεσθαι implies literal children. To reach a more satisfactory explanation we must begin by enquiring after the position of the child in the ancient world. Its culture was not child-oriented as is our Western culture and we ought not to view this passage with our customary emotional sympathy for the child. The Greco-Roman world idealised the mature adult rather than the child; in Judaism the child is 'weak' and not expected to keep the Law until he is bar-mitzwah /32/. In both cases the child is someone who must be trained and educated before he can be viewed as significant. The child is therefore someone who is unimportant and this is emphasised in that he does not belong to the circle of disciples /33/; by implication the disciple ought always to be ready to receive such unimportant people (as in 10.13-16 Jesus receives them) and be their servant ('servant of all', v.35b).

δέχεσθαι can hardly be given the sense 'receive into the church', as if the 'child' was the outsider who is being accepted as a Christian, but means 'receive' in the sense 'welcome, show kindness to' (cf Mk 6.11; Lk. 9.53; Jn 10.45; Col. 4.10; Heb. 11.31; this is a well-established usage of the word going back to classical times) /34/; it can also, but need not necessarily, refer to the reception of missionaries (Mk. 6.11; Mt. 10.40; Lk. 10.8,10; in some of these cases it is the outside world which receives, or does not receive, the missionaries). The disciple, or the 'one with authority' if the Twelve is to be understood as referring to the ministry, shows himself a real διάκονος when he attends to the needs of the unimportant. This is to be done ἐπὶ τῷ ὀνόματί μου This qualifying phrase /35/ can be attached either to the one who is received with the sense 'receive (a child) when my name is confessed, when I am called upon' (where the reference might be to baptism and Christ's name is called over the child) /36/ or in the sense 'for my name's sake' (the one who receives does so because he is a Christian) /37/. Although the 'name' is regularly associated with baptism the second sense is more appropriate here /38/, and is often taken with the added implication 'because I myself have acted in this way' /39/; it is very doubtful if this implication, which involves an imitation of Christ, is actually present; in view of the rarity of the theme in Mark we would expect it to be clearly expressed if it was intended. Christ is Lord, Son of man, Son of God, i.e. on a different plane from the disciple, and the disciple acts because of his appreciation of the difference between himself and Christ, not because of a possible similarity.

This distinction between the disciple or believer and Jesus is implicit in the remainder of v.37 where a unique relationship is set up between Jesus and God. The so-called shaliach principle /40/ is employed here to suggest that Jesus is encountered and helped when the child, who is the least important of all humans, is encountered and helped (cf Mt. 25.31-46). Verse 37b goes far beyond the nature of discipleship in that it indicates the 'reward' of the disciple, though not in crude material terms /41/. The disciple who receives the under-privileged is set in a relationship with Christ and through him with God. He is 'with Christ' (3.14) /42/.

Verses 38f form another brief pericope complete in itself. V.40 was probably an isolated logion at an earlier stage; it appears in antithetical form in Mt. 12.30 = Lk. 11.23; in the present context we note the variation to the first person plural from the second plural and first singular of v.38f; v.40 has the nature of a proverbial saying /43/. Verse 41 has a parallel in Mt. 10.42. At what stage were vv.38f, v.40 and v.41 brought together? Were they already a part of the complex of sayings beginning with v.35 which Mark received in the tradition or did he insert any or all of them into this complex? Matthew omits the whole of vv.38-41 but he has the antithetical form of v.40 at 12.30 and a variant form of v.41 at 10.42; this might indicate that he knew the tradition in a form not containing vv.38-40 or vv.38-41 as well as in its Markan form. But that does not mean that the disputed verses were not in Mark's form of the tradition. There are positive reasons which could have led Matthew to omit the pericope; either he may have objected to its anti-ecclesiastical nature /44/ or he may have followed his general tendency to play down Mark's interest in exorcism. Luke retains Mk 9.38,39a,40 /45/ and drops v.39b and v.41; he also drops the remainder of the complex (9.42-50) though elsewhere he has parallels to portions of it (cf 17.1f; 14.34f).

Verses 38-40 (strictly vv.38f only, but v.40 almost certainly went with them from an early stage) /46/ or vv.38-41 are suspect as part of the logia sequence of 9.35ff both because they have a narrative foundation and because their omission leads to an easier development of the thought. Both arguments are almost certainly true if we are referring to their union with vv.35-37 and vv.41ff (or vv.42ff) in an original setting in the life of Jesus; this however does not prove they were added by Mark; clumsiness of addition and lack of homogeneity with the surrounding material does not of itself prove his hand; they may have come from the original compiler of the sequence. There do not appear in fact to be any positive signs of Mark's activity implying that he added them /47/. Verses 40,41 are both logia beginning with ὅς, a form found widely in Mark (cf 3.35; 4.9,25; 6.11; etc.); but Mark was not responsible for the creation of these sayings and it is unlikely that he changed their form; it is more probable that the source of sayings from which he or the earlier compiler derived them had this uniformity of form within it /48/. The use of γάρ (vv.40,41) /49/ is no sure proof of his hand since he added it to existing sequences of logia /50/. The use of καί at the beginning of v.42 does not necessarily imply a Markan seam; he employs it regularly within pericopae which he received in the tradition. On the other hand there is the presence of catchwords /51/ which is a sign of oral tradition, and any argument that the use of ὄνομα in v.37 led Mark to add a pericope in which it was central applies equally to the compiler of the oral tradition; it is difficult to see any reason for the inclusion of vv.38-40(41) except the catchwords and that again suggests some stage in the oral tradition. Verse 38a is unusual as a Markan introduction /52/.

If now we suppose Mark inserted vv.38-41 he would appear at first sight to have destroyed a good connection between v.37 and v.42: welcoming a child and causing it to stumble /53/. But whereas 'child' and 'little one' do not jar when far apart as they are at present in Mark they would if placed in adjacent verses;

if Mark interpolated vv.38-41 we have also to assume that he added τῶν πιστευόντων and changed the reference from the literal child (v.37) to the Christian (v.42). If the connection between v.37 and v.42 is as good as alleged it is very difficult to see why anyone should have wished to break it up, for vv.38-41 could have been added as easily after v.42. If Mark added vv.38-41 it is difficult to envisage their previous existence as a unit, though vv.38-40 could have been such; v.41 is only linked to vv.38-40 through the use of ὄνομα; this link is much stronger within the sequence of occurrences of the word beginning at v.37. Finally, if Mark added v.41 then with very little alteration he could have brought it into line with vv.38-40 and vv.35-37 by omitting ὑμᾶς, the first ὅτι and ἐστε - 'whoever gives a cup of cold water in the name of Christ, truly I say to you will not lose his reward'.

If we reject the view that Mark added vv.38-41 it may be that he added vv.38-40 and that v.37 was linked to v.41 in the tradition. This is better than the preceding suggestion in that vv.38-40 are a more natural unit than vv.38-41 but inferior in that the connection between v.37 and v.41 is not so strong as that between v.37 and v.42. Schweizer /54/ therefore suggests that v.41 appeared in the pre-Markan tradition in its Matthean form (Mt. 10.42) /55/ and notes that in Matthew the parallels to Mk 9.37 and 9.41 are closely associated at 10.40,42; their conjunction must therefore have preceded Mark. But if the tradition contained v.41 in its Matthean form it is very difficult to see why anyone would have changed it into its present form after inserting vv.38-40. If it was in its present form then the argument for the connection between v.38 and v.41 does not exist. Consequently it is easier to assume that the whole sequence took shape through 'catch-words' in the oral tradition, and we conclude that all of vv.38-41 lay in the tradition received by Mark /56/.

Verses 38-41 clearly bear signs of the influence of the early church: the use of 'your name' (v.38), 'my name' (v.39), 'speak evil of me' (v.39), 'because you are Christ's, (v.41) /57/; and while v.41 in its Matthean form (10.42) may go back to Jesus, probably vv.38f do not /58/. Acts 19.13ff shows that the early church was faced by those who used Jesus' name in exorcism but were not Christians; by the second century his name appears in magical formulae. Our passage is distinguished from Acts 19.13ff in that in the latter the evil spirit is not subject to the exorcists who are thus clearly usurpers of ecclesiastical position or authority. The final words of v.39 link up with 1 Cor. 12.3 in which it is recognised that some people who are not 'in the Spirit' speak evil of Jesus; only those who are in the Spirit can affirm that Jesus is Lord (1 Cor. 12.3; 1 Jn 4.2f; Did. 11.8-12) and cast out demons (Mk 3.22-30). All this sets the pericope firmly within the early church situation.

What is the significance of the incident for Mark /59/? Clearly at some stage vv.38-40 was used to define who were members of the community. If there is a group with common aims and a strong sense of fellowship, as the church had from its beginning, then that group tends to erect a barrier around itself so that it can then more easily define itself over against those who do not belong /60/. This pericope is designed to preserve such a group /61/ but the precise circumstances in which it was first used are now unknown. If this was the original purpose of the pericope, has this been altered in any way by its inclusion within the logia sequence? Since the sequence is held together by catch-words rather than by logic we cannot expect too rigorous a logical progression of thought within it. Certainly there is some relationship in thought between this pericope and the earlier theme of greatness: those who claim to be great must not do so in any exclusive manner; the truly great will not define the borders of the Christian fellowship so that it includes only themselves /62/. The link forwards to v.41 must run somewhat as follows (note the connecting γάρ): vv.38-40 are to be widened from a reference to exorcism alone; if someone whom you do not think to be Christian offers the simplest of services (a cup of water) because you are a Christian (and this implies he thinks he is a Christian), do not despise him for God approves of him and he will receive his reward /63/.

Reploh /64/ prefers to understand vv.38-41 out of v.42; the latter, he argues, pre-supposes a situation of persecution of believers /65/ (and it may be granted that persecution forms part of the situation of Mark's Gospel); those who persecute believers are threatened with a terrible fate (v.42). On the other hand (v.41) the person who assists the Christian who is in such desperate straits that even a cup of water is help will receive a reward, even though he is not a Christian; everyone indeed who does not actively oppose the church may be seen as a secret ally (v.40); the strange exorcist is an example of such an ally (vv.38f). Leaving for the moment the interpretation of v.42, Reploh's interpretation of v.41 is difficult in relation to the phrase 'in the name that (because) you belong to Christ' /66/. Does Mark envisage someone coming to the persecuted Christian and saying 'because you are a Christian I am helping you'? This person would then have to be understood as a secret believer or sympathiser. Verse 40 could be made to fit this, but vv.38f are then almost impossible for the last thing to be said about the strange exorcist is that he acts secretly; Reploh's interpretation also fails to account for his seeming rejection as an ally. Reploh points to κακολογεῖν in v.39 as a sign of persecution but this has as object Christ and not the disciple; it is more easily explained in terms of 1 Cor. 12.3.

Is any particular person intended by the reference to the strange exorcist? J. Weiss /67/ has argued that the exorcist is Paul, and that he was also the 'child' of vv.36f. Mark is then defending him against the official Jewish Christian leadership of the church. It is remarkable, however, to see Paul depicted as an exorcist, an activity to which his letters do not allude, and perhaps even more remarkable to see John and not Peter singled out as his opponent. Was the dispute between Paul and the Jewish-Christian leadership still sufficiently active at the time of Mark's Gospel for any defence to be needed /68/, and if it was needed why is it, as Lagrange wisely remarks /69/, presented so vaguely by such a partisan of Paul as Mark is supposed to be? If Paul is not in mind, is it an attack on the Twelve? Although one of the duties given to the Twelve was exorcism and although they are specifically mentioned in v.35 and John is one of their number it is difficult to be certain that there is any real attack on them. A more plausible case might be put up for taking them to represent the leaders of Mark's community and the passage would then be a rebuke to contemporary leaders. The reference to the Twelve (9.35) belongs to the tradition /70/ but Mark has widened it into a reference to the disciples generally; consequently he is not rebuking leaders as such but the contemporary community as a whole. In support of this we can argue that v.39b, because of its resemblance to 1 Cor. 12.3, would imply that all Christians are intended; charismatic activity, to which exorcism is allied, was not a function only of the leaders in the early church /71/. Moreover v.40 is cast in entirely general terms, and it is easier to take v.41 in this way also. Finally within vv.35-50, vv.42-50 have a completely general reference to believers and not a specific one to leaders; in particular in v.42 it is the simple believer ('one of these little ones') who is made to stumble and v.42 is closely linked to v.41 /72/. The understanding of what constitutes a member is a necessary stage in the evolution of an organisation and ordinary members can be as jealous as leaders over membership and therefore as active in excluding others. The thought bites more deeply when we recall 9.14-29; the 'church' has been given the power to exorcise; it failed; a 'stranger' comes along and succeeds; the church wishes to exclude him; it ought instead to pray (9.28f).

Reploh /73/, as we saw, takes v.42 as an offer of comfort to Christians /74/ because their persecutors will be punished, and from this he interprets backwards to vv.38-41. Quite apart from the moral question whether the punishment of their persecutors ought to comfort Christians, Reploh's interpretation is difficult when we move forward to vv.42-48 /75/ for in these verses it is the disciples and not their persecutors who are threatened with punishment. Indeed even with Reploh's interpretation of v.42 it is not the persecutor as such who is punished but only the successful persecutor, i.e. the one who makes the Christian 'stumble', and by vv.43-8 whoever 'stumbles' goes to hell-fire; the fate of the persecutor will hardly comfort the Christian who has not stumbled, but only his ex-fellow disciple who has, and he will not be caring any longer! Despite this criticism we agree with Reploh in taking v.42 as a continuation of vv.38-41, but we trace the thought in a different way /76/: the rejection of the seemingly unimportant believer ('one of these little ones who believe') who may be exorcising (to the member of the 'official' church he is hardly worth considering since he is μικρός /77/), or giving a cup of cold water will lead to the punishment of the disciple, a member of the official community, who rejects him /78/. We note that the punishment is not visited on an outside secular persecutor but on the disciple himself: this understanding preserves the unity of thought in the whole complex by making it refer to discipleship. The literal child of vv.36f has now become the believer through a perfectly natural extension of the argument.

Verses 43-48 require little comment. If in v.42 the disciple was in danger because he rejected another disciple, here he is in danger because of temptations arising apparently out of his own being. The Matthean parallel (5.29f), which is not derived from Mark, has the sayings about the hand and the eye but lacks the one about the foot; this is appropriate to its sexual context in Mt. 5; the parallel at 18.29f, which is derived from Mark, combines the two Markan sayings about the hand and the foot into one, probably in order to conform to the twofold scheme of the other parallel. There does not seem to be any reason why Mark should have created the saying about the foot; certainly he thinks of discipleship as a journey where feet are necessary but the sacrifice of a foot would not make the journey easier but more difficult! Mark's threefold enumeration accords with the 'three' motif of fairy tales and could either have been original or created at any time in the course of transmission /79/. The ancient world was aware of the demand on the devotees of some religions for the literal sacrifice of parts of the body (e.g. the genitals) but this is hardly in view here, for the sayings are of Jewish origin: the 'evil desire' is set in individual members of the body /80/; καλὸν ... ἢ .. is an Aramaism /81/; Gehenna is an exclusively Jewish term for the place of punishment after death. Yet self-mutilation was a sin to the Jew /82/. Thus from the beginning the sayings (or saying if there was originally only one) can only have been intended as a metaphorical depiction of sacrifice and there is no reason to suppose Mark takes them in any other way. But to say that they are metaphorical does not mean Mark looked lightly on them. They set out the radical nature of discipleship with which nothing within the disciple can be allowed to interfere; they spell out part of what self-denial (8.34) means. They are not a call to asceticism, though they have been used with that implication; the eye, hand, foot are not evil in and of themselves but only when they lead to some activity which is evil; there is thus no automatic requirement to jettison them. In 8.34f the call to discipleship was based on devotion to Christ and the Gospel and had no thought of self; here self has become prominent and radical action is demanded so that the self may preserve itself for entrance into 'life', i.e. 'eternal life' as the contrast of Gehenna shows. Unlike Mt. 5.29f the context is not sexual but that of an offence against a humble believer (v.42) or an outsider who offers a cup of water (v.41) or who exorcises (v.38f); the hand or foot or eye which leads to these offences should be cut off; the sayings thus look outward at others within or outside the community rather than inward at the disciple's thoughts or imagination. To restrict the community by hard and fast lines and to ignore the needs of its simplest members will lead to destruction in Gehenna /83/.

Curiously the need to mutilate a hand, foot or eye is not extended to the plucking out of the tongue though elsewhere Mark writes of the danger which can come from it (7.18-23; cf Jas. 3.6-12). The disciple needs to keep it under control as much as, if not more than, hand, foot and eye. Lack of control can disrupt the community for the sins which are described in 7.21-22 are largely those which would corrupt the mutual relations of disciples. 7.18-23 thus links to 9.35-42 as well as to the more individualistic approach of 9.43-48. Unless he wishes to destroy the community to which he belongs the believer needs to watch carefully what he says.

The final verses (vv.49f) /84/ of our section have long been a puzzle to commentators, though more attention has been given to their origin and original meaning than to their meaning in

Mark. Fortunately we do not need to consider whether they are derived from a Jewish proverb /85/ or were created by Jesus, and, if the latter, in what form /86/. There are similar brief sequences of sayings using the imagery of salt in Mt. 5.13 and Lk. 14.34f. In the former the salt clearly stands for the disciples and the sayings are addressed to them; in the latter it is apparently the crowd which is addressed (cf v.25) /87/. Obviously in Mark the salt cannot represent the disciples since it is people who are 'salted' with fire (v.49) and who can have salt in themselves (v.50c), yet because of their context the sayings must relate in some way to discipleship; certainly they are regarded as addressed to disciples.

In v.49 πᾶς can refer either to every man or to every disciple. Normally in the Gospel γάρ within a sequence indicates that its clause provides the basis or cause for what precedes /88/. The preceding verses have referred to the threat of the fire of judgement for unfaithful disciples and this suggests disciples are in mind here. All are threatened with fire but not all experience it. Perhaps then 'fire' has changed its meaning between vv.43-8 and v.49 (the connection between the two is by catch-word rather than by logical progression of argument) and should be understood as 'persecution': all disciples will suffer persecution. 'Fire' was used frequently as a metaphor for persecution in the early church (1 Pet. 1.7; 4.12; Rev. 3.18; cf. Isa. 48.10. Lk. 12.49 may have this meaning also. If we take it in this way ἀλισθήσεται can hardly be restricted to the simple meaning 'suffer'; since salt is good (v.50a) it probably indicates that the process of persecution is not merely a terror to be endured but also that the very endurance brings benefit to the Christian; this would link it with the conception of fire as a purifying agent (Prov. 27.21; 1 Pet. 1.7; Isa. 48.10). It may however be thought that since salt preserves we should see the image in a slightly different way: persecution preserves true discipleship; in persecution the persecuted gives himself and thereby saves or preserves himself (8.35) /89/.

Yet πᾶς would seem to suggest that v.49 refers to every man and not just to every disciple. But again it is untrue that every man will experience the fires of judgement; faithful disciples will escape. Perhaps on this understanding 'fire' should be regarded as varying its meaning: all will experience 'fire': the unbeliever and the unfaithful disciple, the fire of judgement; the faithful disciple, the fire of persecution.

The meaning of 'salt' appears to change in v.50; this is not wholly surprising if 'salt' is employed as a catch-word and not as a concept to link the verses. V.50ab, καλὸν ... ἀρτύσετε, goes back ultimately to the same original saying as do Mt. 5.13 and Lk. 14.34f but lacks the threat with which they conclude; instead it suggests the need to have salt, which is a 'good', within oneself. If it is difficult to recover the earliest form of this saying it is almost as difficult to be sure what Mark means by it /90/. Perhaps it is best to take salt as that which makes a disciple a disciple, that which distinguishes him from those who are not disciples; without this quality or flavour the disciple is ἄναλος; he ought therefore to seek to have and to hold it (v.50c). Salt is appropriate to describe this flavour since its taste is sharp and biting rather than sweet and pleasant /91/. The flavour itself is that which has been depicted in vv.35-48, and indeed even more widely in all the discipleship passages /92/. This interpretation can only be a suggestion /93/; it is very possible that already by Mark's time the meaning was obscure and that he only repeated these verses because they were part of the complex of logia whose earlier part he wished to use /94/.

The final clause, καὶ εἰρηνεύετε ἐν ἀλλήλοις, can be said to bring us back to the beginning of the complex: if Christians are to preserve the liveliness of their discipleship they will not achieve it through activity directed against one another or against those whom they would wrongly exclude from the community. Is the clause a Markan addition? It is similar in wording and content to 1 Th. 5.13b (cf Rom. 12.18; 2 Cor. 13.11) and may thus have been at some stage a detached logion; there is nothing to indicate that Mark added it; it would indeed have been appropriate to the complex in its pre-Markan stage if it began, as we have argued, at v.35b /95/.

Before we leave the area of individual self-discipline which has been particularly prominent in vv.43-48 we need to look briefly at 2.18-20 which may imply that fasting is a part of the life of the disciple. For our purposes it is unnecessary to trace these verses back to their original form and meaning /96/. Almost certainly vv.19b-20 (and perhaps also v.19a) did not originally belong with v.18, but there are no signs of Markan redaction in their union. We may therefore assume that they came to Mark already joined in the tradition /97/. The only sign of his hand is the periphrastic tense in v.18a /98/. The mention of 'the disciples of the Pharisees' is difficult since the Pharisees did not have disciples. It is unlikely that Mark has inserted this reference /99/ for the complex of controversy stories, normally taken as 2.1-3.6 /100/, is elsewhere directed against Jewish leaders. Probably the reference to the disciples of John the Baptizer predated that to the Pharisees and the latter was inserted when the complex was compiled; its appearance is thus pre-Markan. Were vv.21-22 present in the pre-Markan complex? They are not a controversy story like the other stories in the complex; they have no grammatical link to v.20; they have probably then been inserted by Mark /101/; there are, however, no signs of his hand within them. Whether Mark added them or not there is no reason to dispute the generally accepted conclusion that 2.18-20 and 2.21-22 are meant to be understood together.

2.18-20 are normally regarded as a defence of fasting: while the disciples have Jesus alive on earth with them there is no need to fast; the time for fasting will come when he is dead /102/. But though by Mark's day he is dead the church does not fast continuously; later (Did. 8.1) we find the observance of a twice weekly fast in some parts of the church. Acts 13.2f; 14.23 suggest fasts took place for special purposes but without any connection with the passion /103/. Discussion turns on the meaning of ἐν ἐκείνῃ τῇ ἡμέρᾳ. 'The day' often refers to the last day when the Lord returns (Mt. 7.22; Lk. 17.31); such a meaning would be inappropriate here since the fast relates to his departure and not his arrival. The phrase might be understood quite generally, 'at that time', the time after the death of Jesus; it is doubtful if this is a possible meaning /104/; it is in any case present in τότε and would render the phrase redundant. Mark likes duplicate expressions of which the second qualifies the first /105/; most commentators therefore understand it to refer to a weekly Friday fast but we should not exclude the possibility of a Good Friday fast or a fast on the succeeding Saturday /106/; the use of the singular might be thought to suggest something less frequent than once a week: such a fast would also be more closely associated with the passion.

How now do vv.21-22 help us to understand vv.18-20? The vast majority of commentators see them in terms of the incompatibility of old and new, Christianity being the new and Judaism the old. A few dispute the contrast of old and new /107/. While the contrast may not have been present originally it is dificult to see any other meaning within the complex of controversy stories; nor is it easy to argue that no value judgement is implied between old and new; within the Christian tradition the 'new' is the good (cf Rom. 7.6; Eph. 4.22-24; Col. 3.9f; Heb. 8.13). It is then wholly appropriate to view the contrast as present in the context of a clash between the actions and teaching of Jesus and those of the Jews, or some groups of them, even though the contrast of old and new does not fit exactly to vv.18-20, where the contrast is between sorrow and joy. For believers Jesus, or the Christian faith, is the new wine which cannot be kept in the old bottles of Judaism, and two of the 'bottles' immediately suggested by the context are fasting and the sabbath (2.23-3.5). The new patch (ἐπίβλημα), Christianity, sown into the old garment destroys the old garment of Jewish ways and customs. Thus vv.21-22 suggest that Christian faith rightly understood ends fasting as a religious practice. Is there then a conflict in meaning with vv.19-20?

There is one other point in the N.T. where food and the sabbath are brought into relation (Rom. 14.1-15.6); Paul is writing to the very church from which Mark's Gospel emerged. Admittedly Rom. 14.1-15.6 seems to contrast vegetarianism with the eating of meat, but fasting is not necessarily total abstention from food. Can it be that Mark, inheriting the complex of controversy stories, has inserted vv.21-22 in order to indicate that fasting is not an essential part of Christian faith? He makes his point in such a way that fasting is not declared to be wrong and so like Paul in Rom.14 he avoids taking sides. There is one objection which might be made against the view that v.20 teaches fasting: if Christ is risen he has never been taken away from the church but is continually with Christians; there is no time in which he needs to be mourned /108/. Such a consistency of outlook, however, has never been a strong point with Christians; those who have believed most strongly in Christ's resurrection have usually been the very people who have mourned him most deeply on Good Friday /109/.

If v.20 does encourage fasting /110/, and nowhere does it explicitly lay down fasting as a duty, then that fasting is like all discipleship related to the passion and is not presented as an ascetic or self-disciplinary practice (though this may have been the purpose of whatever fasting John the Baptizer taught his disciples); it is a way of reminding believers as they mourn Jesus of what he has done for them.

Notes

1   This is the majority opinion, e.g. Bultmann, pp.149f; Sundwall, pp.60ff; Taylor; Grundmann; Schweizer; Lane; Reploh, pp.140-156. To the contrary, Haenchen, p.324, who gives no reasons; R. Schnackenburg, 'Mk 9, 33-50'; Pesch, II, 101f; Ambrozic, pp.171-177. Kuhn, pp.32ff, is uncertain but inclines towards a Markan compilation.

2   ὄνομα (vv.37,38,39,41); δέχεσθαι (vv.36,37); παιδίον-

μικρός (vv.36,37,42); βάλλειν and καλόν ἐστιν (vv.42,43,45,47); σκανδαλίζειν (vv.42,43,45,47); πῦρ (vv.43,48,49); ἅλς (vv.49,50). Verses 43,45,47 are obviously parallel formations.

3   P.34; cf. Schnackenburg (as n.1).

4   E.g. 4.21f and 4.23f. This unity was probably pre-Markan, cf. Best, 'Mark's Preservation of the Tradition'. Schnackenburg (as n.1) instances 8.34-38; but as we have seen this was pre-Markan, cf. pp.30f.

5   P.129

6   Cf Black, pp.169-71,218-222; A. Vaganay, 'Le schématisme du discours communautaire'.

7   Schnackenburg (as n.1) argues that Mark regularly joins sayings together with γάρ (cf vv.40,41,49) even where there is no logical connection; we have however seen that Mark inserts γάρ into already existing sequences, e.g. 8.34-38. Its addition in our sequence has helped to create some kind of logical connection.

8   Cf Best, 'Mark's Preservation of the Tradition'. The difficulty commentators seem to find in relating the verses of our sequence to one another and to their context is an indication that Mark is using material of which only a part, the first part, was really suitable for his purpose. As often, instead of dropping the less relevant material, he preserves the whole unit.

9   To argue that most of vv.33-50 existed as a unit prior to Mark is not to assert that it goes back as a unit to Jesus. The extensive use in it of ὄνομα is post-resurrection; ὅτι χριστοῦ ἐστε (v.41) cannot come from Jesus; the way in which many of the individual logia appear in different forms and contexts in Matthew and Luke confirms that they were not originally linked. The logia were not then put together by Jesus for easy instruction but by the early church, probably in Palestine.

10   Cf Légasse, pp.23f.

11   For a detailed discussion of Mark's redaction at this point, see Best, 'The Twelve'. In this paper I have disputed the frequent assertion that a reference to the Twelve is a necessary sign of Markan redaction.

12   D.R. Catchpole, 'The Poor on Earth and the Son of Man in Heaven', takes Capernaum to be from the tradition because it would not have lain on Jesus' direct route to Jerusalem. But for Mark Capernaum was probably only the name of a town which occurred regularly in the tradition and which he picked up and used because he wanted a place name in Galilee. Elsewhere he does not reveal such a full knowledge of Palestinian geography as Catchpole's hypothesis pre-supposes.

13   This is Matthew's argument for he connects 18.1 and 18.3f with the reference to the Kingdom of heaven; Luke does the same by his addition of 9.48b. Codex Bezae omits v.35; perhaps Matthew and Luke knew Mark without it, but it is more likely that D harmonises with Matthew and Luke.

14   Cf P.S. Minear, Commands of Christ, pp.86f.

15   So Schnackenburg (as n.1).

16   Meye, pp.180f, argues that the reference to the Twelve is redactional because of the peculiar appropriateness that those who were given authority (6.7) should be instructed in greatness. This however would still be true if the reference to the Twelve was part of the tradition; it does not then necessarily derive from Mark, though he may have agreed with it. Meye determines what is redaction and what tradition in Mark more by a series of guesses than by any accurate study of the text; he never discusses in vv.33-35 what may be Markan and what not.

17   This transition would be easier if the tradition Mark used did not include the final words of the logion, 'servant of all'. Haenchen, ad loc., thinks they are an addition intended to make Jesus' sayings apply more directly to the church. διάκονος however, is essential to 10.43f which is a pre-Markan unit and a variant of 9.35; its presence in 9.35 will therefore be pre-Markan.

18   Mark has made clear the reference to greatness by writing vv.33f; it is not a necessary understanding of v.35b taken by itself. The association was present in the tradition of 10.43f.

19   Cf Haenchen.

20   Ad loc.

21   Note also the use of πάντων; contrast the use of ὑμῶν in the parallels (cf Stock, pp.119f). The believer is related to the world rather than the 'official' to the community.

22   Schnackenburg (as n.1) followed by Reploh, suggests that the passage from v.35b to v.36 has been assisted by the association of ἔσχατος with the child, who is the 'last' or least important member of the community.

23   It is found also in Prov. 6.10; 24.33.

24   P.143; cf Haenchen, p.326.

25   Matthew and Luke modify the phrase to remove its clumsiness. Whatever the phrase means it does not mean 'an adult who is like a child'; it is children themselves who are intended (cf Légasse, p.26, n.3).

26   Such vivid concrete detail is not an indication that the material derives from an eye-witness; preachers regularly add such detail.

Chapter 8: Mark 9.33-50

27   Cf Légasse, p.27; Catchpole (as n.12), p.366. Apart from
this one word there is nothing else in the verse which is
characteristic of Mark and would imply that the verse was his
composition. Both Matthew and Luke repeat, with unimportant
modifications, all of the verse except this clause. M. Black,
'The Child in the Midst', suggests that Aramaic talya underlies
both 'child' and 'servant' and so makes the transition easy;
Schnackenburg (as n.1), p.186, n.3, doubts this.
28   So Knox, I, p.24.
29   P.146.
30   For a discussion of the various views and for full literary
references see Légasse, pp.101-4. Légasse himself, drawing on
an identification of the μικροί in v.42 with believers, inclines
to the view that the children represent the missionaries of the
early church; he does not however accept Loisy's view that this
is intended as a defence of Paul as a missionary; see A. Loisy,
Les Evangiles Synoptiques, vol. II, pp.69f.
31   παιδίον is used of the Christian in 1 John 2.13,18 and in
view of the use of the re-birth imagery in the early church it is
a natural metaphor to describe the Christian.
32   Cf A. Oepke, TDNT, V, pp.639-48; Billerbeck, I, pp.569f,
607,780ff; II, p.373; Légasse, pp.276ff, cf pp.168ff; P. Ariès,
Centuries of Childhood; The History of Childhood (ed. L.
deMause).
33   Cf E. Wilhelms, 'Der fremde Exorcist'.
34   Ambrozic, pp.155-7, goes too far when he includes an
element of 'subjection' in δέχεσθαι on the grounds that it is
required by διάκονος; this might be true if δοῦλος had been
used. On the meaning of διάκονος, willingly offered service,
see pp.126f. The sense we have adopted for δέχεσθαι
harmonises with that of διακονεῖν understood as 'table-service'
(cf Stock, p.121).
35   There is probably little difference in the use of ἐπί and ἐν
(cf v.38) in this phrase; cf S. New, 'The Name, Baptism, and the
Laying on of Hands', especially p.123, n.3.
36   Cf Hauck, ad loc., who takes the child to represent the
believer.
37   For the two senses see Bauer, s.v.
38   So Billerbeck; cf Schlatter, Das Evangelium nach Markus,
ad loc., who gives the sense 'in obedience to my command'.
39   Cf Reploh, p.145; Grundmann.
40   Cf Billerbeck, III, p.2; K.H. Rengstorf, TDNT, I, pp.414ff;
T.W. Manson, The Church's Ministry, pp.31-52. We are not
intending to imply anything here about the origin of the
apostolate through this principle. Cf G. Klein, Die Zwölf

93

Apostel, pp.30-2.

41   Haenchen, pp.326f, suggests that it makes finding God in children more important than loving them, i.e. that the disciple will receive the child because this is a way of receiving God. The danger of such an interpretation must be recognised, but it is not very apparent in the text.

42   Cf Stock, p.122.

43   Cf Bultmann, p.81.

44   W.L. Knox, I, p.24, n.1, describes it as 'a saying so shocking to all sound ecclesiastical feeling that Matthew had to omit it'.

45   He changes the first plural in Mark to a second plural, possibly to minimise the contradiction with his 11.23 (first singular).

46   Contra Reploh, p.149, who finds in the γάρ the indication that Mark united them. But see pp.30f. Wilhelms (as n.33) is clearly correct in his view that in vv.38-40 the stress lies on v.40; vv.38f is a concrete illustration of its basic principle.

47   The asyndetic introduction at v.38 might appear Markan (cf C.H. Turner, JTS 28 (1926/7) 9-30) but if Mark added the pericope we should expect an introductory καί. Many of the Markan asyndeta occur within the tradition.

48   Cf Best, 'An Early Sayings Collection'.

49   Pace Schnackenburg, Reploh.

50   See pp.30f. He could have added it here in v.40 though v.40 was connected to vv.38f in his Vorlage.

51   See above, n.2.

52   Cf Schmidt, p.236, ἔφη is non-Markan.

53   Cf Bundy, p.319.

54   Ad loc.

55   Cf Kuhn, p.33, n.133. Légasse, pp.81f, considers the Markan form more original, because ἐν ὀνόματι ὅτι represents an Aramaic idiom 'because ...', and 'one of these little ones' is Matthean. The variant reading which adds μου shows the difficulty of the Greek of the Markan form.

56   Cf Légasse, p.82. Knox, I, p.21, includes vv.38f in his 'Twelve'-source because of the mention of John. We see no reason to accept the existence of that source. It was natural to attach vv.38f here after the reference to the Twelve in v.35 since it mentions one of them. Reploh considers that Mark compiled the whole complex up to v.43. We fail to find sufficient signs of Mark's activity and so prefer to place the compilation earlier; nor do we believe that Mark elsewhere carried out this kind of wholesale editorial activity.

57   Schweizer points out that our pericope also presents the disciples as a group which can be thought of independently of

Jesus, and they did not become this until the period of the post-resurrection church. Luke's alteration of 'followed us' to 'followed with us' slightly ameliorates this difficulty.

58 If a name is to be used in exorcism (as the Jews used Solomon's, cf Josephus, Ant. 8.46f) then it must be well-known both to the healer and patient for its power to be effective; Jesus was hardly as well-known as this in the brief period of his ministry (cf Haenchen, p.327). Nineham's argument (p.253f) that the pericope must be late because if the church had always possessed it, it could hardly have acted in an intolerant way later (e.g. Acts 19.15ff) is hardly valid. The saying has certainly existed since the time of Mark's Gospel and the church has not always been tolerant since then! Schnackenburg (as n.1) and Wilhelms (as n.33) on the other hand take its tolerance as a sign of an early date. We must allow that the pericope might go back to Jesus (so Pesch, II, p.109) in a modified form: the disciples tell him of a Jewish exorcist, but not one using his name, and Jesus says, in effect, 'if a man is defeating evil he is on our side'. Also in favour of an early Palestinian origin is the linking with a definite person (John) and the fact of the exorcism itself, for exorcisms took place more regularly in the Jewish world than the Hellenistic. Schweizer, ad loc., suggests that the saying arose from a Christian prophet answering the question, 'What would Jesus have decided in this matter?' It does not appear that at this stage Jesus was regarded as a 'pattern' to be imitated and the question would therefore not have been formulated in this way.

59 It might be argued that it would have no significance for Mark since, though he took over the complex 9.35-50, he was only interested in the first incident 9.35-37. But if 9.38f relates to discipleship, as it does, and this is the general theme of the Gospel at this point, then 9.38-41 will have been of interest to Mark.

60 The exclusiveness that overtakes closely knit communities is illustrated by the change from Jesus' original 'Love your neighbour (i.e. everyone) as yourself' (Lk. 10.27) to 'Love one another' (i.e. fellow-Christians; Jn 13.34; 1 Jn 4.11; 1 Pet. 1.22; 1 Th. 4.9); the earlier form, of course, did not disappear (Rom. 13.8; Gal. 5.14).

61 Note the 'who did not follow us' where we would expect 'who did not follow you' (i.e. Jesus). The group is concerned about those who belong to it and not those who belong to Jesus.

62 The 'child' in vv.36f was from outside the circle of disciples: cf Wilhelms (as n.33).

63 Cf Nineham (p.254), 'In its Marcan context it must

presumably be interpreted as an example of how those who have not formally thrown in their lot with the Christians may yet be "for them"'. The strange exorcist is not formally a member of the Christian community, yet he is doing good (and perhaps to Christians), and therefore he will receive his reward, i.e. be numbered by God in the company of the saints. Perhaps we should also see some connection back to v.37: the person who helps the disciple in reality helps Christ and therefore helps God (cf Lane); God will reward such a person.

64 Pp.149-154.

65 Reploh, pp.149-153, argues that Mark has added τῶν πιστευόντων to an earlier form of Mk 9.42 which, lacking it (cf Lk. 17.1f), was therefore more general.

66 It is unlikely that either Mt. 10.42 or Mk 9.41 is the original form of the logion; this is probably irrecoverable. Légasse, pp.76ff, considers that Mk 9.41 is nearer the original. Reploh prefers Mt. 10.42; on this supposition it is difficult to see why Mark introduced 'in the name that you belong to Christ' if he wished it to be understood as Reploh sees it.

67 Das älteste Evangelium, p.258; cf Loisy, Les Evangiles Synoptiques, II, pp.69f,74f.

68 That Weiss argues that the incident only appears in the revised, and therefore later, edition of Mark makes it all the more difficult to accept his view.

69 Lagrange, p.247.

70 See Best, 'The Twelve'.

71 If the pericope has been modelled on, or influenced by Num. 11.26-29 we must note that Moses expects 'prophecy' to be a characteristic of every Israelite and not confined to leaders alone.

72 See below.

73 P.153.

74 τῶν πιστευόντων is clearly an ecclesiastical addition, but it is impossible to determine whether it is pre-Markan or not.

75 We agree with Reploh that there should be no break between v.41 and v.42 as in many printed texts, but we also think that there should be no break between v.42 and vv.43-8 in the way his theory demands.

76 Cf Lane, p.345.

77 Schmidt, p.234, remarks that the exorcist is regarded as someone μικρός in faith. This does not mean that we ought to see here a connection with the 'weak' brother of Rom. 14.1ff; 1 Cor. 8.10-12; 9.22 (so Taylor); the official church does not believe that the exorcist is a Christian at all but the 'weak' brother is still a believer in their eyes.

78 '...subversive forces are already at work within the church and have already claimed their victims' (Bundy, p.321).

79 Originally there could have been one, two or three sayings and the number varied according to situation and use. On their form see G.F. Snyder, 'The Tobspruch'.

80 Cf Billerbeck, I. p.302f.

81 Cf J.H. Moulton and W.F. Howard, A Grammar of New Testament Greek, Vol. II, p.442; Black, p.117.

82 Cf W.D. Davies, The Setting of the Sermon on the Mount, p.227, n.2.

83 Cf Trocmé, p.202.

84 We assume that the reading of Codex Vaticanus is original here, that the reading of Bezae arose under the influence of Lev. 2.13 out of the difficulty of the original, and that the reading of Alexandrinus is a conflation of the two. The reading of it[k], which Lohmeyer prefers, is so ill-supported that we must reject it. Cf Metzger, pp.102f.

85 For the proverb, 'Salt, if it becomes putrid, wherewith shall it be salted', (b. Bekhoroth 8b) see Billerbeck, I, p.236 and I. Abrahams, Studies in Pharisaism and the Gospels, II, p.183.

86 In addition to the commentaries, see O. Cullmann, 'Qui signifie le sel dans la parabole de Jésus?'; T.J. Baarda, 'Mark IX.49'; Black, pp.166f; W.R. Hutton, 'The Salt Sections'; D.R. Griffiths, 'The Salt Sections in the Gospels'; Reploh, pp.154-6; W. Nauck, 'Salt as a Metaphor'.

87 Cf J. Jeremias, The Parables of Jesus, pp.168f.

88 See p.51 n.81 for reference to literature.

89 This interpretation corresponds largely to that of Taylor and many other commentators. It is difficult to sustain a connection with baptism (F.C. Burkitt, The Gospel History and its Transmission, p.17; cf Baarda, as n.86) for this would involve a total non sequitur from vv.43-8. The attempt of Trocmé (p.202, n.4) to relate vv.49f to the general theme of an 'open' community is insufficiently based on a detailed exegesis of the passage. Grundmann takes 'salt' as God's gift of his Word (the Law was likened to 'salt' by the Rabbis); but how could the 'Word' lose its flavour?

90 On the meaning in Mark see most recently C.E. Carlston, The Parables of the Triple Tradition, pp.174-80.

91 Nineham (p.257) writes of 'astringent qualities' which the disciple ought to possess. Reploh's interpretation (p.155) that the disciple is to go on his way in the same spirit as Jesus went to the Cross is not unsimilar.

92 This accords with the meaning implied by the context of Lk. 14.34f; cf Cullmann, as n.86.

93 Taylor's remark (p.413) about v.49, 'no one will wish to speak with too much assurance' (of its meaning), is applicable to both verses.

94 Cf Best, 'Mark's Preservation of the Tradition'.

95 Reploh, pp.154-6, takes it as Markan since he regards most of the early part of the complex as a Markan construction.

96 In addition to the commentators see, for example, A. Kee, 'The Question about Fasting'; J.B. Muddiman, 'Jesus and Fasting (Mark ii.18-22)'; Roloff, pp.223-237.

97 So almost all commentators.

98 See Pryke, pp.103ff.

99 So, e.g., Taylor, ad loc.

100 Kuhn, pp.53-98, does not include 3.1-6; Cook, pp.47f, constructs the complex very differently but with the Pharisees included on every occasion.

101 Kuhn, p.89, n.26, leaves the issue open.

102 The inappropriateness of the metaphor need not detain us; bridegrooms are not taken away.

103 As do the variant readings at Mk 9.29; 1 Cor. 7.5. The fast of Cornelius (Acts 10.30, again a variant reading) was not a Christian fast.

104 See Kuhn, pp.64f.

105 Cf Neirynck.

106 Kuhn, pp.66f, lists those who have held the various views.

107 This is argued in great detail by A. Kee, 'The Old Coat and the New Wine'.

108 See below, ch.31.

109 Sorrow and joy can co-exist; cf Phil. 1.23 and 1.19; 3.1; 4.4.

110 To allegorise fasting is an evasion of the difficulties and not a solution.

Chapter 9
MARK 10.1-12

The movement from 9.33-50 to 10.1-12 is at first sight somewhat surprising. 9.33-50 developed 9.30-32 in the direction of discipleship: the disciple accepts all who work in the name of Jesus whether they appear to be outside the Christian community or are unimportant members within it, and, in a more remote development of the theme which already lay in the pre-Markan material, the disciple examines himself carefully lest he stumble and no longer be able to be considered a member of the community. 10.1-12 seems to be much more like a 'rule' for the community than an expansion of a call to discipleship /1/. Did Mark introduce 10.1-12 at this point, and, if so, with what purpose? It has been suggested /2/ that all that lies between the second and third passion predictions, 9.33-10.31, was originally a pre-Markan complex which he modified and enlarged. The material has not sufficient homogeneity for this, as the subsequent discussion will show.

If then 10.1-12 did not belong to 9.33-50 in the pre-Markan tradition and if therefore 10.1-12 was introduced at this point by Mark, was it previously an isolated pericope or part of a complex consisting of some or all of the pericopae in 10.1-45? Elsewhere we have discussed this in detail and need only give our conclusions here /3/. We believe that Jeremias /4/ is basically correct in viewing 10.1-31 as a pre-Markan complex dealing with 'marriage, children, possessions', though we disagree with him in many details and particularly with his view that vv.13-16 have a baptismal orientation. All three pericopae (vv.1-12,13-16,17-31) cohere because they deal with discipleship in relation to an external factor: the marriage partner, children of the marriage, possessions. The early church put together the sayings of Jesus without much regard for logical consistency; it did the same here with these three pericopae, though, of course, there is a certain amount of affinity between them; this affinity was probably greater in the pre-Markan stage, for the changes Mark made in respect of the second /5/ and third /6/ sections decrease their coherence. If he saw some common element in them, even in their present form, and brought them together (which is the alternative to his finding them together in the tradition), then it is even more probable that someone prior to him should have observed their affinity and brought

99

Following Jesus: Discipleship in Mark

them together.
Turning now to 10.1-12 itself it needs to be examined for
signs of Markan redaction. Verse 1 is largely, if not entirely,
his. The first half καὶ ἐκεῖθεν /7/ ἀναστὰς /8/ ἔρχεται /9/ εἰς
τὰ ὅρια /10/ τῆς .. is almost verbally identical with 7.24a; both
are Markan seams. In the second half his hand is seen in the use
of πάλιν /11/, in the historic present συμπορεύονται and in the
reference to Jesus as teaching which appears regularly in
redactional verses /12/. The crowd plays no part in the
subsequent story and acts only as a foil to prepare the way for
the secret teaching of the disciples in vv.10-12; if not Markan it
has been emphasised by Mark /13/. The first half of the verse
was constructed by Mark to show Jesus as one step further on
his journey towards Jerusalem - the journey which began at
8.27. At 9.30,33 he was in Galilee, now he is reaching Judea
/14/, a stage nearer to the cross the goal of his journey.
There are few signs of Markan editing within vv.2-9 /15/ and
it is generally taken to be from the pre-Markan tradition /16/.
Verses 11,12 represent the adaptation of the original discussion
to the Roman environment where women could divorce their
husbands. It is unlikely that Mark has created this extension
which makes the original logion of Jesus cover both sexes /17/;
it almost certainly represents the rule of the Roman church.
But has Mark added it to the tradition at this point /18/ or was
it already united to vv.2-9 /19/? Verse 10 is largely Markan: the
reference to the house /20/, the private instruction of the
disciples /21/, the simple union through καὶ to what preceded,
the use of πάλιν /22/ (linking back to previous private
instruction) and ἐπηρώτων, /23/, probably influenced on this
occasion by its use in v.2. That v.10 is largely or wholly Markan
/24/ does not mean that vv.11f were not previously linked to
vv.2-9 /25/; if these verses and the pericope were known to the
Roman community they would have been associated at least in
thought. Mark, then, has probably not brought them together
but has re-written the link so that vv.11f are seen as private
teaching of the church and therefore of importance to it. If so
this confirms our rejection of Kuhn's hypothesis /26/ that Mark
used 10.2-12 only because it was already attached to 10.35-45
and not because he himself was interested in it.
Why has Mark included this pericope in his Gospel at this
point where he is dealing with the nature of discipleship and
relating it to the passion of Jesus, especially since in v.1 he has
either deliberately introduced the crowds or stressed their
presence as the recipients of Jesus' teaching /27/? In the
sexually permissive world of Rome some teaching on marriage

was necessary and the Christian claims in this respect (as seen in vv.2-9) would have borne heavily on those who were contemplating entrance (the crowds are the uncommitted /28/) into the church. It is not then surprising to find such a section in the Gospel, and in particular in relation to discipleship seen from the point of view of the cross. The prospective disciple is warned that his present sexual ethic will have to be abandoned and a new and rigorous attitude adopted, an attitude where he will almost certainly have to take his cross and deny himself. Mark's sexual teaching is as absolute as the cross itself.

So far this seems satisfactory. But since Mark has introduced the disciples at v.10 he implies that there is also special teaching (vv.11f) for them. What is this special teaching? Does it differ from the teaching of vv.2-9 or is it explanatory of it? Elsewhere in the Gospel when Jesus has taught the crowds and goes on to give special teaching to the disciples this private teaching either explains the previous teaching (4.10-12) or draws out its consequences more explicitly (7.17-23; 9.28f; 10.23-31) /29/. Verses 2-9 begin with the question of the possibility that a man might divorce his wife but the answer of Jesus, based on Gen. 1.27; 2.24, says that husband and wife are 'one flesh' and cannot be put apart because God has joined them /30/. This conclusion actually forbids divorce to both husband and wife, though within the original context of vv.2-9 the extension to the wife was not envisaged. The addition of vv.11f makes this extension explicit, and this was necessary for the Roman church in whose area wives could divorce their husbands /31/. It is true that vv.11f appear only to condemn re-marriage after divorce whereas v.9 forbids divorce itself but in their present context vv.11f re-inforce the view that marriage is indissoluble /32/ but names the sin, viz. adultery, which in Christian eyes almost invariably resulted in pagan society when a marriage was broken up by one partner.

The distinction between vv.2-9 and vv.11f has been seen in another way by Baltensweiler /33/ who regards vv.2-9 as a demand which is made on the crowd while vv.11f represents a church law /34/ for disciples. But this is not the kind of distinction which Mark makes between teaching to the crowds and teaching to the disciples and he does not elsewhere set down church laws for the guidance of members. If vv.11f once functioned as a 'church law' in independence of vv.2-9 it does not continue to do so in Mark. Caught up now in the discipleship section it explicates what discipleship involves in relation to marriage as vv.17-31 will do in relation to wealth.

Notes

1   The suggestion of R.H. Lightfoot, The Gospel Message of St. Mark, p.114n, that Jesus is here conceived as the bridegroom of his people, who is faced with the necessity to decide whether he will maintain his union with his people or divorce himself from them, is too fanciful.

2   H. Baltensweiler, Die Ehe im Neuen Testament, p.73.

3   'Mark 10.13-16: The Child as Model Recipient'. Kuhn, pp.146-191 (cf. Pesch, II, pp.128-130), has argued in great detail that the original complex contained the pericopae about marriage (vv.2-12), wealth (vv.17-31) and service (vv.35-45) on the grounds that we have three pericopae (a) which are similar in form, (b) which had a similar Traditionsgeschichte, (c) which deal with community problems of behaviour. Mark, he alleges, wished to use only the final pericope but retained the first two because they were in an existing complex. Our reasons for rejecting Kuhn's view are stated in the article referred to at the beginning of this note and will also appear from time to time in our detailed discussion of the passages.

4   J. Jeremias, Infant Baptism in the First Four Centuries, p.50; cf. Schweizer, ad loc.; Légasse, pp.36f, 206-18; Grundmann, ad loc; Reploh, pp.174, 186.

5   See pp.106-8.

6   See pp.110ff.

7   Cf. 6.1; 9.30; 7.24 (all seams).

8   Cf. 1.35; 7.24 (both seams), and Doudna, pp.55f.

9   Note the use of Mark's favourite historic present.

10   Cf. 5.17; 7.24,31 (bis; the last three are seams).

11   17-28-3-43.

12   E. Schweizer, 'Anmerkungen zur Theologie des Markus', pp.37ff.

13   The text is uncertain in both v.1 and v.2 in relation to the crowd and the Pharisees and it is difficult to account for the reference to both. The singular ὄχλος, which Mark uses everywhere else, is read in various ways by D W θ faml it syrs copsa The reference to the Pharisees is omitted by D ita,b,d,k,r(l)syrs Orig. It is possible that D ita,b,d,k,r(l) syrss retain the original reading: καὶ συμπορεύεται (συνέρχεται) πάλιν ὄχλος πρὸς αὐτόν ... καὶ ἐπηρώτων αὐτὸν...The plural ἐπηρώτων would accord with Mark's normal practice of using a plural after the singular ὄχλος. The plural 'crowds' would have appeared under the influence of the plural verb and the reference to the Pharisees would have come from Matthew (cf. the note by B.M.M. and A.W. in Metzger, ad loc., for the second suggestion). If however the plural ὄχλοι is taken as original

then Mark will probably have found this in the tradition which will have read, 'The crowds came to Jesus and according to his custom he taught them and they asked him', and the reference to the Pharisees will be either a Markan addition or a later assimilation to Matthew. Elsewhere in Mark it is the Pharisees who usually try Jesus with questions.

14   So Reploh, p.178.

Whether καί is to be read before πέραν is doubtful (see the thorough discussion by Taylor, ad loc.) because Mark's travel data are not always geographically accurate (cf. 7.31; 8.10; see Reploh, p.175); a firm conclusion either way would not in any case affect our argument.

15   Cf. Reploh, pp.181f; see also K. Niederwimmer, Askese und Mysterium, p.15. If the reference to the Pharisees in v.2 is not original ἐπηρώτων may be a Markan impersonal plural.

16   The view of B.K. Didericksen, Den markianske skils-misseperikope, pp.116ff (cf. Haenchen, pp.338-41), that vv.2-9 were composed by Mark or a Gentile Christian (probably a Roman) has been effectively refuted by A. Isaksson, Marriage and Ministry in the New Temple, pp.119,121 and Baltensweiler (as n.2), pp.52f. We can add the non-Markan allusion to the failure of the Pharisees or crowds (depending on the reading; see n.13) to understand (σκληροκαρδία); with Mark it is disciples who fail to understand; cf. K. Berger, 'Hartherzigkeit und Gottes Gesetz'. On the essentially Jewish background to the pericope see Daube, pp.71-9. Berger argues that v.9 contains nothing to which a Jew would object (pp.536f); he takes the original pericope to have consisted of vv.1,2,9 (p.552). 10.2-9 may contain an attack on the Jewish Law (Suhl, pp.72-6), but this is not Mark's primary interest.

17   Cf. Isaksson (as n.16), p.72; Baltensweiler (as n.2), pp.59,66; G. Delling, 'Das Logion Mark. X.11'; Kuhn, pp.161ff. The changed form of v.12 shows that it is secondary to v.11 (Berger, pp.557f, claims that v.11 is more Semitic) and represents its further adaptation to a new situation where women could divorce. This extension to women is implied in 1 Cor. 7. Taylor's attempt (ad loc.) to argue for the reading of D fam 13 syr^s, even if correct, does not establish v.12 as belonging originally to a Jewish context (cf. Kuhn, pp.162f; Baltensweiler (as n.2), pp.66f). It is just possible that v.12 could reflect a Jewish situation; cf. E. Bammel, 'Markus 10.11f und das jüdische Eherecht'. Berger, p.534, argues that the teaching of v.9 is to be distinguished from that of v.11 since the latter unlike the former deals with re-marriage.

18   So Schweizer, ad loc.; Niederwimmer (as n.15), p.20.

103

19 So Kuhn, pp.160f. Kuhn does not, of course, believe that vv.11f were united with vv.2-9 in the earliest form of the tradition and refutes Daube, pp.141-150, on this point. Mt. 5.32; Lk. 16.18 show that v.11 had an independent existence.

20 See below, ch.28. The use of εἰς for ἐν is Markan; see Turner, JTS 26 (1924/5) 18f.

21 Cf. 4.10-12, 34; 7.17-23; 9.2-13; 10.23-31; etc.

22 17-28-3-43.

23 8-25-17-2.

24 Kuhn, p.167, (cf. Suhl, pp.72f; W. Marxsen, 'Parabeltheorie') disputes the Markan nature of the verse and regards only the reference to the house as his. He argues: (i) οἱ μαθηταί without αὐτοῦ is unusual in Mark; it does, however, occur at 9.14; 10.24; 14.16 (the Western and Byzantine traditions add αὐτοῦ) in redactional passages (14.16 with its parataxis reads very much like Mark's composition); (ii) καὶ λέγει αὐτοῖς (v.11) is not normally Markan. Admittedly in most of its appearances in the Gospel it came from the tradition (2.25; 3.4; 6.50; 11.2; 12.16; 14.13,34,41) but it is Markan at 1.38; 6.31; 7.18; 9.35, and 4.13 may be Markan (cf. Räisänen Die Parabeltheorie im Markusevangelium, pp.102ff.). Even if it is pre-Markan in v.10 the reference of αὐτοῖς to the disciples is created by Mark if he introduced the disciples into the account; it would have referred originally either to the Pharisees or to the crowd; (iii) ἐπερωτᾶν is not generally used by Mark for questions asked by disciples; it is, however, found in this way at 7.17; 9.11; 9.28; 9.32; 13.3, all of which are Markan passages; it is also a favourite Markan word, cf. n.23.

25 Many scholars think Mark united the sections: Bultmann, pp.26f; Sundwall, p.63; Reploh, pp. 179-85; Knox, I. p. 69. Reploh (p. 184) argues that v.12 in fact comes from Mark, for only when vv.6-9 are present can v.12 be deduced from v.11. If however, vv.11f were joined in the pre-Markan tradition to vv.2-9 then any case for seeing v.12 as Mark's addition falls to the ground.

26 See n.3.

27 πάλιν ἐδίδασκεν clearly points forward to vv.2-12 showing that it is to be understood as teaching for the church.

28 Cf. pp.28f.

29 Lagrange (ad v.10) sees vv.10-12 as an application of the principle of 4.34.

30 That Jesus is seen in v.9 to present a 'better' argument than Jewish legal arguments may represent polemic against the Jewish Law but belongs to the pre-Markan stage (cf. Berger, pp.537,561).

31   The distinction between vv.2-9 and vv.11f is similar to that between 7.1-15 and 7.17-23. In each the earlier public instruction is based on the O.T. and the later private elucidation is given in simple and direct teaching.
32   Didericksen (as n.16), pp.91ff.
33   (As n.2), pp.74f.
34   Cf. Haenchen, pp.337, 341; Baltensweiler (as n.2), p.75.

Chapter 10
MARK 10.13-16 /1/

We have already argued /2/ that in the pre-Markan material
10.13-16 belonged with the pericopae which precede and follow
it. The Markan seams connecting them are slender consisting
only of a simple καί at v.13 and little more at the junction with
the story of the rich man /3/. Though at first glance it might
seem as if our pericope took place in the house of v.10 because
v.17 speaks of Jesus 'going out' this is not necessarily true; even
if it were it would not affect the understanding of the story
since we know nothing about the 'house' of v.10 and since it is in
any case clear that the crucial saying of v.15 is addressed to
the disciples and not to the crowd, or (even primarily) to those
who brought the children. The subject of προσέφερον (v.13) is
not the disciples; it is easier to regard it as an impersonal plural
('children were brought to Jesus') than to assume that the
inhabitants of the house brought their children. The verb itself
is non-Markan /4/ and probably formed the original introduction. In v.13b ἐπιτιμᾶν is a Markan favourite /5/ but some
rejection of those who bring the children is essential to the
story and the idea at least must be pre-Markan; it is
conceivable that he re-wrote this and introduced an explicit
reference to the disciples using his favourite word.

Verse 15 breaks the smooth connection between the first
narrative portion of the pericope and its climax in v.16 and
probably did not originally belong here /6/. Also when it is
present the three sections of 10.1-31 do not form a simple set
of instructions on marriage, children and possessions so that if,
as we have argued, this was a pre-Markan complex of
pericopae, v.15 cannot have belonged to it when it was first
compiled. It is likely that it had an independent existence as an
isolated logion (cf. Mt. 18.3 /7/; Jn 3.5 /8/); once introduced it
makes v.16 unnecessary, a fact which Luke clearly realised
since he omitted it (cf. 18.15-17). At what stage, then, was v.15
added? Before we consider this we must also examine v.14c,
τῶν γὰρ τοιούτων. It hangs together with v.15.

Without both v.14c and v.15 we have a straightforward
incident in which children are brought to Jesus so that he may
touch them; they are repelled by the disciples who in turn are
rebuked by Jesus; he then finally touches and blesses the
children /9/. Verse 14c is more easily explicable as inserted into

this subsequent to the addition of v.15 than prior to its addition, for v.14c is a typical Markan γάρ clause /10/. Within it τῶν τοιούτων can either have its classical meaning, 'the kingdom belongs to those similar to children', in which case it means much the same as v.15, or its occasional Hellenistic meaning, 'the kingdom belongs to these (= τούτων) children', i.e. to these particular children or children as a class /11/. If v.14c predates v.15 then this second meaning must be accepted; if v.14c was a Markan insertion it must have the first meaning; but even if v.14c predated v.15 once the latter is present the first meaning seems the more natural. Finally, if, as we have argued, v.14c is Markan, then it serves to emphasise v.15 rather than the original meaning of the pericope. If Mark added v.14c then since it is a comment on v.15 it is probable that v.15 was present in the pre-Markan tradition, though not in its earliest form: the 'catch-word' παιδίον probably led to its insertion at this point.

If then we eliminate both v.14c and v.15 we have a simple account: children are welcomed by Jesus. In the ancient world children were easily ignored as an unimportant section of the community /12/. The disciples wished to ignore them but Jesus would not; he had time for children and to show it he is ready to bless them. Given this interpretation we can see how the pericope came to be attached to that on divorce (10.1-12) in the oral tradition; it follows the latter just as children follow marriage and it answers the question of their relationship to the church - a question which certainly agitated some Christian circles (1 Cor. 7.14). But it is unlikely that any defence of infant baptism was intended at this stage /13/. Even if there was there is certainly none intended in its use by Mark /14/. The addition of vv.14c,15 changed the meaning of the pericope; attention is no longer directed to the need to bring children to Jesus in baptism or in some other way, but to the need to be like children in receiving the kingdom. This meaning is appropriate to the main drive of the Gospel at this point, viz., the understanding of discipleship. To say that discipleship meant bringing one's children to Jesus in baptism would be incongruous as an explication of taking up the cross, denying oneself or losing one's life.

If then the pericope is to be understood in relation to discipleship and if vv.14c,15 form its true climax, what does it mean? The child is clearly the model but is the kingdom to be received as a child is received or as a child receives /15/? We reject the former solution because: (i) In the ancient world children were not honoured and surely the kingdom is something

107

which is to be honoured by receiving it. (ii) Neither Matthew (see 18.3) nor John (see 3.5) can be made to have this interpretation, which suggests it was not the original. (iii) V.14c blends more easily with v.15 on the assumption that children are the models of how to receive /16/. We conclude that the kingdom is to be received in the way children receive, which is the interpretation generally accepted by commentators, though the way in which they have viewed this on the part of the child has varied. We must dismiss from our minds any attempt to romanticise the child for this would have been foreign to the ancient world. Rather, just as a child trusts an adult and receives from him what he offers, so the disciple is to trust God and receive from him the kingdom. But the kingdom is not a 'thing'; it is God's active rule; the disciple has therefore to allow God to rule in his life. He does not achieve this all at once when he becomes a disciple; it is a gradual process; hence our pericope fits appropriately into a discussion of the nature of discipleship. The disciple who does not receive God's rule now into his life will never enter the future kingdom (cf. 9.47; 10.17,21,23,25,30).

In its earliest form, lacking vv.14c,15, the story could have been used to set out Jesus as an example of the way in which the disciple ought to receive one of the least respected members of society, the child. This understanding is impossible in the Markan form and position of the pericope. Here Jesus has a special position. The children are brought to him and he blesses them; the disciple who receives the kingdom will also be the recipient of Jesus' blessing. Jesus is not just another disciple but is in a category all of his own.

Notes

1   For a fuller discussion of this pericope see Best, 'Mark 10.13-16; The Child as Model Recipient'.
2   See ch.9 and the reference in n.1 here.
3   See the discussion in the next section.
4   15-3-4-2. Pryke, pp.107-9, takes the impersonal plural as a sign of redaction. Mark may have varied the form of the verb used in the tradition.
5   6-9-12-0. In Mark the word almost always appears in redactional passages.
6   Cf. Bultmann, p.32; Légasse, p.38; J. Jeremias, 'Mc 10. 13-16'; J.I.H. McDonald, 'Receiving and Entering the Kingdom'.
7   Cf. Légasse, p.43.
8   Cf. Légasse, pp.33-5; W.L. Knox, II, p.16,n.1; Ambrozic,

pp.136-8. But contrast W.G. Thompson, Matthew's Advice to a Divided Community, pp.76-8, 136f.

9   The pericope would thus originally have been an apophthegm or pronouncement story whose climax was an action and not a logion of Jesus. It probably goes back to Jesus himself; it was certainly not composed as a setting for v.15 (cf. Bultmann, p.32). The reception and blessing of children would not be exceptional in a Jewish environment; cf. J. Jeremias, Infant Baptism in the First Four Centuries, p.49; Billerbeck, I, pp.807f.

10   See p.51, n.81; cf. Pesch, II, p.132. Pryke, p.133, for no apparent reason regards it as coming from the tradition.

11   Cf. N. Turner, pp. 46f; Légasse, p.39; Bl-Deb, §304.

12   Cf. p.93, n.32.

13   The view that the pericope relates to the baptism of infants has in recent times been upheld principally by J. Jeremias (as in n.9), pp.48ff, and O. Cullmann, Baptism in the New Testament, pp.25f,71ff, and opposed by G.R. Beasley-Murray, Baptism in the New Testament, pp.320ff; K. Aland, Did the Early Church Baptize Infants? pp.95-9; cf. Légasse, pp.210ff.

14   For a more detailed discussion see Best (as n.1). M. Smith, Clement of Alexandria and a Secret Gospel of Mark, pp.167ff, has argued that Mk. 10.13-45 was a baptismal lection (he includes with it the portion of the 'longer text' of Mark which he found in a letter of Clement of Alexandria). We find his argument unconvincing; see Best (as n.1) for discussion.

15   The various ways of understanding vv.14c,15 are discussed in great detail by J. Blinzler, 'Kind und Königreich Gottes (Markus 10,14f)'. He does not however allow for possibilities of redaction.

16   For fuller discussion see Best (as in n.1). Ambrozic, pp.152ff, provides a variant of this view; we have discussed it in that article.

Chapter 11
MARK 10.17-31 /1/

We have already seen·that there was a pre-Markan association of 10.17-31 with the pericopae about divorce (10.2-12) and children (10.13-16) but this section has undergone much more Markan redaction than either of the other two. It divides into three distinct paragraphs: (i) vv.17-22; (ii) vv.23-27; (iii) vv.28-31. While the primitive Christian teaching may have associated instruction about marriage, children and wealth, (iii) has little direct relation to the theme of wealth and only part of (ii) has. We require to examine all three paragraphs to determine both the extent of Markan redaction and whether any portions of them were united in the pre-Markan tradition.

We commence with vv.17-22. Though this short narrative may have been altered during transmission there is little of Mark's hand to be detected in it /2/ apart from the opening and conclusion. A simple καί unites it to the preceding incident; ἐκπορεύεσθαι is a favourite Markan word /3/ and when Jesus calls disciples, as he calls the man here, he (Jesus) is normally seen as in motion (1.16,19; 2.14); Mark regularly begins pericopae with a participle (1.16,19,29,35; 2.1 etc.) and he favours the genitive absolute /4/; ὁδός is used by Mark to depict the way that Jesus goes and the way of discipleship /5/. The first five words of v.17 are thus Markan /6/. Probably the final clause to the whole incident (v.22b) is also since it is a typical Markan γάρ clause /7/ and uses the periphrastic imperfect /8/ which Mark likes. The clause serves to intensify the drama of the occasion, and gives a reason for the man's rejection of Jesus. For Mark the rich man is a potential disciple /9/; the kind of ties which may have held back such enquirers from full commitment are given in vv.29f.

In the second paragraph, vv.23-27, v.23 relates to wealth, v.24 generalises it omitting the reference to wealth, v.25 again returns to deal explicitly with wealth /10/, v.26 expresses the astonishment of the disciples (as had v.24a) and ends with a question from them to which v.27, again without any reference to wealth, is the answer. In v.26b, σώζειν belongs to the vocabulary of the early church and the question is hardly therefore original. The logion of v.27 is a theological maxim based probably on certain O.T. passages (Zech. 8.6; Job 10.13; 42.2; Gen. 18.14: see in each case the LXX) /11/ and would

110

sound more at home on the lips of Paul than of Jesus. Verse 27a betrays signs of Mark's hand: the use of βλέπειν and its compounds and synonyms in seams (cf. 8.33; 10.23; 11.11, and contrast Matthew and Luke), the historic present λέγει /12/. Verse 26a also is probably Markan: περισσῶς appears only twice in the N.T., here and in Mk 15.14 /13/; πρὸς ἑαυτοὺς is Markan /14/. We conclude that Mark, employing a logion current in the early church /15/, has added vv.26,27 to vv.23-5 /16/. The effect of this addition has been to change a saying about the difficulty of entering the kingdom (with special reference to the difficulties created by wealth) into a theological statement expressing the impossibility of becoming a Christian except by the grace of God. Mark is but the first to have turned the edge of a 'hard' saying by transforming it into a theological proposition! We must thus attribute the core of vv.23-25 to the pre-Markan tradition for he would hardly have added vv.23-5 to vv.17-22 and then immediately changed their meaning /17/.

This, however, is not to argue that all of vv.23-5 is pre-Markan; these verses need to be examined in more detail. At first sight v.23a appears to come from Mark's hand because of its use of περιβλέπειν but Kuhn has pointed out that the construction of v.23a (καὶ + participle + subject + λέγει + object in the dative) is characteristic of the tradition rather than of Mark /18/. Verse 23a may then belong to the underlying tradition, but whether it does or not its logion surely does. However v.24 /19/, which generalises v.23, is probably Markan for in emphasising the astonishment of the disciples we have a Markan theme expressed through a Markan word /20/. There is nothing in the next clause, 'And Jesus said ...', which can be viewed as either particularly Markan or non-Markan; it serves to introduce the logion which concludes the verse. From where does this logion come? It is perfectly general, lacking the reference to possessions of v.23b. It is most unlikely that both are original; we therefore give the preference to v.23b which is specific and concrete, and thus much more likely to have originated in some actual situation (it probably goes back to Jesus). The logion of v.24 has then been created out of v.23b and since Mark's hand can be detected in at least part of v.24a it seems fair to conclude that he created all of v.24 /21/, perhaps as a foil to vv.13-16; its unrestricted nature forms a preparation for the general statements of vv.26f, which we have seen were added by Mark. We are now left with v.25; there is no reason to suggest Mark created it; at no point does it bear any sign of his hand; its vivid nature is reminiscent of the genuine logia of Jesus /22/. We conclude that v.23b, if not all of this verse, and v.25 came to Mark in the tradition.

The total result of the additions Mark has made in vv.24,26f has been to generalise discipleship from a precise reference to the abandonment of wealth to discipleship in and of itself /23/. It is as impossible to become a disciple as to become a little child (10.15; cf. Jn 3.3,5, which imply it can only take place through the Holy Spirit); to become a disciple is to be the object of God's miraculous activity. Similarly in 1.16-20; 2.14 Jesus calls and without psychological preparation men immediately rise to follow him leaving their work and homes. Clearly Mark has not worked out the philosophical question of man's freedom (he probably never realised it existed!). For the rich man has been called but unlike the fishermen brothers and Levi he has been able to withstand the divine call, and vv.28-30 clearly imply a conscious decision on the part of the individual to follow. Leaving aside the philosophical question the pericope could be used to explain why some men were not disciples; they had been preached to and yet they had turned down the good news: the sacrifice was too great. The church is thus supplied in this pericope with an explanation of the failure of the gospel to come home to some to whom it was preached /24/. A psychological explanation is not necessary when disciples accept the call, for in their own eyes it has been the compelling voice of Christ, but they require some explanation when others reject; later thought attributed this to the devil; Mark has not developed the concept of the devil in this way.

If vv.24,26f generalised the difficulty of a rich man becoming a disciple into that of any man becoming one, vv.28-31 /25/ generalise the idea of abandonment. Obviously there were not many wealthy people whom the early church was regularly challenging with the Gospel but there were always those who had some possessions and even more those who felt themselves tied by their family relationships which they might be unwilling to give up. Thus while vv.28-31 have some connection with vv.17-22,23,25 there is an abrupt break in thought after vv.26f. Because vv.28-31 do not deal with wealth alone they will not originally have followed v.25 (assuming vv.23,25 belonged with vv.17-22 from an early stage of the growth of the tradition).

Has then Mark joined vv.28-31 to the rest of the material or was this paragraph appended after v.25 in the pre-Markan tradition? Verse 28a with its use of ἄρχεσθαι /26/ as an auxiliary and its reference to Peter /27/, in whom Mark appears to take a special interest, is almost entirely Markan, but he may have written v.28a either to introduce vv.28b-31 or to re-connect them to vv.17-25. If vv.28-31 had followed directly on v.25 there would have been an abrupt break, not because vv.28-31 widen the theme of abandonment but because they contain the idea of recompense which is foreign to vv.23,25 (though the idea was already present in v.21; this makes easier the attachment of vv.28-31 to the whole section). The presence of vv.26f serves to soften the jar between vv.28-31 and v.25. We assume then that Mark added vv.28-31 at this point, and, as we shall see, nothing in our analysis of his internal modification of this paragraph will cast doubt on this provisional conclusion.

Not only did Mark compose v.28a but everything suggests that he also wrote v.28b, though vv.29f may have previously had some form of introduction /28/. V.28b corresponds to 1.18 in the combined use of ἀφίημι and ἀκολουθεῖν in relation to Peter, and the second of these words is a Markan favourite /29/. In v.29 the list is disjunctive: to abandon any one of house, brother, etc. will bring a reward; but in v.28a πάντα is total: everything must be abandoned. Mark has thus made the demand universal and absolute, going far beyond that made on the rich man. Unlike 6.6b-13 where instructions are apparently given only to missionaries /30/ we have a duty here laid on all in Mark's community; the call for renunciation is made to the disciples (Christians) as disciples (Christians)/31/.

As well as appearing in the Matthean parallel to our passage v.31 is also found in different contexts in Lk. 13.30 and Mt. 20.16. It was thus an independent logion which has been added here, probably by Mark but certainly at a late stage of the tradition /32/. In its present context the point of the logion lies in its final clause, for there was nothing in the earlier verses to suggest that the rich or mighty of this world are to be cast down /33/. It is the new position of the disciple which is at issue. The disciples who have abandoned all will receive eternal life and become the 'first'; v.31 has a basic eschatological orientation and therefore cannot refer to the recompense 'now in this time'. It was probably added at a stage later than the insertion of the reference to eternal life (v.30), or possibly simultaneously with it. This reference to eternal life carefully balances the initial question of the rich man (v.17). Either, then, this reference was introduced into the tradition in vv.28-30 when it was added to vv.17-27 by Mark in order to round off the material /34/, which as we shall see is the more probable, or it was its existing presence which was one of the factors leading to the use of vv.28-30 at this point. The contrast between 'in this time' /35/ and 'in the coming age' is Jewish and was probably added to the earliest form of the saying (which we take to have stopped at ἑκατονταπλασίονα

/36/ and not have included 'for my sake and the gospel's sake') by the Jewish-Christian community. Without it the saying could be taken as wholly eschatological; with it the saying distinguishes between present and future rewards, a distinction which would become more necessary as the interval before the parousia was seen to lengthen. The addition of νῦν adds nothing to the meaning but accords with Mark's love of dual statements /37/ and so we may attribute it to him.

In v.30 the list of v.29 /38/ is repeated /39/ with one omission, 'father', and one addition, 'with persecutions'. The omission clearly implies a Christian situation for the Christian could not have many 'fathers' since he has one alone, God /40/. The addition /41/ harmonises with the way in which Mark has depicted discipleship: following Jesus (cf. ἠκολουθήκαμεν, v.28) in terms of the cross /42/. Occupying the position of emphasis at the end of the list it removes any temptation to 'follow' for the sake of reward; despite his ultimate recompense the Christian cannot escape persecution /43/. The re-appearance in v.30 of the list of v.29 is clumsy and unnecessary; both Matthew and Luke omit it. It was probably added by Mark and the other evangelists then omitted it either because they saw its clumsiness and 'flatness' or because they knew the saying without it in the oral tradition. By its repetition Mark identifies the reward that comes in this life; this probably led him also to identify the reward of the coming age as eternal life; the contrast with persecutions is fitting (cf. Lk. 6.22f; Mt. 5.10-12; 1 Pet. 4.14). Perhaps the process actually worked in the opposite direction: adding 'eternal life' to balance the question of v.17 he had also to add an internal balance in v.30 and so created the list.

What is the recompense of the Christian in this age? When he is converted ties of kinship, home and occupation may be severed (cf. 13.11-13; Lk. 14.26f; 9.59-62) but these ties will be replaced a hundredfold by new ties with fellow-Christians; he will find that he has many brothers, sisters, mothers /44/; there will be many 'homes' in which he will be received as a member /45/; he will share in the corporate possessions of the church ('fields'; although the 'communism' of the early Jerusalem Christian community may have been rapidly abandoned what we know today of the way small sects look after the financial needs of their impoverished brethren suggests the same would probably have happened in the Christian community in Rome) /46/.

In v.29 Mark has probably made one other addition: 'for the gospel's sake'. We have seen how he did this in 8.35, and he has probably introduced it here for the same reasons and to produce the same effect /47/.

We can now see that Mark has widened the pericope in two different ways: (i) By the addition of vv.24,26f he implies that it takes an act of God to make a man a Christian. (ii) By the addition of vv.28-31 he implies that (a) total renunciation (πάντα in v.28 is Markan) is required from the Christian, (b) this renunciation is recompensed now through the fellowship of the community and in the future through eternal life, and (c) the path of the Christian lies through persecution (he has added 'with persecutions'). If the original unit of tradition emphasised the keeping of the Law (v.19) /48/ this stress has disappeared in Mark; for Mark discipleship ('following') is not related to the Law but to the person of Jesus. Thus Mark uses vv.17-22 because of the demand of v.21, and the extensions he makes in vv.23-7 and vv.28-31 are not attempts to argue against the importance of the Law.

Notes

1   For a fuller treatment of this pericope see Best, 'The Camel and the Needle's Eye'. To the literature quoted there add P.S. Minear, 'The Needle's Eye' and Commands of Christ, pp.98ff; Kuhn, pp.146-91; Ambrozic, pp.158-71; M. Lehmann, Synoptische Quellenanalyse, pp.90-102.
2   Our pericope is often used as an argument for the existence of an Ur-Markus since there is quite considerable agreement between Matthew and Luke in their omissions from Mark. These omissions however can be explained quite satisfactorily in terms of the editorial habits of Matthew and Luke; cf. Haenchen, ad loc.; N. Walter, 'Zur Analyse von Mc. 10.17-31'. See also Lehmann (as n.1), pp.90-102, in relation to the theory of E. Hirsch.
3   6-11-3-2; of the Matthean occurrences four (3.5; 15.11,18; 20.29) are derived from Mark, one (4.4) is in an O.T. quotation, and the sixth (17.21) is textually uncertain; of the three Lukan usages one (3.7) may be dependent on Mark (1.5) but the others (4.22,37) are not.
4   Cf. Pryke, pp.62ff.
5   See pp.15-18. The absence of the article could cause some doubt on it as deriving here from Mark's redaction.
6   It is just possible that the remainder of the verse up to γονυπετήσας is also Markan since it is missing from Matthew and Luke and has the vivid detail which Mark appears to like. Pesch, II, p.135, takes v.17a to be the pre-Markan link to v.12.

7   Berger, pp.402f, suggests that v.22b makes the connection between vv.20-22a and vv.24b,25 through v.23 because vv.24b,25 had no original reference to riches. But Mark does not use γάρ clauses to make connections and it is very doubtful if v.25 was originally entirely general.

8   Cf. Taylor, p.45; Pryke, pp.103ff.

9   Potential disciples are also seen in Lk. 9.57-62.

10   On the variant readings, see Linton, 'Evidences for a Second-Century Revised Edition'.

11   Cf. Schweizer, ad loc.

12   Cf. Taylor, p.46.

13   Mark alone also uses ἐκπερισσῶς (14.31) and ὑπερπερισσῶς (7.37) for neither of which is there any pre-biblical evidence. The second of these is again associated with ἐκπλήσσεσθαι at 7.37 which is probably also a redactional passage.

14   0-5-2-0; Cf. 9.10; 11.31; 12.7; 14.4.

15   Perhaps vv.26b,27 were a question and answer drawn from the instruction of catechumens.

16   The language and style of vv.26f is analysed in great detail by Kuhn, pp.171-3, who concludes that of themselves they do not prove Mark composed these verses.

17   It is not necessary for us to determine whether they originally belonged with vv. 17-22. I have discussed this in 'The Camel and the Needle's Eye'.

18   Cf. Kuhn, pp.149f. It is not possible to accept his further point that περιβλέπειν is non-Markan because it is not found in Markan seams. In retelling stories Mark seems to like to make a reference to Jesus and others 'looking'.

19   For a discussion of the difficult textual question in relation to this verse see Best, 'The Camel and the Needle's Eye', where it is argued that א B W give the correct reading.

20   θαμβεῖσθαι is used by Mark alone of the evangelists; 0-3-0-0 (cf. ἐκθαμβεῖσθαι 0-4-0-0); cf. Walter (as n.2). For the theme as Markan see Tagawa, pp.99ff; Minette de Tillesse, pp.264ff.

21   Cf. Pryke, pp.99,100,112.

22   Cf. Minear, 'The Needle's Eye'.

23   Here we differ from Ambrozic (pp.170f) who, since he takes vv.23,25 to be Markan additions, regards Mark as moving from a general statement to emphasis on the perils of wealth for disciples.

24   Other interpretations of the reasons why men reject the gospel are given in 4.11f and 4.14-20.

25   For a discussion of textual variants and of Markan priority see M. Goguel, 'Avec des persécutions'.

26   Cf. Taylor, pp.48,63f; Pryke, pp.79ff; Doudna, pp.51-3, 111-117.

27   Peter is inappropriate in the present context since in the list of v.29 the reference is not to boats or nets but to fields. Note also the omission of 'wives' from the list (contrast Lk. 18.29); while it is possible that this is due to the genuine memory that Peter as apostle had not left his wife (1 Cor. 9.5; cf. Mk 1.29-31) it is more probably explained by the 'hundredfold': the disciple as possessor of a hundred wives would suggest the wrong idea!

28   ἔφη ὁ ᾿Ιησοῦς probably was the pre-Markan introduction (there are similar phrases at 9.12; 10.20; 12.24; 14.29; cf. Reploh, p.202). Both v.28 and v.29 begin asyndetically, which suggests that Mark is not merely adding material but also composing; cf. C.H. Turner, JTS 28 (1927) 9ff.

29   Cf. pp.36f.

30   Cf. Chapter 22.

31   Not only has the logion not been conformed to Peter's occupation as fisherman but it has not been adapted to suit the urban Roman community to which Mark was writing; this could have been achieved through the omission of 'fields' and the insertion of a general reference to 'possessions'. The emphasis lies, in any case, more on 'family' than on property.

32   This is much more satisfactory than the view of Walter (as n.2) that Luke and Matthew derived the logion from Mark but placed it in other contexts. This implies that Matthew used it twice, once in the Markan parallel and once at 20.16; it does not appear to be his habit to use material twice in this way. We must admit that it is possible that v.31 was already linked with vv.29,30a in the pre-Markan stage but this is unlikely for the reasons given in the text.

33   Bultmann, p.111, takes the logion to have been originally minatory in intention; it cannot have this flavour in our context. Pesch, II, p.135, points out that it balances 9.35b; the latter follows after the second prediction of the passion as 10.31 immediately precedes the third; in this way the section 9.33-10.31 is held together.

34   So Walter (as n.2). The phrase 'eternal life' is rare in synoptic material and is not Markan. However the repetition of a concept already in the material would not be un-Markan (cf. Neirynck, p.128).

35   In vv.17-22 the reward is 'future' (v.21) without a 'present' reference.

36   Thus many commentators from Wellhausen onwards. We cannot agree with Berger, p.405, that a statement of reward in

order to be effective must spell out the reward in detail.

37   Cf. Neirynck, p.95.

38   The content of the list in Luke (18.29) is different; we cannot say what its earliest form was; disjunctive lists of this type are easily subject to alteration. Luke's reference to 'wives' would not go happily with Mark's 'hundredfold'. Trocmé (p.204), however, thinks Mark makes no reference to wives because the problem of separated missionary couples must have been acute in his community and points to the closeness (10.1-12) of the reference to divorce.

39   Neirynck, pp.96,99.

40   '... the gap in ... the Christian's spiritual family is filled by God himself' (J.M. Robinson, The Problem of History in Mark, p.81, n.1). While this is probably the reason for the absence of 'father' it is also true that the 'father-child' relationship was known to the early Christians (cf. 1 Cor. 4.15; 1 Thess. 2.11). That Mark retained the reference to the father in v.29 shows his respect for the tradition he received.

41   We note that the form 'with persecutions' differs from the others in the list (it should have been διωγμούς). This suggests it was added at the time when the list was created. Its form as well as its position creates the contrast with the list of 'new possessions'.

42   Cf. Reploh, p.204.

43   We cannot accept the view of Goguel (as n.25) that the list of 'possessions' is intended ironically and that only 'persecutions' is to be taken seriously. For the possible background in Jewish mission literature, cf. Berger, pp.421-39; see also T. Job 4.6f.

44   There is no need to view this as a spelling out in a Christian context of the fifth commandment (see H.-H. Schroeder, Eltern und Kinder in der Verkündigung Jesu, pp.125ff). For the enriched sense of personal fellowship in the early church see Rom. 16.13; 1 Cor. 3.22; 4.15; 2 Cor. 6.8-10; Philm 10; 1 Tim. 5.2f; Jn 19.28f.

45   This interpretation is preferable to that which sees here a reference to 'house-churches'.

46   If Mark's form of the list in v.29 goes back to the 'communism' of the primitive community this may explain the absence of any reference to 'wives'. Luke's list would then represent a later modification. (See also n.38).

47   Cf. p.40. Bultmann (pp.110f; cf. Schweizer, Hauck ad loc.) holds that the Lukan phrase 'for the sake of the kingdom of God' represents the original wording which Mark has altered, but Marxsen (pp.79ff), followed by Walter (as n.2), correctly argues that Luke avoids the term 'gospel' (he uses the verbal form) and

therefore replaced it by 'the kingdom of God', one of the ruling
terms of the passage.
48   Cf. Berger, pp.431ff.

Chapter 12
MARK 10.32-34

The third passion prediction is fuller than the other two and even quite conservative scholars recognise it as <u>vaticinium ex eventu</u>. Did Mark compose it or did he obtain it from the tradition? It follows fairly closely the account of the passion in his Gospel and could therefore have been composed by him /1/. But since Mark's passion account was presumably derived from that of the Roman church the prediction could have been formulated from it in the Church in Rome, or even at some earlier stage during the handing on of the passion narrative. Certain differences between it and the Markan passion narrative can be accounted for most easily if the prediction came from the tradition /2/: e.g. the omission of the 'elders', the false witnesses and the ill-treatment of Jesus by the Jewish authorities. On the other hand most of v.32 is redactional as we see from the use of 'the way', 'the going up to Jerusalem' (drawn from the tradition of vv.33f), the periphrastic imperfect, the theme of fear. Probably the prediction was introduced in the tradition by a reference to the Twelve which Mark has widened by writing v.32a so that the teaching which follows can be seen to be for all disciples and not just for the Twelve alone. In v.32a Mark intends us to see only one group at whose head Jesus goes and which follows him /3/. Elsewhere Mark has stressed separately the fear and amazement of the disciples; now he brings both themes together.

What caused their fear and astonishment? Would it not have come better after vv.33f? Mark's readers, however, know that Jerusalem is the place of Jesus' death, even if this is the first time it is mentioned as the goal of his journey, and ἐν τῇ ὁδῷ through its use in association with the other predictions recalls to them that he is going there to die. The disciples are amazed at him going this way; they are afraid as they follow because the end for them may be the same. This implies that at this point they understand what is about to happen to Jesus, whereas at 8.31-33 Peter simply did not believe that Jesus could suffer. Verses 35-45 show that they still do not understand what it will mean for themselves; Bartimaeus (10.46-52) is the first who is depicted, howbeit symbolically, as understanding /4/. Mark may not be wholly consistent in the way he speaks of the amazement and fear of the disciples but we need to remember that he is not 'historicising' the disciples but using them in order to instruct his own church. The church knows of the death of Jesus and should be amazed at it; its members need to realise what the way of Jesus means for them and this may lead them to fear.

Both the fear and amazement of the disciples is regularly associated with the 'uncanny' in Jesus and his deeds (4.41; 6.50; 16.5,8) and it may be that Mark sees something of this in the picture of Jesus 'at the head'. If so we should be careful not to read into this any idea of Jesus as the strong young hero who strides manfully at the front of his disciples to the sure fate that awaits him while they tail along fearfully behind /5/.

Finally we should note the urgent sense of movement in these verses; it is clearer than in either of the other predictions. They go up to Jerusalem /6/; they follow Jesus; he goes ahead of them. The same word is used here as in 14.28; 16.7; as the risen Jesus goes ahead of his people in mission so the earthly went ahead of them in suffering; unless they go with him to Jerusalem, they cannot be with him in Galilee /7/.

Notes
1   E.g. Taylor, p.438; cf. Strecker, 'The Resurrection and Passion Predictions ...'; Hahn, p.37; Cook, p.55. It is viewed as pre-Markan by Tödt, pp.171-5; Reploh, p.108.
2   For further details of the redaction and tradition in vv.32-34 see Best, 'The Twelve'; cf. R. McKinnis, 'An Analysis of Mark X 32-34'; Pryke (see his index of passages quoted).
3   We take δέ in οἱ δέ to be continuative; cf. Thrall, Greek Particles, pp.51f. The references which she gives to δέ-continuative relate to its use with the article acting as a demonstrative pronoun. There are many more instances; it is only the context which enables us to decide whether it is used in continuation or adversatively. 10.50 provides a clear example of the continuative use in which, as in 10.32, we have article, participle and finite verb. See also Meye, pp.162f.
4   See ch.14 (b).
5   This 'psychological' interpretation has even been expanded in relation to the attitude of supposedly different groups in their following of Jesus by A. Menzies, The Earliest Gospel, p.197.
6   ἀναβαίνειν was used cultically of going to the/a temple both in Jewish and secular Greek; cf. J. Schneider, TDNT, I, pp.519-22. Mark's readers might not know of the elevation of Jerusalem above Jericho but they would pick up the word's

'pilgrimage' overtones. Its regular use in Jewish Greek may have occasioned its presence in v.33; this would support Schweizer's view (ad loc.) that vv.33f were formulated in a Jewish-Christian context.

7   Cf. Best, pp.173-7 and ch.23 below.

Chapter 13
MARK 10.35-45

We have already rejected Kuhn's theory that this pericope together with those on divorce and wealth formed a pre-Markan complex /1/. We therefore assume that Mark introduced 10.35-45 at this point in order to follow up the third passion prediction. But did 10.35-45 exist as a pre-Markan unit? We note: (i) Verses 35-40 relate to the position which John and James hope to attain in Christ's glory and therefore have an eschatological reference whereas vv.41-5 relate to those who hold positions of authority in the present age and in this world. The answer to the original question of v.35 is given in v.40 /2/. Verses 42ff criticise those who already exercise power either for exercising it at all or for exercising it in the wrong way and not just for the desire to exercise it as in vv.35-40 /3/. (ii) Verses 42b-45a are found in another form in Lk. 22.24-7 showing that they possessed independent existence at some period in their transmission /4/. (iii) Verses 35-40 is basically narrative /5/ but vv.42b-45 consists of a sequence of logia, and while it is not impossible that two such diverse sections should have belonged together in the tradition it is unlikely /6/. (iv) Verses 41,42a are in large part, if not entirely, Markan: ἄρχεσθαι is employed as an auxiliary /7/ and we have a participial form of προσκαλεῖσθαι with a verb of saying /8/. (v) While vv.42b-45 may have their meaning elucidated by a reference to a dispute they do not require such a context to be understood. We conclude that it was Mark who united vv.35-40 with vv.42b-45. He may have been led to do this since 'sitting' (v.37) and the exercise of authority are associated or because of the reference to the death of Jesus both in v.38 and in v.45.

The two sections now need to be examined individually. We commence with vv.35-40. There is nothing at its beginning other than καί suggestive of Mark's hand; the incident had its own introduction which required no alteration when it was placed after the passion prediction. This implies that the names of John and James were present prior to Mark; indeed had Mark introduced them there would have been no need to identify them as the sons of Zebedee since this had already been made clear twice (1.19; 3.17). Within the incident vv.38,39 are generally regarded as an addition to its original form /9/ for the question asked by James and John is not answered until v.40

123

/10/ and the two intervening verses add little to its elucidation. Furthermore an independent tradition at Lk. 12.50 embodies the 'baptism' theme of vv.38f showing that at one time this existed apart from the question of James and John. Did then Mark introduce vv.38f? There is nothing distinctively Markan about v.38a /11/; it is not his habit to add 'splinters of tradition' in this way /12/; we have already seen that he added vv.41-5 but there is no obvious common theme between it and vv.38f. We therefore conclude that vv.38f were inserted into vv.35-7,40 prior to Mark /13/.

Within its context Mark vv.38f may be understood either literally in relation to martyrdom or sacramentally /14/. I have argued elsewhere /15/ for the latter: on this view James and John feature as typical believers; all believers participate sacramentally in the passion of Jesus; there cannot then be special seats in glory for special believers /16/. If, alternatively, we assume the reference is to literal martyrdom, then we can either regard the verses as an explicit allusion to a supposed martyrdom of James and John or to them as examples of martyrdom to the church in Rome with the actual fact of their martyrdom left as relatively unimportant. Setting aside the question of the historicity of John's early martyrdom it is difficult to see any reason why Mark should wish to emphasise the fact of their death other than as example. There is no reason to think of James and John as special heroes of the Markan community, and if their position were being attacked we would expect it to be done more clearly, for v.40 /17/ does not exclude their possession of a special position in glory. That, however, they may be presented as examples certainly fits in with the general theme of the passage: in 10.32-4 Jesus has predicted his death; then as in the movement from 8.31 to 8.34 we go on to the death of disciples; James and John are types who have gone the way of the cross; they wish to follow Jesus to his kingdom but have not understood that the way to it is the way of the cross. It is not 'heavenly places' which are important for Mark but present following of Jesus, and this involves suffering /18/. Thus if we understand vv.38f of literal martyrdom, or suffering, nothing essential is added to the way in which Mark has presented discipleship in 8.31,34, but the point made there is driven home with renewed emphasis. If, however, we adopt the sacramental interpretation of the verses, implying a participation in the death of Jesus, a new element is introduced which relates the life of the disciple to the sacraments of the community. This leads on more adequately to vv.42-5 where the sacramental dying to or with

Christ is developed as a daily dying in service to him and to men, whose basis is his death (v.45b); if so the flow of thought follows a pattern of early church catechesis. On the supposition that vv.38f refer to literal suffering or martyrdom vv.42-5 must be regarded as Mark's reinterpretation of this as daily service to Christ and men; in that case vv.42-5 could have followed directly after the third prediction and there would have been no need of vv.35-40; yet Mark has introduced both sections. This confirms the view that Mark intended the sacramental understanding of vv.38f.

We turn now to vv.42b-45. We have already concluded that vv.41,42a are mainly Markan and designed to introduce vv. 42b-45. How did this sequence of logia begin in the pre-Markan tradition? Since Mark in writing his seams often incorporates existing introductions to pericopae we may assume that the logia sequence commenced with either 'Jesus said' or 'Jesus said to ...'. In view of the second plural in vv.43f it is probable that some group was identified and it would presumably have been either the disciples or the Twelve. Since we find 'The Ten' in v.41 it is easier to assume it was 'the Twelve'; the mention of 'the Ten' is not strictly necessary; had the group been 'the disciples' Mark would have written 'the other disciples'. Moreover, contrary to the view of some scholars, we have not elsewhere discovered any particular desire on the part of Mark to introduce the Twelve /19/. Thus we conclude that the pre-Markan tradition began 'Jesus said to the Twelve'. In support of this conclusion we can adduce the independent but parallel piece of tradition in Lk. 22.24-7 which, because of its setting in the Last Supper, has as its audience the Twelve (cf. 22.3,30). This section of Luke is introduced by a reference to a dispute among the Twelve about who was greatest and it is possible, but by no means probable, that vv.42b-45 had such a reference in their pre-Markan setting; if they had, Mark's use of vv.35-40 rendered it unnecessary.

Verses 42b-44 /20/ cohere but there is a break at v.45 caused by the introduction of the term 'Son of man'. Did then v.45 belong with the preceding logia in the pre-Markan tradition? This question has to be taken further, for a break also exists between v.45a and v.45b created by the introduction of the reference to 'ransom', so that it is possible that v.45a belonged with vv.42b-44 but v.45b did not. We begin with v.45a, and we assume that Lk. 22.24-7 was not derived from Mark but represents an independent but parallel strand of the same tradition. Lk. 22.27b introduces a reference to the service of Jesus; it is not significant that it is couched in the first person singular and not the third referring to the Son of man for we sometimes find the same saying appearing in both forms /21/. This implies that the tradition underlying both Luke and Mark concluded with a saying speaking of Jesus' own activity /22/. But, since the Lukan passage has no parallel to Mk 10.45b, that clause must be a later addition to the sequence /23/. Was it added by Mark /24/? Mk 10.42b-45a is more Palestinian in colouring than Lk. 22.24-27 /25/; Mk 10.45b is also Palestinian in colouring /26/. It is therefore inherently probable that the two came together during the Palestinian period of transmission; it is unlikely that an isolated fragment /27/, such as v.45b would have been, would retain its Palestinian colouring until the time of Mark and then be added. There are, moreover, no signs of Markan redaction /28/.

Following Bultmann /29/ vv.42b-44 can be described as a community rule; this does not mean that it was a rule devised by the community /30/ and enforced on its members; such enforcement would probably be self-defeating. In these verses the Christian concept of greatness is opposed to that of the secular world /31/; strictly the contrast is not between two ways of exercising authority, a good way (that of Christians) and a bad way (that of secular rulers) but between authority good or bad and service; two terms are employed to make the distinction clear: διάκονος, δοῦλος. These are not necessarily synonymous; the latter can refer to the status of an individual and the former to a particular kind of unimportant or degrading service, viz. serving at table /32/, but within the present context they approximate in meaning. Either can be applied to a position of importance within the church and the first is certainly used in this way in Phil. 1.1 and the second possibly /33/, but although Mk 10.42-44 may deal with the behaviour of those who claim to hold some position of authority in the Christian community this has hardly occasioned their present use. In their context they describe how a Christian, or a Christian leader, ought to behave and they do not assert the status or official position of leaders within the community /34/. Thus while Paul regularly uses the root διακον-to describe his own ministerial activity (Rom. 11.13; 2 Cor. 3.3,6; etc.), especially in relation to the collection for the saints (Rom. 15.25,31; 2 Cor. 8.4; etc.), a more satisfactory parallel to its use in our passage is found in the way the root is used in the Gospels of the service of women (Mk 1.31; 15.41; Lk. 8.3; 10.40; cf. Mt. 25.44) /35/; this is service of a personal nature freely offered. It is surprising that this root is used, for it has no real biblical background. Secular ways of exercising authority are rejected and a secular word with a basic meaning 'to wait at table' is actually employed to describe Christian behaviour. Just as it does not refer to ecclesiastical office in our context no more does δοῦλος imply legal status; it indicates the nature of the work that one who is important in the church must be doing, work which would normally be accounted proper for a slave. Just as John the Baptizer was ready to attend to the sandals of the one who was to come after him, the follower of Jesus must be ready to treat in the same way, not merely the Lord if he should appear, but any fellow-Christian (cf. Mt. 25.31-46). In the secular field pre-eminence is associated with public honour and position (v.42b); in the church it emerges in humble, unrewarded service (vv.43f).

When v.45 was added to the community rule of vv.42b-44 it brought this humble service of the community's members into relationship with Christ. The same root, διακον-, now describes his behaviour and καὶ γάρ links v.45 causally with vv.42b-44. Here the theme of the imitation of Christ /36/ makes one of its rare appearances in Mark. While in 2 Cor. 8.9 and Phil. 2.6-11 /37/ imitation is related to Christ's example in becoming man, it is related here to his behaviour on earth. Verse 45b serves to focus this not only on his day by day activity (v.45a) but also on his once-for-all death, an emphasis often found elsewhere in the N.T. (Eph. 5.2,25; 1 Pet. 2.21; Heb. 12.2f; in Jn 13.34; 15.12 Christ's love is probably to be seen both in his incarnation and death /38/). But v.45b does more than increase the appeal for the imitation of Christ by recalling the depth of love displayed in his death; it supplies the foundation on which imitation must be based. Jesus' love in dying may be an example for men but 10.45b isolates an element of uniqueness in his dying: it has redemptive significance. In the theology of Mark no one other than Jesus can give his life a ransom for others. For Mark Christianity is not the imitation of Jesus, if it were the theme would appear more often, but redemption through Christ, and it is only on the basis of this redemption that imitation becomes possible. If the underlying connection between vv.42b-44 and v.45b is the table-fellowship of the Eucharist /39/, then this interpretation is confirmed in that the death which the Eucharist celebrates is the foundation of the community.

Verse 45b offers a suitable ending to the long section on discipleship which commenced at 8.27, for it brings the death of Christ back into the centre of the picture; the discussion began from the first prediction of that death (8.31). Moreover in providing an interpretation of the death it opens up the way for the final journey to Jerusalem and the passion itself. If v.45b provides the basis for discipleship, v.45a relates the life-style of the disciple to that of his Lord; the disciple is always tempted to link his life-style to that of those who appear important in the world (v.42b). If then, vv.42b-45 was a unity prior to Mark, as we believe it was, we can see why he picked this particular pericope to conclude his instruction of the members of his church on the nature of their discipleship: discipleship can only be understood in the light of the cross and must be based on redemption through the cross.

Assuming then that Mark wished to end this section of his Gospel in this way, we can also see why he inserted the pre-existing unity of vv.35-40 here. Both it and vv.42-5 deal with the assessment of success. John and James wish to measure it by the position they will attain in the future eternal kingdom, where a position of importance would bring them honour from others. This is only one example of how men ordinarily reason about success, but as such it comes under the same general rebuke (vv.43f) as Jesus gives to any who seek it in the style of v.42b. In addition vv.42b-45 require some setting; they may have been prefaced in the tradition with some reference to a disagreement among the disciples; if so the substitution of vv.35-40 sharpens their point. Consequently the third prediction of the passion (10.32-4), as the earlier two, leads on to teaching about discipleship, but unlike them it is brought speedily to a climax in v.45. The very speed with which this climax is reached throws into strong contrast what Jesus has done and the ease with which believers forget it and devote themselves to building up their own positions.

Possibly there were other reasons assisting in the association of vv.35-40 and vv.42b-45: (i) Both v.45b and v.38 /40/ provide interpretations of the meaning of the death of Jesus. (ii) Verse 40 indicates that a decision on position within the kingdom can only be made by God, presumably in the light of what he sees of a disciple's total behaviour, and the total behaviour on which judgement is made is indicated by vv.43f. (iii) Given the sacramental understanding of vv.38f both it and v.45 relate the activity of believers to the death of Jesus; participation in his death (vv.38f) provides the ground on which daily dying (vv.43f) can alone take place.

There may however be another and quite different deduction to be drawn from Mark's collocation of vv.35-40 and vv.41-45. John and James ask after an apocalyptic position (cf. 1 Cor. 4.8) and are refused it; to reign is to serve (vv.41-45) /41/. In a sense Mark is denying the application of Dan. 7.27 to his community. Chap. 13 has much to say about the sufferings which face Christians in the end period but nothing about how they will reign. The nearest we come to this is in 10.30, and yet all that is promised there for the post-parousia period is eternal life and not honoured positions.

Finally we need to enquire after the role of the Twelve in vv.35-45; the Ten of course were as guilty as James and John. Does the passage deal generally with the service of all disciples or specifically with that of the leaders of the community? We saw in vv.32-4 that Mark deliberately widened an original reference to the Twelve; has he then here narrowed the reference back to the Twelve alone? James and John belonged to the unit which Mark used in vv.35-40; this of itself would quite easily draw in a reference to the remainder of the Twelve, i.e. the Ten (vv.41-5); this supports our view that the Twelve were already mentioned in the pre-Markan introduction to vv.40-5. It is therefore probable that Mark did not introduce the Twelve into vv.35-45 but used them because he already found them there; thus he did not deliberately narrow the wider reference he created in vv.32-4.

Yet this does not fully answer our question for, though the content of vv.42-5 deals with the nature of greatness, it explicitly introduces those who exercise authority in the secular sphere and by implication deals with authority in the Christian community. If Mark was written for the benefit of that community in Rome, how well established was a form of leadership there when he wrote? 1 Clement, written probably about twenty-five years after Mark, though it does not indicate any particular officials in Rome, certainly implies their existence by the type of argument it uses against dissidents in Corinth; at this time there must have been some fairly clear line of demarcation between 'ruler' and 'ruled'. Paul's letter to Rome, written at most fifteen years prior to Mark, is much less definite. No leaders are picked out in the address (1.7; contrast Phil. 1.1); the terms used in 12.6-8 relate to function rather than to position. Mark must fit in somewhere between these two; it is difficult to know at what stage rulers holding a permanent position will have emerged. But the desire to be considered important does not necessarily relate to being a 'ruler' in what we would ordinarily recognise as ruling situations: the glossolaliacs of Corinth (1 Cor. 14) desired primary positions in the community. Observation shows that anyone who works within a community or organisation seems to wish to have his work acknowledged by his fellows. As at 9.33ff we would probably go too far if we were to assume that Mark was only attempting to rebuke 'rulers' in his community /42/. But even if he intended it as a rebuke to the rulers we cannot extend this to mean that he was rebuking the historical Twelve; in the instruction they received he offers them as examples to the community's leaders; he is not waging war against them or any party which adhered to them /43/. The same holds for the way John and James are used in vv.35-40; there is no attack on a party linked to their names.

Notes

1   See ch.9, n.3.
2   Cf. Bultmann, p.24; Reploh, pp.157f, etc. Contrast Dibelius, p.51; R.H. Lightfoot, History and Interpretation, pp.119f.
3   S. Légasse, 'Approche de l'Episode préévangélique du Fils de Zébédée'.
4   H. Schürmann, Jesus Abschiedsrede: Lk 22.21-38, pp.63-98, V. Taylor, The Passion Narrative of St Luke, pp.61-4, and T. Schramm, Der Markus-Stoff bei Lukas, pp.50f, all argue for the independence of the Lukan passage with respect to Mark. H.J.B. Combrink, Die Diens van Jesus, pp.13-38 contests that position. Cf. E. Arens, The ΗΛΘΟΝ Sayings, pp.117-134.
5   Bultmann, p.24, classifies vv.35-40 as an apophthegm, Dibelius, pp.43,60 as a paradigm.
6   9.38f is exceptional; 'catch-words' probably led to its insertion; see discussion of 9.33-50.
7   Taylor, pp.48, 63f; Doudna, pp.51-3, 111-117; Pryke, pp.79-87.
8   προσκαλεῖσθαι 6-9-4-0. The construction with the aorist participle followed by a finite verb of speech is common in Mark, cf. 3.23; 7.14; 8.1; 8.34; 12.43 and here; all of these are in redactional passages with the possible exception of 12.43. At 3.13; 6.13 we have a finite form of the verb. Kuhn, pp.159f (cf. Pesch, II, p.161), disputes the conclusion that vv.41,42a are Markan for ἄρχεσθαι appears as an auxiliary in non-Markan material (2.23; 10.47) and προσκαλεῖσθαι is similarly non-Markan in 12.43; 8.1; 15.44. Whether he is right or wrong in his particular instances of non-Markan passages (and we would dispute some of them), Kuhn does not allow for the joint appearance of these two Markan characteristics. Meyer, I, pp.144f, attributes all of 10.32b-45 to his 'Twelve-source' and appears to exclude any significant Markan redaction.
9   Cf. Bultmann, p.24; Reploh, p.157; Légasse (as n.3); G. Braumann, 'Leidenskelch und Todestaufe (Mc 10.38f.)'.
10   Since this logion implies no position of importance for

Jesus (cf. 13.32) but asserts that God allots the places of glory it is probably early.

11   W. Wrede, p.106, suggested that v.38a with its reference to the ignorance of the disciples (cf. 4.13; 9.6; 14.40) should be attributed to the evangelist and Reploh argues that it was formed by Mark employing αἰτεῖσθαι from v.35. These views are correctly contested by Légasse (as n.3), p.162, n.1. The theme of ignorance appears in the pre-Markan material; the misunderstanding of Peter probably lay in the tradition of the transfiguration (see discussion of the passage) and its presence in the present context is perfectly natural.

12   Cf. Kuhn, p.158.

13   Cf. V.P. Howard, Das Ego Jesus, p.100.

14   We do not need to determine whether the saying is a piece of the genuine teaching of Jesus or to seek its place in the life of the pre-Markan church. On the meaning of the imagery used, see, most recently, R. le Deaut, 'Goûter le calice de la mort'; A. Feuillet, 'La coupe et le baptème'; Légasse (as n.3).

15   Pp.152-7. See also F.G. Cremer, 'Der "Heilstod Jesus"'; Feuillet (as n.14); Braumann (as n.9). For other references and a critical rejection see Légasse (as n.3), p.176, n.3.

16   Lane, p.378, comments that John and James have an inflated understanding of their own position; it is not only church leaders among Christians who have this.

17   The reading ἄλλοις (v.40) is weakly attested and probably arose from a failure to divide ἀλλ' οἷς . ἡτοίμασται is passive; God is to be understood as its subject, a point which some MSS make explicit through harmonisation with Mt. 20.23; cf. Metzger, ad loc.

18   Cf. Reploh, pp.156ff.

19   Cf. Best, 'The Twelve'.

20   Verses 42b-44 was not the original unit of tradition; something similar to vv.43b-44 will have preceded it as the parallels in 9.35; Lk. 9.48b; 23.11 indicate (cf. Schulz, p.253, n.4). But vv.42b-44 were certainly a pre-Markan unity as Lk. 22.24-7 shows.

21   Cf. J. Jeremias, 'Die älteste Schicht der Menschen-sohn-Logien'; F.H. Borsch, The Christian and Gnostic Son of Man, pp.5ff.

22   Mark may have introduced γάρ as in the pre-Markan sequence 8.34-8, but this does not mean he added 10.45a.

23   It is conceivable that it was present in Luke's source and that he omitted it, for in his interpretation of the death of Jesus he does not stress its soteriological value but its nature as God's act. If this possibility is allowed it would strengthen our

argument that v.45a and v.45b were already joined prior to Mark. Combrink (as n.4), p.161, argues that their union goes back to Jesus.

24 Cf. Klostermann, ad loc.; Trocmé, pp.124f.

25 Cf. J. Jeremias, 'Das Lösegeld für Viele (Mk. 10,45)', pp.216-29, and New Testament Theology, pp.292-4; E. Lohse, Märtyrer und Gottesknecht, pp.117ff; see also Schürmann (as n.4), pp.79ff; he argues only for the greater originality of Lk. 22.27 over against Mk 10.45a.

26 Cf. Lohse, (as n.25), pp.118f; Jeremias, as n.25, 'Das Lösegeld'; W.J. Moulder, 'The Old Testament Background and Interpretation of Mark X.45'. For our purposes it is unnecessary to determine whether v.45b depends on Isa. 53; those who reject Isaianic dependence do not deny Jewish colouring; cf. M.D. Hooker, Jesus and the Servant, pp.74-79; C.K. Barrett, 'The Background of Mark X.45'; Suhl, pp.114-120; Best, pp.140-4. For a discussion of all the issues see, most recently, Combrink (as n.4), passim. If 10.45b draws on the picture of the Maccabean martyrs then the saying may come from a Hellenistic Jewish Christian environment (cf. Dautzenberg, pp.98ff).

27 It may not originally have been a Son of man saying but become so through its present context; cf. Tödt, pp.203ff.

28 Cf. J. Roloff, 'Anfänge der soteriologischen Deutung des Todes Jesu (Mk. x.45 und Lk. xxii.27)' at p.51.

29 P.146.

30 We should not picture the early Christians as armed with a rule-book or a constitution.

31 The variant ἔσται (v.43) is a natural correction of ἐστιν and is almost certainly wrong. Mark is not thinking about the historical Jesus laying down rules for the future but of their application to his own community. K.W. Clark, 'The Meaning of [ε το]κυριεύειν', has argued convincingly that the translation of this word as 'lord it over' is much too strong and that it means no more than 'exercise authority'. Rulers display their greatness in the secular world by the exercise of authority but in the Christian community by service.

32 Cf H.W. Beyer, TDNT, II, pp.81ff; K.H. Rengstorf, TDNT, II, pp.261ff; W. Brandt, Dienst und Dienen im Neuen Testament; Combrink (as n.4), pp.39-109.

33 Cf G. Sass, 'Zur Bedeutung von δοῦλος bei Paulus'; Best, 'Bishops and Deacons: Philippians 1.1'.

34 The ὑμῶν of v.43 prevents us drawing a sharp distinction between a group (the Twelve?) which rules and a group which is ruled.

35 Cf Combrink (as n.4), pp.87-106.

36   Cf Schulz, pp.260ff; Kuhn, pp.156f; Pesch, II, pp.162f.

37   Whatever the original meaning of the Christological hymn it seems to carry some idea of the imitation of Christ in its Philippian context.

38   Schulz, pp.302ff, classifies in relation to literary form the passages where the theme of imitation is found in the N.T. Cf also Roloff (as n.28).

39   The Lukan parallel to vv.42a-44a appears in the context of the Eucharist. See Tödt, pp.209f; Roloff (as n.28).

40   Cf Best, pp.152-7.

41   This provides another argument for rejecting an apocalyptic interpretation of Mark.

42   Reploh, pp.169f, leaps too quickly to this conclusion.

43   Cf Best, 'Mark III, 20,21,31-5', and 'The Role of the Disciples', for discussions of the general way in which Mark uses historical figures as illustrative material for his own community.

We have seen that two inter-related themes run through
8.27-10.45, viz. the nature of Christ and his mission, the nature
of discipleship. The whole is constructed as a journey from
Caesarea Philippi to Jerusalem and is preceded and followed by
healing miracles in which blind men have their sight restored by
Jesus. Blindness is a common symbol for lack of understanding
and its recovery for the opening of the mind. We need then to
examine these two pericopae about blindness so that their
symbolic meaning can appear. Both are transition sections /1/.
Almost all the miracles recorded by Mark are found in 4.35-
8.26; so a miracle with a symbolic meaning about discipleship
(8.22-6) fittingly concludes the miracle section and leads into
the section on discipleship /2/. 10.46-52 takes us from the
discipleship section where discipleship is related to the cross of
Jesus to the story of the cross itself (11.1ff) by means of a
disciple who is prepared to go the way of the cross with Jesus.

Notes
1   While many commentators associate 8.22-6 with what
precedes and 10.46-52 with what follows, D.J. Hawkin, 'The
Incomprehension of the Disciples', links both the miracles to
8.27-10.45.
2   Cf Best, 'Miracles'.

(a) 8.22-26
8.22-6 follows directly on a passage, 8.14-21, which has been
constructed by Mark /1/ and whose principal theme is the
blindness of the disciples. In 8.27-10.45 the disciples are taught
the true understanding of Christ and of discipleship and thus
given the possibility of sight. 8.22-6 with its story of the
restoration of sight to a blind man comes between the later
passage and 8.14-21. The emphasis in 8.22-6 does not then lie on
the actual healing but on its symbolic meaning: the restoration
of sight to disciples. The pericope has been carefully positioned
by Mark and is not the result of his adoption of two parallel
pre-existing complexes (6.30-7.37; 8.1-26); these 'parallel' com-

plexes are probably a scholarly fiction /2/.

It is generally agreed that there is little Markan redaction within 8.22-6; the initial clause (v.22a) καὶ ἔρχονται /3/ εἰς βηθσαϊδάν probably comes from him /4/, though the original tradition may well have contained the place name /5/. Although v.26b /6/ appears to contain a command to silence it is probably better not to take it as redactional for it is not the way in which Mark formulates such commands /7/. It is just possible that καὶ ἐνέβλεπεν τηλαυγῶς ἅπαντα (v.25) is his for it is typical of the way he repeats himself. It may be, however, that the clause introduces a new point if its imperfect tense is to be contrasted with the preceding aorists: the man having had his sight restored continues to see clearly. Moreover though Mark does use ἐμβλέπειν redactionally at 10.27 /8/ it can hardly be described as one of his favourite words /9/. But even if Mark did not write these words he must have accepted the very great stress laid by them on the complete restoration of the man's sight. Verses 22b-26 are then almost entirely from the tradition. There is a close association of our passage with 7.31-37; the two may have formed a doublet in the tradition, a link which Mark has broken for his own purposes.

While it is unnecessary to examine vv.22b-26 in detail /10/ the three compounds of βλέπειν are noteworthy /11/. After the first attempts at healing the man's sight returns (ἀναβλέψας) /12/; as the sequel shows, the man does not yet see normally. After Jesus' second attempt he does so: διαβλέπειν can carry the sense 'see clearly, distinguish' /13/, ἐμβλέπειν the sense 'see into, understand' /14/ and the accompanying context implies that his sight, symbolic of his understanding, is now perfect, and will continue to be so (imperfect tense).

When we enquire into the significance of this healing for Mark it is essential to take seriously the two stages in which it is carried through; it is the only healing effected by Jesus which is not immediately complete. If recovery of sight means the attainment of understanding and if this refers to the disciples then the lesson must be that the disciples did not immediately attain full understanding. We cannot therefore see the confession of Peter at Caesarea Philippi, the immediately succeeding event, as the fulfilment of the symbol contained in the miracle /15/. The confession of Jesus as the Messiah would be formally correct but gravely inadequate /16/, for Peter does not understand that the Messiah, the Son of man, has to suffer and die. 8.27-10.45, as we have seen, is wholly taken up with the teaching that the way of Jesus is the way of the cross and that anyone who would be his disciple must realise that this is also the way for the disciple, a way not of triumph but of suffering /17/.

But it can be objected here: (a) the disciples have already some sight from the time of their call, otherwise they would not have become disciples. (b) They never attain full sight within the Gospel; right through 8.27-10.45 they continue to misunderstand Jesus' teaching (cf 9.6,10,32; 10.32,37); in the passion itself they are still unable to see (14.29,37,50,66-72). Thus they are as blind at the time of the death as they were in 4.10-13; 6.52; 8.14-21; there has been no change.

But that is not the full story and we must add: (c) Surprisingly Mark does not bring out in any way the insight of the disciples at the time of their call; Jesus calls and they respond; the accounts are devoid of psychological detail. (d) We find for the first time in the Gospel in 8.27-10.45 a true and full explanation of the necessity of Jesus' passion and of the nature of discipleship; at its conclusion, that is after full instruction, we have the healing of another blind man who immediately follows Jesus 'on the way', i.e. he is regarded as a true disciple /18/. Consequently we can conclude that Mark views true discipleship with real understanding as a possibility after 10.45, and indeed the structure of the Gospel implies that he finds this in the centurion (15.39).

But this still does not deal with the actual disciples and their failure to respond even after instruction. To appreciate the point more fully we need to take a wider perspective. Mark is writing for the Roman Christian community and is seeking to lure them away from a false view of Christ, possibly one which laid the emphasis on his miraculous powers so that he is seen as the one who heals physically, mentally and morally, and from whom the community primarily benefits in these kinds of ways. He wishes them to see Jesus on his cross as challenge; the disciple is not just the recipient of blessing but one who must take the gospel to the world, even though it will involve him in taking up his cross, denying himself, losing his true being, serving the least important members of society, being at the beck and call (the one who waits at table) of all. In order to achieve his purpose Mark uses the disciples as examples /19/; they represent in the Gospel the church of his own day, as the crowd, by and large, represents the unconverted mass /20/. The disciples are within (4.11f); they receive the mystery; they are given the essential teaching; and this is precisely what Mark is giving to those in his own church. Theoretically Mark should show the disciples responding to the teaching of Jesus and therefore gradually losing their blindness and gaining insight into his mission; but had he done this there would have been a serious conflict with the facts. Everyone knew the basic traditions about the disciples: Judas had betrayed Jesus, Peter had denied him and the remainder had fled when he was arrested. Mark cannot then show the disciples as receiving their sight prior to the resurrection, but by giving the relevant teaching which ought to produce sight he can help his own community who, unlike the historical disciples, are in the position of knowing of the resurrection. He preserves the basic accuracy of the tradition in relation to the actual blindness of the disciples and yet at the same time instructs his own people in the nature of Jesus' suffering and the necessity of their own. He can only do this symbolically. Thus the two stage healing of 8.22-6 is a picture of what ought to happen. Outsiders may be attracted to the church by the charismatic activity of its members in Rome (cf Acts 3.1ff; 14.8ff); once within they need to be brought to see the place of the cross in the life of Jesus and in their own lives. In the case of the historical disciples the second stage of their healing only took place after the resurrection and could not therefore be narrated in the Gospel; it is, however, told symbolically in 8.22-6 (and 10.46-52). For the church in Mark's day the first and second stages ought to take place more or less simultaneously but if in fact only the first has been achieved it is urgent that the second should be also. In actual fact the second is a stage to which the church needs to be continually brought back; men see and understand the cross for a time, and then forget. Mark's education of his church in this is a process which must continually be carried on so that the members have always the cross at the centre of their faith.

Both Matthew and Luke omit this pericope and their omission is often attributed either to the oddness of the healing (in two stages) or to the use of material means (spittle) to effect it. While these may be partial explanations there is in each case a deeper motive. In Matthew's Gospel the confession of Peter is a true confession, for Peter terms Jesus not only Messiah but also 'son of the living God' and the confession itself is attributed to God's revelation. In Luke's Gospel the failure of Peter to understand Jesus' prediction of his passion disappears. In neither case is there any reason for preserving a story which rejects immediate complete understanding on the part of Peter.

Notes

1   Cf Taylor, Schweizer, Best, p.78, T.A. Burkill, 'Mark

6.31-8.26: the context of the story of the Syrophoenician woman' in his New Light on the Earliest Gospel, p.50, Q. Quesnell, pp.103ff, Reploh, pp.76f.

2   Cf Taylor, pp.628-32; Lohmeyer, p.154; Nineham, pp.206f; Cranfield, pp.204f; Burkill (as n.1) pp.48-50.

3   On the variant readings here and elsewhere in the pericope see Linton, 'Evidences for a Second-Century Revised Edition'.

4   The evidence has been examined in great detail by E.S. Johnson, 'Mark 8.22-26'; cf G. Theissen, Urchristlichen Wundergeschichte, pp.130f. The impersonal plural of v.22b may also be Markan, caused by his re-writing of the introduction; cf C.H. Turner, JTS 25 (1924) 382. Mark has also used his favoured φέρειν; so Turner, JTS 26 (1924/5) 13.

5   The journey in 6.1-8.27 is geographically tortuous and it is difficult to be sure that the information is reliable; cf Johnson (as n.4).

6   We accept the reading of Codex Vaticanus; see Metzger, pp.98f. The command to silence is explicit in the reading of it^k; cf C.H. Turner, JTS 26 (1924/5) 18.

7   In fact there is no explicit command to silence in v.26b. Commands to silence are found at 1.25,34,44; 3.12; 5.43; 7.36; 8.30; 9.9 and are normally formed with a verb of command or prohibition followed by a clause introduced by ἵνα; cf Johnson, as n.4.

8   At 14.67 and 10.21 it belongs to the tradition; it may be its use in 10.21 which led to Mark using it again in 10.27.

9   2-4-2-2.

10   Verse 24b is difficult although the meaning is reasonably clear; see the commentators and Black, pp.53f.

11   Johnson (as n.4), has worked this out in great detail. I am indebted to him for the references of nn.12-14.

12   Cf Isa. 42.18; Tob. 11.8 (א); 14.2 (א B); Herodotus 2.111; Aristophanes, Pl. 95,117,126,866; Plato, Rep. 10.621b.

13   Cf Mt. 7.5; Lk. 6.42.

14   Job 2.10; Sir. 42.18; Xenophon, Mem. 3,11,10; Plato, Chrm. 155D; Polybius, Histories 15.28,3; Josephus, BJ 3.385; 7.341; Mart. Polycarp 9.2. It can also be used of spiritual vision: Philo, De Sobr. 1.3; 1 Clem. 19.3.

15   As do Lightfoot, History and Interpretation, pp.90f; P.Achtemeier, 'Towards the isolation of pre-Markan miracle catenae', pp.286f; R. Beauvery, 'La Guérison d'un aveugle à Bethsaïde'; A. Richardson, The Miracle Stories of the Gospels, p.86. Nineham, pp.217f, thinks of a more gradual opening of the disciples' eyes of which the second phase is found in 8.27-10.45. Koch, pp.68-72, rejects all connection with the context.

Schenke, pp.308f, accepts a connection but does not discuss the two stages of the healing. Johnson (as n.4) includes a thorough examination of the views of others.
16 Cf ch.4 (b).
17 Cf A. Kuby, 'Zur Konzeption des Markus-Evangelium'; Luz, 'Das Geheimnismotiv'; Minette de Tillesse, pp.272f; Best, p.108 and 'Discipleship in Mark: Mark 8.22-10.52'.
18 See Ch.4 (b).
19 For further discussion of the role of the disciples in the Gospel see Best, 'Mark III 20,21,31-5', and 'The Role of the Disciples in Mark'.
20 See pp.28f. It is possible that the 'house' (v.26) should be understood to refer to the church (house-church; cf Ch.28) and the village to the place of the 'crowd', i.e. the non-Christians. Since the man now sees, he should join the community and not return to his non-Christian associations.

(b) 10.46-52

The second of the pericopae about the restoration of sight like the first consists largely of pre-Markan material. It probably began with the statement of Jesus leaving Jericho /1/; since he had not previously indicated his presence there Mark composes the brief introductory καὶ ἔρχονται εἰς 'Ιεριχώ (v.46a) /2/ in which the link made with καί and the plural verb followed by the singular participle are signs of his hand /3/. The two references to Jericho stress again the sense of movement; Jesus is 'on the way'. They also serve to bring him one stage further on the road to Jerusalem and the cross. In v.52b we may attribute to Mark the connecting phrase καὶ εὐθύς /4/ and the reference to Jesus as 'on the way' /5/; ἀκολουθεῖν is a term he likes. In Mark ὕπαγε (v.52a) normally has the sense 'go away from' /6/ and this clashes with the statement that the man 'followed' Jesus. The reference to the restoration of sight (ἀνέβλεψεν) is redundant after v.52a but could express an original reference to the restoration of sight which Mark has re-written; restoration of sight could also be implied in the ability of Bartimaeus to walk after Jesus (without help, cf Acts 9.8). Indeed since the usual final characteristic of miracle stories, viz. the amazement of the crowd, is missing, v.52b may be a substitution by Mark for it; in itself it provides the verification of the healing.

What signs of Mark's hand are there within the story? Certainly there are clear indications of modification of the original material but most of this, if not all, is pre-Markan. Burger /7/, however, argues that Mark was responsible for the whole middle section (approximately vv.47-9); vv.46b + 50-52a were the pre-Markan tradition and as such form a coherent story; Mark introduced the command to silence (v.48), for it resembles other such Markan commands (e.g. 1.25; 3.12; 8.30); 'Son of David' (vv.47f) clearly implies a different Christology from ραββουνι (v.51) and is appropriate to the entrance of Jesus into Jerusalem which follows immediately and in which 11.9f imply a similar Christology, as does 12.25-7; indeed it is in order to make this preparation for 11.9f and 12.35-7 that Mark has made this drastic amendment to the original pericope; the repetition of the cry in vv.47f shows his great interest in the title. Over against this view we would argue: (i) Substantial evidence is lacking to show that Mark extensively rewrote narrative pericopae; on the contrary he had a real respect for the tradition /8/. (ii) Verses 47-9 lack sufficient Markan characteristics of vocabulary and style to sustain a claim that he wrote them: ἄρχεσθαι (v.47) is not used as an auxiliary in typical Markan fashion but is given its more normal sense 'begin', as the blind man's repeated shouting in v.49 shows /9/; φωνεῖν while used regularly in Mark is not the word he normally employs in the sense 'summon' (it is προσκαλεῖσθαι) /10/. (iii) 'Son of David' is not an important title for Mark's Christology /11/ nor does its use here correspond properly to 11.9f which does not speak of the Son of David. In 8.27-33 Peter is rebuked for using the equivalent title 'Christ' because it does not give an adequate understanding of Jesus. Matthew makes the correspondence complete between our passage and the entry. (iv) It is not true that vv.46b,50-52a form a coherent whole by themselves. Verse 46b supplies no reason why the man should throw away his cloak and run to Jesus; the question of Jesus (v.51) hangs oddly without the previous persistent attempts of the man to get to Jesus. (v) The command to silence (v.48), though it uses Markan terminology, differs from the other commands which are attributable to him in that: (a) it is the crowd and not Jesus who issues it; (b) it is not the use of the title which is silenced /12/ but the attempt to draw the attention of Jesus /13/; (c) it is not certain that all the other commands to silence in the Gospel derive from Mark; some lay in the tradition /14/; Mark did not create the theme but extended and developed it. (vi) It is perhaps significant that the man uses the title 'Son of David' while he is blind, just as Peter used 'Christ' at the time when he could not see properly /15/.

There is one further possible Markan addition, viz., the

reference to the disciples and crowd in v.46b /16/; it is joined rather clumsily to a singular participle (ἐκπορευομένου) /17/. The crowd is essential to the story in v.48 and was therefore almost certainly introduced in a pre-Markan stage of transmission /18/. It is difficult to see why the disciples are mentioned at all; they play no part in the story. In the Markan context they are present in vv.35-45 and the plural of v.46a continues their presence. Probably therefore they were mentioned in the pre-Markan introduction and Mark has retained them. They might be accounted for on the supposition that 10.46-52 adhered to 11.1ff in the pre-Markan tradition and were mentioned to prepare the scene for the entry /19/. But Mark might have introduced them to create a 'discipleship' /20/ atmosphere.

In arguing that vv.47-9 were pre-Markan /21/ we are not intending to imply that they are original; there are clear evidences of the development of tradition within the story: (i) The translation of the blind man's name implies a stage when it did not need to be translated, i.e. a setting in the Jewish Christian church /22/; the translation is not due to Mark; for elsewhere he introduces his translations with ὅ ἐστιν /23/ and translates whole expressions (here only Bar is translated). (ii) The use of the title 'Son of David' is hardly original since there was little of the expectation implied by the present form of the story that the coming Son of David would perform miracles /24/; the title must then have been added during the period of transmission in the Jewish Christian community /25/. (iii) ραββουνι (v.51) will clearly represent a very early stage of the tradition; it is certainly non-Markan; he would have used διδάσκαλε. (iv) There is a slight inconsistency between vv.47f where the crowd appears to be round the blind man and vv.46,50 which imply it was with Jesus and some distance away. It is not necessary for our purposes to trace the tradition-history of vv.46-52 /26/ but only to show that most of the development was pre-Markan /27/.

In the form in which it existed directly prior to Mark's use the story ended with the saying of Jesus, 'Go, your faith has healed/saved you', where there is play on the double meaning of σώζειν with the sense 'save' being brought forward through the accompanying use of πίστις /28/. There is no reason to suppose that Mark was unaware of this symbolic meaning; it appears in other parts of the material he uses (5.23,28,34) /29/. The story is then a symbol of the unbeliever who as such is blind but who is saved when his 'eyes' are opened. Salvation and sight are, of course, closely related (Exod. 14.13; Ps. 91.16; Isa. 40.5; 1QS

11.2f; Lk. 3.6; Jn 9) /30/. The incident will also have carried Christological emphasis in that it is Jesus who heals the man /31/. The Markan redaction serves to draw out further the element of discipleship, turning attention from the act of becoming a disciple into the meaning of discipleship itself. This Mark achieves by positioning the story at the point where the passion begins and by the addition in which he makes Bartimaeus follow Jesus on his way to the cross.

But is this argument not vitiated if the story originally was either connected to 11.1ff or contained the name Jericho /32/? We consider the latter objection first. In view of Mark's total scheme which only brings Jesus to Jerusalem at the end of his ministry there was no other place where he could insert the story and therefore the idea that it drives home his theory of discipleship will not hold water. But if Mark had wished to use it only to show that as Jesus gave sight to physical eyes so the gospel gives sight to the spiritually blind he would have used it earlier with the other miracles and simply dropped the name Jericho, or if he had retained Jericho he could have placed it almost anywhere in the Gospel because his plan of the movements of Jesus is difficult to follow throughout almost the whole Gospel. Furthermore Mark did not need to use the story in its present position unless it fitted his scheme; he could simply have omitted it as he presumably omitted many stories of Jesus. But having used it he has stressed the element of discipleship by his addition of v.52b. The objection that 10.46-52 was attached to 11.1ff in the tradition may seem more serious. It is difficult to see why the tradition would have brought these two incidents together. Where we find complexes they are linked by some harmony of content and form, e.g. the parables in 4.1-34, the miracles in 4.35-5.43, the instruction on marriage, children and wealth in 10.1-31, the day in the life of Jesus in 1.20-34. In the present case we have two incidents whose form and content are different. Even if it were true that they reflect a similar Christology this would not be sufficient to hold them together for in each the Christology is implicit rather than explicit. Did then the name 'David' act as a catch-word to bring them together? But where we have found catch-words used to create links in material they have been found closer together in it and they have normally been in collections of the teaching of Jesus. We cannot then accept the view that these two pericopae were united in the tradition. We must however allow that it was fortunate for Mark that he should find an incident about a blind man ready to fit into his journey at the right point, but we cannot really know how fortunate Mark was, simply because we do not know the total extent of the material available to him. Certainly on this occasion he realised the potential within the pericope as it existed in the tradition for the purpose he had in mind.

When Mark took up the incident he will have been aware of its existing symbolic meaning - restoration of physical sight means the creation of spiritual insight - but by his addition of v.52b he has introduced a new symbolic meaning: 'to see' is to go with Jesus to the cross. The emphasis lies no longer on a new disciple finding faith but on the disciple as following Jesus in the way which he goes, i.e. the theme is discipleship /33/, and the way of discipleship is the way of suffering.

Notes
1   Cf Reploh, p.222; Roloff, p.121: E.S. Johnson, 'Mark 10.46-52'.
2   Note how v.46a resembles 8.22a. For καὶ ἔρχονται with subject unstated but carrying on a supposed previous subject as a Markan redactional connection see 2.3,18; 8.22; 11.15,27; 14.32. Matthew omits any reference to entering Jericho; Luke transfers the healing to the time of entry rather than departure; cf Achtemeier, ' "And He Followed Him" '.
3   Cf 1.21 (variant reading); 5.1; 11.15,27; see Bultmann, p.344; C. H. Turner, JTS 26 (1925) 228ff.
4   Used as an adverb 7-42-1-3.
5   See pp.15-18. Note that once again Matthew and Luke omit the expression. παρὰ τὴν ὁδόν (v.46b) is probably pre-Markan.
6   Cf C.H. Turner, JTS 29 (1928) 287ff.
7   C. Burger, Jesus als Davidssohn, pp.59-62. V.K. Robbins, 'The Healing of Blind Bartimaeus', takes a similar view. Koch, pp.126-130, Johnson (as n.1), Achtemeier (as n.2) strongly reject such views. Schenke, pp.357f, opts for v.48 alone as Markan.
8   Cf Best, 'Mark's Preservation of the Tradition'.
9   Pryke, pp.79,81, takes it as redactional and though providing little evidence leaves a pre-Markan rump that could hardly have had independent existence.
10   See p.130 n.8.
11   Cf Best, pp.165f; Johnson (as n.1); E. Lohse, TDNT, VIII, p.485; Achtemeier (as n.2).
12   Robbins (as n.7), assumes without evidence that it is the title as such which the crowd dislikes; yet he links 10.46-52 strongly to 11.9f and implies that the title is present there also; in 11.9f the crowd favours the title.
13   Even Wrede (pp.278f) does not class it with the passages in

which he finds the Messianic secret.
14 Probably 1.25,43f; 5.7; 8.26b.
15 See also Theissen, Urchristlichen Wundergeschichte, p.146.
16 So Burger (as n.7), p.43; Reploh, p.223.
17 Matthew (20.29) changes the singular into the plural; Luke omits at this point the reference to the crowd and the disciples.
18 ἱκανός (3-3-9-0) is not a Markan word; at 1.7 it comes from the tradition and this is probably true also of 15.15. To indicate the size of a crowd Mark regularly uses πολύς (5.21,24; 6.34; 8.1; 9.14; 12.37; many of these are redactional). Luke, however, uses the word to denote the size of a group of people (7.12; 8.32; Acts 11.24,26; 12.12; 14.21; 19.26).
19 So Hahn, p.273, n.110; Kertelge, pp.180f. Even if this unlikely hypothesis were true, Mark by writing a new introduction (v.46a) and conclusion (v.52b) to the story has broken the connection and, as we shall see, changed the emphasis from Christology to discipleship.
20 Cf Achtemeier (as n.2).
21 See also Johnson (as n.1).
22 Names are unusual in the healing stories; it is impossible to determine if 'Bartimaeus' belonged to the earliest layer of the tradition. Kertelge, pp.179f, argues for its historicity.
23 Cf 3.17; 7.11,34; 12.42; 15.16,42. In 5.41; 15.22,34 Mark employs the fuller form ὅ ἐστιν μεθερμηνευόμενον.
24 Cf Burger (as n.7), p.46; Hahn, pp.189f; Fuller, p.111. It is, however, denied by K. Berger, 'Die königlichen Messiastraditionen des Neuen Testaments', who argues that healing power was associated with Solomon, son of David, and a type of the Messiah. But see the criticisms of Johnson (as n.1), n.24.
25 Fuller, pp.111f and Hahn, pp.253-5 attribute it to the Hellenistic Jewish Christian community, W. Trilling, Christusverkündigung in den synoptischen Evangelien, pp.151f, to the Palestinian Christian community.
26 Cf Hahn, p.272, n.88; Roloff, pp.121-3.
27 Achtemeier (as n.2) argues that in an earlier stage the story functioned as that of a call of a disciple.
28 Apart from Mark's own use see Lk. 17.19; Acts 4.9. Cf W. Foerster, TDNT, VII, p.990. For Mark's use see Best, pp.109f.
29 For Mark's understanding of the miracles generally as symbolic see Best, 'Miracles', and for this miracle in particular see Achtemeier (as n.2).
30 For the evidence in detail see Johnson (as n.1).
31 Lohmeyer goes too far when he points out that in this pericope attention is focussed not on Jesus but on Bartimaeus, with the implication that in the tradition it was used not to

disclose the nature of Jesus but of discipleship, and that when Mark uses it he is extending this main theme. Those who make the effort to become disciples and persevere in it find that faith saves (cf Trilling, as n.25, pp.156f). While the lesson may be true it is doubtful if it was the original emphasis. Jesus appears in the story as one who can save; the soteriological and christological element is quite as prominent as that of discipleship.

32 Many commentators hold that it was this geographical reference which led Mark to insert the pericope at this point; cf Schmidt, p.245; Grundmann, p.220; Roloff, pp.121ff; Burger (as n.7), p.63; Schenke, pp.351f. Pesch, II, pp.167f, believes it was connected to 11.1ff in the pre-Markan passion account.

33 Cf Reploh, p.225.

Chapter 15
CONCLUSION WITH RESPECT TO THE JOURNEY

With 10.52 the discipleship theme of the central section reaches its climax. The way which Jesus goes, the way of the cross, has been clearly laid out since 8.27. By means of an artificially constructed journey he has progressed steadily nearer Jerusalem; in the course of this journey its goal has become clearer - a death for others. 10.45b, the ransom saying, finally enunciates this plainly. There remains now only the cross itself, and the way in which Mark has compressed the material so that all the events take place in less than a week brings us quickly to that climax; and as the way of the cross for Jesus has become clearer so has the way of discipleship for his followers. They have followed him in amazement, misunderstanding and fear as they realised that it requires the denial of self, expressed in a readiness and willingness to take the cross, lose themselves, accept the seeming outsider, serve the unimportant, even the child, and count themselves the servants of all. Now that the final step is about to be taken by Jesus one man, Bartimaeus, instead of leaving him when he is healed, as indeed Jesus instructs him to do (v.52a), follows him 'on the way'. This phrase thus provides a climax to the long section on discipleship and at the same time leads on to the passion story itself.

8.22-6, the first healing of a blind man, was a transition section between two large blocks of material: 4.35-8.21 narrated the mighty deeds of Jesus and increasingly emphasised the disciples' blindness in face of them (cf. 6.52; 8.14-21); 8.27-10.45 predicts the way Jesus will go and the way his disciples must follow if they are to be his disciples. In between a blind man is healed, but not all in one action. Throughout 8.27-10.45 the disciples see, but not as they ought to. Now at the end of this section there is another transition paragraph. Between the section that predicts the way Jesus will go and the section (11.1ff) which describes how he goes, there is the story of another blind man who is healed instantaneously and who, already 'beside the way' (10.46), follows Jesus 'on the way'. Disciples are able to follow the way the Jesus goes.

Chapter 16
WATCHFULNESS

Outside the main section 8.27-10.45 there are a number of smaller sections where we find discipleship set directly into the context of the cross, e.g. Gethsemane, 14.32-42; its theme of the need for watchfulness by the disciples is linked to the same theme in 13.33-7, and we therefore consider these two pericopae together, and associate with them the neighbouring pericope, 12.41-44.

Opinions vary greatly as to the pre-Markan form of 14.32-42. Some scholars think Mark has united two pre-existing but differing accounts of the one event /1/ but others argue he has reworked, more or less heavily, one original account /2/.

In v.32 the linking words καὶ ἔρχονται /3/ are typically Markan but the remainder of the verse is not. The place name must be traditional; the way it is introduced is non-Markan /4/; some narrative must have been attached to it; it is difficult to see any story of Gethsemane beginning without something like v.32b; a group of observers is necessary to what follows. Verse 32 then, apart from its initial two words, is pre-Markan /5/. Verse 33 contains one characteristic of Markan style in the use of ἄρχεσθαι /6/ and one Markan favourite word in ἐκθαμβεῖσθαι /7/. Mark has an interest in the Three, Peter, James and John /8/. In the sequence of the story only Peter is important. This suggests that either the reference to the disciples or that to the Three is non-traditional. In view of the Markan appearance of v.33 and the fact that once the disciples have been mentioned (v.32) it is natural enough to refer to Peter later in the story we attribute the mention of the Three to Mark /9/. Thus all v.33 comes from him /10/. At the beginning of v.34 καὶ λέγει αὐτοῖς is resumptive but this is no reason for denying that the verse belongs to the tradition /11/; it can be easily attached to v.32. Within the words of Jesus in v.34 there is nothing which is peculiarly Markan /12/. Verse 35 would come in somewhat surprisingly if it had not been prepared for by v.34. Verse 35 itself has little Markan in it /13/; as Rom. 11.13 shows there is no reason why ἥ ὥρα with an eschatological reference should not be pre-Markan. However εἰ δυνατόν ἐστιν may be a Markan addition to the verse /14/. The word δυνατός recurs in v.36 where the content of the prayer is repeated in the direct speech which Mark prefers; this verse

147

may then derive from him /15/. It is however unnecessary to make a final decision whether v.35 or v.36 is Markan for the conclusion would have no bearing on the discipleship theme.

What now of the threefold departure of Jesus to pray and his threefold return to the disciples? There can be no doubt that the tradition will have contained one reference to Jesus' departure and return, but is the threefold repetition Markan? It is true that Mark likes a threefold schema /16/ but since this is also true of folk literature generally it is of no help to us in reaching a decision. The paratactic nature of v.37a is Markan but the use of 'Simon' instead of Peter /17/ and of ἰσχύειν instead of Mark's favourite δύνασθαι /18/, suggests tradition /19/. Mark has probably re-written tradition at this point. If, as we argued, v.34 with its use of γρηγορεῖν is pre-Markan then the use of the verb somewhere in vv.37-40 will be also. The γάρ clause in v.40 is a favourite construction of Mark /20/ but these clauses usually presuppose an existing text into which they are inserted /21/. Other Markan features in vv.37-40 may be: πάλιν /22/ (vv.39,40; but the word is found within pericopae, cf. 8.25; 11.3; 12.4; if there were three returns of Jesus then they had to be distinguished in some way; Mark could have used the word to emphasise the threefold return if this was a pre-Markan feature); paratactic καὶ + historic present (v.37); καὶ οὐκ ἤδεισαν .. (v.40), which is very similar to 9.6 and stresses the Markan theme of the ignorance of the disciples. Can the 'sleep' motif be attributed to Mark? Kelber /23/ points to the association of ἔρχεσθαι, εὑρίσκειν and καθεύδειν in 13.36; 14.37a,40a and implies that therefore all three words are supplied by Mark on each occasion; but, as we shall see, 13.36 probably lies in Mark's application of the parable of 13.34 and either 14.37a or 14.40a arises from the threefold schema and would come from whoever (Mark or the tradition) introduced it. Moreover at least one occurrence of each of the three words in our pericope is quite natural; 'sleep' is already associated with 'watchfulness' in 1 Th. 5.6,7,10 in relation to eschatological expectation and is present in v.37b, the address to Simon, which as we have seen comes from the tradition. One or other of v.37a and v.40a, or both, is therefore traditional. Linnemann /24/ argues that the reference to Peter only obtains its significance from its context in Mark where it follows 14.31; but Mark clearly has an interest in Peter right through his Gospel and even without 14.31 the point of the Gethsamene account would not be lost, and unless we assume that Mark invented Peter's denial, that denial would be known and form part of the background information about Peter /25/. We conclude that in vv.37-41a the certain traditional elements were a return by Jesus to the disciples and a rebuke to Peter about his lack of watchfulness and his sleeping. Whether the pre-Markan narrative had the threefold schema may seem more doubtful /26/; if it did possess it then Mark emphasised it with his use of πάλιν /27/.

In vv.41f attention is turned back from the disciples to Jesus. Verse 41 is difficult /28/. In what way is καθεύδετε .. ἀπέχει to be construed? If it lay in the earlier tradition the first two verbs could have been understood as statements, commands or questions; in their present context with ἐγείρεσθε and ἄγωμεν (v.42) they are most easily taken as questions. The command in v.42 would contradict any supposed command they may contain and would also militate against reading them as statements because of the adverbial τὸ λοιπόν which would imply some sense of lengthy continuity ('you are going on and on sleeping') or finality ('you are sleeping for ever'). If, as is almost certain, v.42 is Mark's link to what follows then it is tempting to suppose that the difficulties in this part of v.41 arise not because Mark wrote it but because he is taking over a statement from the tradition. But does this also apply to v.41b? ἦλθεν ἡ ὥρα · could have been formed from the previous reference to the 'hour' (v.35) which we saw lay in the tradition; ἰδοὺ παραδίδοται repeats part of 9.31; if 9.31 is traditional then this could also have been traditional, or Mark may have created it out of 9.31; yet interestingly παραδίδωμι is used in two different ways in v.41 and v.42 /29/; in the latter its use is 'historical' referring to Judas's betrayal of Jesus; in the former 'soteriological'; clearly the two are related but the double use suggests either two layers of tradition /30/ or one of tradition and one of redaction; this is confirmed by the difference in meaning between ἦλθεν, which is eschatological, and ἤγγικεν, which is geographical /31/. Apart from the parataxis and the two historic present tenses at the beginning of v.41 there is nothing else in it which is characteristically Markan; probably therefore most of it comes from the tradition. If, however, it was not merely from the tradition but was also part of the pre-Markan pericope it is difficult to see it as addressed to Peter (or all the disciples) if Jesus only made one visit back to them; this then would imply that the threefold structure was pre-Markan. If that is so /32/, then Mark has re-written the narrative in respect of the elements of 'movement' within it as the historic present tenses show. The use of tenses in the pericope is not consistent; historic present tenses are mixed with past tenses. This is a characteristic of Mark where he

149

retells a longer narrative, cf. 2.3-12; 3.1-5; 4.35-41; 5.1-20, 35-43; etc. It is not surprising, for most people in retelling stories shape them partly but not entirely into their own style. But the threefold schema may well be Markan.

Is v.38 Markan? The logion in the second half is certainly not his composition since he rarely employs the μὲν ... δὲ .. contrast /33/ but is a kind of Christian proverb which he could easily have inserted (cf. 10.15,27). The prayer to avoid entering into πειρασμόν could have come from liturgical tradition (cf. Mt. 6.13; Lk. 11.4; the change of person in our clause would necessitate the change of verb from that in the Lord's Prayer); the reference to watchfulness could have been taken from v.37; there has been no previous reference to 'prayer'; the ἵνα clause has a future rather than a present reference /34/. The pre-Markan narrative would have read much more straight-forwardly and directly if v.38 were omitted. It is a Markan comment and this probably goes also for the final clause of v.40 (cf. 9.6).

Thus we see that in relation to the original story and in respect of the disciples Mark has introduced the reference to the Three, has added v.38 and v.40bc thus emphasising (v.40bc) their sleep and failure to understand and giving (v.38) clear instruction on how this failure may be avoided /35/. His addition of πάλιν, if he has not created the threefold schema, brings out the repetitiveness in the incident and underlines the failure of the disciples and the need for watchfulness and prayer (v.38a). The introduction of the Three also serves to some extent to weaken the rebuke to Peter: v.38 is plural and addressed to the Three and, more ultimately, to Mark's own readers (note the future reference of v.38a); v.40, also plural, does not refer to Peter alone. Thus Mark has widened what he has to say to include all Christians /36/.

The incident makes a strange double impact. Given the triple withdrawal by Jesus and the impasse in which he is said to find himself in the first prayer we would expect a resolution of his conflict at or after the third prayer; instead attention swings to the behaviour of the disciples. This serves yet again to indicate the relation of discipleship to the behaviour of Jesus. In fact the resolution of Jesus' conflict is clearly shown through his behaviour at his trial and crucifixion; in 1.12f we are not told that Jesus defeated Satan but deduce it from what follows; similarly we are left to make our own deduction here. The attention, then, which is given to the disciples shows that in this case at any rate they are not just the background against which Jesus' agony is played out. But equally it should not be taken to indicate that Mark is not interested in Jesus in this pericope; Mark's use of the 'cup' theme elsewhere (10.38f; 14.24) disproves such a view.

The disciples sleep while they should wake. In his interpretation of this sleep Mark introduces a direct reference to 'eyes' and thus to the sight of the disciples. To sleep is in effect to fail to see adequately. Mark's verb καταβαρύνειν has not been found elsewhere in relation to the eyes. It carries as basic significance 'to burden' /37/ and is used metaphorically of life as a burden. It needs to be distinguished from total blindness. If Mark had wished to indicate this he would have said that the eyes of the disciples were closed or that they did not see. The word he uses suggests rather difficulty in sight: we may compare the case of the man who received his sight in two stages (8.22-6). As yet the disciples have not passed beyond half sight to full sight. As in 8.27-10.45 their lack of sight is related to the passion as we see both from the placing of the Gethsemane account and from the inner struggle of Jesus. The disciples know as little what to say (v.40) in face of the cross as they did in face of the glory of Jesus (9.6).

In 8.27-10.45 attention was concentrated on the nature of discipleship; this is continued here in the idea of watchfulness but a new factor is introduced: the disciples are told how they may be helped to attain at least one aspect of true discipleship. This was implicit in the relationship to Jesus which underlay 8.27-10.45 (it almost becomes explicit in passages like 8.35,38; 10.45) for through this relationship men could achieve true discipleship. It is now explicitly expressed but in a different way through watchfulness, prayer and the Spirit. The reference to prayer, if not that also to the Spirit, comes from Mark and may be understood as an explanation of the meaning of watchfulness /38/, and how it may be attained.

Before we go on to the other passage on watchfulness we need to examine briefly the meaning for Mark in our context of πειρασμός. Originally, as in the Lord's Prayer, it may have had a purely eschatological orientation with the significance, 'Do not let us fall victim to temptation' /39/, but this can hardly be the way to understand it in the context of 14.38. There must be some comparability between the prayer and situation of Jesus and that of the disciples. Before him lies the cross; death and persecution may also threaten them. This is part of the meaning of the cross in 8.34, but as we saw there the cross also has a much wider reference and this holds probably here also. The reference will still be outward, relating to the various afflictions with which others might attack Christians. For Mark and his readers these could never be fully separated from the final eschatological woes /40/. Afflictions can only be truly accepted and overcome when the passion of Jesus is fully understood. Real discipleship means a true understanding of the passion. Hence the reference to sight and understanding in our passage (v.40).

What then does it mean to be watchful or alert? This theme re-appears in 13.33-7. Through its context this passage is closely related to the discussion of the End. The initial question of 13.4 indicates that Mark's community desired some clue about the timing of the End. Signs and portents are discussed but the final answer does not provide an exact time but dissolves into an assertion of ignorance (13.32,33b,35a) and a related exhortation to watchfulness (13.33-7).

The centre of this exhortation is a parable (v.34) for which Mark has supplied an introduction (v.33) /41/. The parable as we have it has been taken over from the tradition either through its creation from material similar to that in Lk. 12.36ff or through the modification of an existing parable /42/. The considerable number of unevennesses which it contains demonstrates that Mark was using tradition in some way or other and not just creating freely /43/. Probably there was an existing parable to which Mark added τὴν ἐξουσίαν /44/, if not also the whole phrase δοῦς ... ἔργον αὐτοῦ /45/. Within the context which Mark gives the parable the key word is γρηγορεῖτε and the key thought 'watchfulness'; these are underlined in the introduction to the parable by ἀγρυπνεῖτε /46/. The first two words of v.35, γρηγορεῖτε οὖν, with the change into the second person plural clearly intimate the application of the parable and are almost certainly Markan /47/; the remainder of v.35 with v.36 is probably his also /48/; it relates the parable to its position in the chapter. 'Sleep' is introduced quite naturally for it balances the theme of watchfulness (cf. 1 Th. 5.6,10).

Finally v.37 should be attributed to Mark /49/. Within the context of the chapter the teaching of Jesus was addressed only to the four, Andrew, Peter, James, John, who were with Jesus. Verse 37 widens the application and Mark will have intended his readers to see themselves as included in the πᾶσιν /50/. The instruction which comes from the tradition is ultimately aimed not at the historical disciples but at the contemporary Christian church.

If the parable has been widened in Mark who are the servants other than the doorkeeper (he was probably its original centre)? What ἐξουσία has been given to them? ἐξουσιά is an important word in Mark both in relation to Jesus and to the Twelve or the 'missionaries' /51/ (3.15; 6.7). In 3.15; 6.7 it refers to authority over the demonic world. The reference in our pericope is wider and the restriction to 'missionaries' seems unnecessary. The word fits the parable and suggests responsibility as given to each church member; 'to each his work' generalises the reference to the doorkeeper /52/ and is not an application to the work of officials or ministers in the church. This is brought out again by v.37. The parable is not then for the 'ministry' /53/ of the church but for all the members /54/.

In the parable the need for watchfulness appears to be met only in relation to the parousia. Is watchfulness then unrelated to the theme of the great central section (8.22-10.52) where the disciple is called to take up his cross, deny himself and be the servant of others? This distinction is more apparent than real. The persecution and suffering which Mark implies in the central section as the lot of the disciple was an eschatologically oriented suffering. We, with our settled civilisation, may dissociate the call to carry the cross from eschatological suffering but such a distinction as this was probably impossible for Mark and his community. Even if they did not believe that they were already in the midst of the final messianic woes they certainly believed that any suffering which came might be these final woes. Watchfulness in relation to the End would fit in most appropriately with the call to take up the cross /55/. It is relevant to note that it is during the night that the disciple is to stay awake. Travellers, least of all the master of the house coming from a considerable distance /56/, would not arrive suddenly at night; people avoided travelling by night; the parable is improbable at this point. 'Night' must therefore have symbolic meaning: it signifies this age of evil, the age in which the Christian lives /57/ and which presents him with the perils that would lure him from watchfulness in respect of the way of the cross. In addition we should note the close connection through language ('sleep', 'watchful') between our passage and the Gethsemane story. Both 'sleep' and 'watchfulness' are set firmly in the latter in a passion and not a parousia context; the 'hour' is not the 'hour' of the return but of the cross. Should we not then interpret the 'watchfulness' of 13.33-7 in terms of that of Gethsemane? The failure of the disciples to be watchful is seen directly after Gethsemane in Peter's denial and in the flight of all of them at the time of the arrest. Finally we should note the passion context of the whole of Mk 13, which Lightfoot first indicated so clearly /58/.

This may be looked at from another angle. The watchfulness

153

which is desired is not one which looks out for the Lord on his return but a watchfulness about oneself so that no matter when the Lord returns those who await him will be alert /59/: thus while the unpredictability of the householder's return is stressed (v.35) it is in their sleep that danger lies for the watchers. It is required of them that they be alert disciples and the Gethsemane incident shows that a sleeping disciple lacks alertness in relation to the cross.

But there is no reason why a disciple should not be alert: (i) he may pray; (ii) he has the Spirit to assist him even though his 'flesh' is weak /60/. There is little elsewhere in Mark's Gospel about either prayer or the assistance of the Spirit, but both concepts would call to the mind of the Christian disciple all that prayer and the Spirit meant in the early church. Where prayer is mentioned elsewhere it is usually in relation to individualised activities: in 13.18 it is directed to the parousia and is not shown as a part of the disciple's daily life; in 12.40 the prayers of hypocrites are in mind; in 9.28f it is a means of obtaining help to exorcise, and something similar appears to be the case in 11.23-25. In a similar way the help of the Spirit is assured in persecution (13.11). But we may assume from these individualised references that prayer must be used more generally and that the Spirit will be given in many situations. Thus the reference to prayer and the Spirit implies that the disciple is not left to his own resources in contending with sleep. Watchfulness and prayer are associated; Jesus prays and remains awake. In this he is an example to the disciples /61/. If they pray they will be able both to understand, and to go the way of the cross. A vast amount of teaching has already been given throughout the Gospel on what the cross means; at this point, after all the teaching has been given, the disciple is assured that God will help him both to understand and to carry his understanding into the practice of his life. Premonitions of the supernatural help available to the disciple were already found in the deliverance from trial in the sea-miracles (4.35-41; 6.45-52) and in the food (teaching) of the feeding-miracles (6.30-44; 8.1-10) /62/. Yet it is these very mighty deeds of Jesus which the disciples have failed to understand (cf. also 5.31 and 9.18). Related to this is the instruction to those who are healed not to spread abroad news of their healing (1.44; 5.43; 7.36). Concealment from the crowds, i.e. the unevangelised, and failure to understand Jesus' and their own full capability suggests on the one hand the rejection of miracles as a sole or even principal way of advancing the mission of the church, but on the other the need to accept the full power of Jesus within the community. Mark's community may not merely be rejecting the cross as the way of discipleship but also be unwilling to allow themselves to be upborne by the power of Jesus.

There is one further passage (12.41-44) which relates discipleship to the apocalyptic situation; in 12.41-44 the widow who gives her last two coins to the temple is presented as an example to the disciples. Most of vv.41f are necessary if the story is to be told at all but in v.41 πολλά is a Markan favourite /63/ and the whole of the clause to which it belongs may come from him. ἐλθοῦσα (v.42), a redundant participle, is another sign of his hand /64/; this may indicate that he has rewritten the story, for v.42a is an essential part of it. The final words of the same verse, which relate the widow's two coins to a known coin of the Roman world, are certainly not original, and probably come from Mark. The use of προσκαλεῖν in v.43a is Markan /65/ and suggests that Mark explicitly introduced or deliberately drew attention to the disciples at this point. The concluding γάρ sentence (v.44) could also be Markan since it is explanatory; it is also rather clumsily expressed /66/. Taken with the redactional emphasis on the disciples it sets before them the example of generosity rather than the need for total commitment to God ('giving up all'), though the latter is necessarily implied. Love is to be expressed (12.28-34) in the same way as the widow has expressed it. Her willingness to give all she has contrasts acutely with the attitude of the rich man (10.17-22).

If sacrificial generosity is taught by the Markan redaction of the story another lesson lies in the place he has given it in the Gospel /67/. It is improbable that it was originally attached to the earlier part of the chapter. 12.13-37 /68/, or a longer section beginning further back and ending at v.37 or v.40, has often been recognised as a pre-Markan unity /69/. If this ended at 12.37, vv.38-40 may well be Mark's attempt, through the use of a piece of tradition, to discredit the scribes yet again in advance of the crucifixion. The slender verbal connection of 'widow' in v.40 with vv.41-44 is hardly enough to have led to the introduction of the latter passage. There is a better link forwards to chap. 13. Jesus praises a woman who gives her all to the temple which is about to be destroyed (13.2). The two passages are connected through the clause καὶ ἐκπορευομένου αὐτοῦ ἐκ τοῦ ἱεροῦ: Mark, as here, regularly uses a genitive absolute in such seams /70/. The situation is threatening to his readers; they believe they are in the last days; Mark not merely wishes to restrain them from being too sure about this (13.32) but also wishes them to realise that however threatening things may be this should not change their basic ethical response; no matter what is happening, or about to happen, the need for generosity remains. The woman is commended because in a possible apocalyptic situation she does what in any case she ought to have done. No matter what may threaten or happen believers are not to neglect the deep demands that Jesus makes on their behaviour. 2 Thess. 3.6-13 shows the ever present danger that these demands may be neglected. The two main points we have detected in the story are not unrelated: an apocalyptic atmosphere easily produces a determination to stand firm and in this situation steadfastness rapidly replaces love as the ultimate virtue: the next section, chap. 13, stresses steadfastness; this incident sets love in the centre.

Notes

1   See K.G. Kuhn, 'Jesus in Gethsemane', followed by T. Lescow, 'Jesus in Gethsemane' and R.S. Barbour, 'Gethsemane in the Tradition of the Passion'. For earlier attempts see Bultmann, pp.267f; W. Bussmann, Synoptische Studien, I, pp.193ff; Knox, I, pp.125-9, and, for a more recent attempt, W. Schenk, Der Passionsbericht nach Markus, pp.193-206.

2   See E. Linnemann, pp.11-40; W.H. Kelber, 'Mark 14,32-42'; W. Mohn, 'Gethsemane (Mark 14.32-42)'; L. Schenke, Studien zur Passionsgeschichte des Markus, pp.461-560.

3   Cf. 1.40; 3.20,31; 8.22; 10.46; 11.15,27.

4   Cf. Kelber (as n.2), Schenke (as n.2), p.462.

5   Possibly v.32b, since it duplicates v.34, may be Markan.

6   The verb could possibly have its normal significance here, cf. Lagange, p.xciii.

7   0-4-0-0.

8   5.21-4,35-43; 9.2-8; cf. 3.16f. Kelber (as n.2) points to the association of the verb παραλαμβάνειν with the Three in Markan redaction at 9.2. 10.38-40 and 14.29,31 highlight their present failure (cf. Lane, p.515).

9   Cf. Schenke (as n.2), pp.480-5; V. Howard, Das Ego Jesu, p.126.

10   ἀδημονεῖν is non-Markan (1-1-0-0; it appears only three times in the N.T.) and may represent a pre-Markan reference to the agony of Jesus; Mark, then, has re-written the reference in v.33b in order to emphasise it. On Mark's use of the Three, cf. Schmahl, pp.128ff.

11   Verse 34 does not presume v.33 as Mohn (as n.2) supposes. It is only natural for Mark to use a favourite historic present (λέγει) when picking up the connection. There would have been

no clause introducing the words of Jesus when v.34 followed v.32.

12 Kelber (as n.2) assumes that the use of γρηγορεῖν is Markan. It is only found in Mark in 14.32-42 and 13.33-7; neither incident nor parable could be told without it. Its use is certainly pre-Markan in the catechetical tradition of the church in an eschatological context (1 Th. 5.6,10). The assumption that Mark introduced it is gratuitous and implies an utterly sceptical attitude to the pre-Markan tradition. Schenke (as n.2), pp.485-93, argues that it is from the tradition since it is a necessary preparation for v.37 which is traditional.

13 προέρχεσθαι (1-2-2-0) is probably redactional at 6.33 but this proves little about its use here since it was used with a different sense there and the total number of occurrences is small. ἵνα does not introduce direct speech here (Mark does not use it in that way) but a final clause. Cf. Mohn (as n.2), p.198, who defends the pre-Markan nature of v.35.

14 Mark likes δύνασθαι (27-33-26-36) and δυνατός (3-5-4-0).

15 So Mohn (as n.2), p.198. On the other hand would Mark have drawn Αββα ὁ πατήρ from the liturgical tradition to place it on Jesus' lips? It is the address used for God by every Christian (Rom. 8.15; Gal. 4.6) but Mark does not classify Jesus with 'every Christian'. He sees Jesus as possessing a special sonship, as his use of 'son' in respect of Jesus clearly shows.

16 As Kelber (as n.2), p.170, correctly points out.

17 Kelber (as n.2), p.184, thinks the use of 'Simon' is part of a general attack by Mark on the disciples: Peter has lapsed to the position he had before Jesus made him one of the Twelve and so his original name is used (cf. Klostermann and Swete ad loc.). But if Mark intended this interpretation he would have continued to call him Simon throughout the remainder of the Gospel, and in particular at the time of his denial of Jesus.

18 Cf. n.14 above. By comparison ἰσχύειν is only used four times (4-4-8-1).

19 Cf. Schenke (as n.2), pp.507-512.

20 Note also the periphrastic tense; cf. Pryke, pp.103ff.

21 We must therefore reject Schenke's tentative suggestion (as n.2), p.535, that this clause is pre-Markan.

22 17-28-3-43.

23 (As n.2), p.170.

24 (As n.2), p.25.

25 If the Gospel was written in Rome and if Peter had been there it is highly probable that the church would have had a cycle of stories about him.

26 To say that the threefold scheme in prayer is Jewish does

not help us in deciding if the scheme is Markan here; at best it would imply it was pre-Markan; but threefold structures are widespread in popular literature.

27 Schenke (as n.2), pp.525-539, argues convincingly against the original nature of the threefold prayer but not so convincingly as to its Markan character.

28 The textual variants indicate the difficulty the verse caused to scribes; see Metzger ad loc. We accept the reading of ℵ A B etc. On ἀπέχει see G.H. Boobyer, '"Απεχει in Mark xiv. 41'.

29 For the use of the verb see N. Perrin, A Modern Pilgrimage, pp.94-104.

30 Bultmann, pp.267f, argues that 'the hour is come' forms a fitting climax to the story. This may have been so at a very early stage of the tradition but the following clause expresses the meaning of the story in clearer Christological terms (cf. K.G. Kuhn, as n.1, pp. 273f).

31 Cf. K.G. Kuhn (as n.1), p.262.

32 It is not present in Luke's account and if this, as is probable, represents a separate strand of the tradition, then it would not have formed part of the earliest form of the tradition.

33 Only elsewhere at 12.5; 14.21; in neither of these verses is it used in the same way as here.

34 Cf. Schenke (as n.2), pp.512-525; he however regards v.38b as part of the pre-Markan tradition.

35 Cf. D. Dormeyer, Die Passion Jesu als Verhaltensmodell, pp.136f.

36 By implication we have rejected the two-source theory of K.G. Kuhn (as n.1), and Schenk (as n.1), pp.193-206. Our conclusion that Mark has stressed the place of the disciples in the pericope would remain true even if we had accepted Kuhn's view for in it the threefold schema which draws attention to the role of the disciples arises from the unification of the sources and therefore is in part Markan. It serves to stress the paraenetic nature (Kuhn, p.284; Barbour (as n.1), pp.233f) of the B-source. Kuhn does not consider whether the two sources might not have been united in the pre-Markan tradition. Schenk, however, argues that Mark united them; his analysis would also imply that Mark stresses the role of the disciples.

37 Cf. Bauer, s.v. Kelber, 'The Hour of the Son of Man', in Kelber, p.49, also notes the connection between 'sleepiness' and lack of sight.

38 Cf. Schenke, (as n.2), pp.513f.

39 Cf. Jeremias, New Testament Theology, I, p.202.

40 Cf. Barbour (as n.1), pp.236,243.

41   Cf. R. Pesch, Naherwartungen: Tradition und Redaktion in Mk. 13, pp.195f; J. Lambrecht, Die Redaktion der Markus-Apokalypse, pp.241ff. See also A. Weiser, Die Knechtsgleichnisse der synoptischen Evangelien, pp.131f; J. Dupont, 'La parabole du maître'.

42   For a discussion of various interpretations see Lambrecht (as n.41), pp.243ff,250(n.2), 251(n.2); Pesch (as n.41), pp.196ff; Dupont (as n.41). Weiser (as n.41) opts, probably correctly, for adaptation of an existing parable.

43   Cf. Lambrecht (as n.41), pp.243-5; Pesch (as n.41), pp.197-9; Weiser (as n.41), pp.132-41.

44   So Pesch (as n.41), p.198.

45   So Weiser (as n.41), pp.136-9.

46   Pesch (as n.41), p.195, believes it was taken over from the parable as found in the tradition; Lambrecht (as n.41), pp.243-9, is more doubtful.

47   The motif of 'watchfulness' was, however, widespread in the early church; cf. 1 Th. 5.6,10; Mt. 25.13; 1 Pet. 5.8; Rev. 3.2f.

48   Cf. Pesch (as n.41), p.200; Lambrecht (as n.41), p.246. οὐκ οἴδατε γὰρ πότε repeats v.33b; it contains a typical Markan γάρ clause; the 'man' becomes ὁ κύριος; ἔρχεσθαι links back to v.26; the 'watches' are named according to the Roman terminology appropriate to Mark's readership. Weiser (as n.41), pp.139f, holds that the core of vv.35f is traditional but was originally in the singular and applied to the 'doorkeeper'.

49   Cf. Lambrecht (as n.41), p.248; Pesch (as n.41), p.202; Weiser (as n.41), p.144.

50   Lambrecht (as n.41), p.248, balances πᾶσιν with κατ' ἰδίαν (13.3); if the latter is redactional so is the former. Pesch (as n.41), p.198, sees the reference to all believers already present in the use of δοῦλοι in v.34.

51   See chs. 22, 23.

52   Cf. Weiser (as n.41), p.151.

53   Minear, Commands of Christ, pp.156,160, would see the exhortations of both 13.33-37 and 14.32-42 as addressed to church leaders. In particular in 13.33-7 they have been set in charge of the house (= the church) as doorkeepers and must be watchful for the sake of all within. In 13.3 Mark has certainly introduced κατ' ἰδίαν(see n.50 supra) and it serves to indicate that the teaching which follows is private teaching for the community rather than public teaching for all; in v.37 Mark clearly indicates that he intends the parable to be obeyed by all Christians. It is only if we stress the responsibility of the doorkeeper that we could argue a reference to the ministry, but

as we have seen Mark is interested in all the servants rather than the doorkeeper alone. Finally there is little in 14.32-42 to support Minear's view apart from Mark's introduction of the Three and this seems to be designed more to remove the sting from any rebuke to Peter (cf. Best, 'Peter') than to advance their 'ministerial' claims; they finally merge into the whole group of disciples either at the end or even before its end without any special attention being given to this merging.

54 Cf. Carlston, The Parables of the Triple Tradition, pp.197-202.

55 F. Bursch, Zum Verständnis der synoptischen Eschatologie, p.48, argues that Mk 13 is a spelling out of 8.34ff, i.e. the trials which are depicted in Mk 13 show what is involved in the taking up of the cross (cf. T.J. Weeden, pp.83f, who adds 10.23-30 to 8.34ff). This could only be wholly accurate if Mark envisaged his readers as at last launched into the final eschatological woes, but on the one hand the parable's emphasis on watchfulness seems to suggest that there are woes still future and on the other our interpretation of 8.34ff has shown that it (and all 8.22-10.52) deals with far wider and deeper issues than the threat of death alone. Yet, of course, the eschatological woes will require the disciple to carry his cross and to that extent Bursch is correct.

56 As is implied by ἀπόδημος.

57 Cf. E. Lövestam, Spiritual Wakefulness in the New Testament, pp.78-91.

58 Gospel Message, pp.48-59; cf. G.R. Beasley-Murray, Jesus and the Future, pp.216-20. Lightfoot, p.53, relates the four watches of v.35 to the events of the Passion. The parable and the Gethsemane account are also related not only through the theme of watchfulness and the coming of the Lord but also through the use of 'the hour' and the reference to prayer in 13.33, if that is the true reading there; the joint evidence of B D it[a,c,d,k] cop[fay] coupled with the possibility of contamination from 14.38 must make it unlikely.

59 The change produced by Mark's redaction of the original form of the parable from emphasis on the doorkeeper to that on all the servants supports this interpretation.

60 We accept E. Schweizer's interpretation of πνεῦμα in 14.38; cf. TDNT, VI, pp.396f; see also his Mark ad loc; cf. Pesch, II, p.392; Lane, p.520. But even if we understand the word here of the human spirit the Godward reference remains in the summons to prayer.

61 In so far as Jesus is shown in prayer elsewhere in the Gospel (1.35; 6.46) little is done to emphasise him as a pattern

for disciples in praying (contrast Luke's picture of Jesus).

62   Mark may intend to draw this out by his use of 'on the way' in 8.3; the people are 'weak' as they go 'on the way', the way which is later seen to be that of the cross, but are strengthened with the supernatural food Jesus supplies (cf. Best, 'The Miracles in Mark').

63   Pryke, pp.70,72.

64   Pryke, p.100.

65   Cf. p.130 n.8.

66   Pryke, p.134.

67   In Pesch's pre-Markan passion narrative it was already joined to 13.1 (Pesch, II, pp.265,269).

68   Cf. Daube, pp.158ff and 'Four Types of Question'.

69   From Albertz, Die synoptischen Streitgespräche, Berlin, 1921, onwards. Cook, p.49, includes vv.38-40.

70   Pryke, pp.62-4.

Chapter 17
CONCLUSION

As Quesnell has pointed out /1/ almost all of Jesus' teaching on behaviour in respect of the general situation of believers and not of their particular or accidental situations (e.g. tax-paying in 12.13-7) is contained in the long section 8.27-10.45. This concentration reinforces our view that it is the main discipleship section. Yet in describing discipleship as the way of the cross and in limiting our discussion up to this point to Mark's understanding of it in terms of the cross we have neglected two other areas which must be drawn in. (i) The disciple and the world outside. If the disciple were wholly taken up with his own inner life as this is portrayed in 8.27-10.45 he might still fail to be a disciple in the terms of 8.35; in his concern about his own Christian discipleship he might lose himself. So he must look outward: What is his commission as disciple? We examine this in Part II. (ii) The disciple and his fellow disciples. The way of the cross can only be a lonely way; as the disciple sees Jesus tread it to the cry of dereliction he cannot but be frightened, and Mark depicts him as frightened, not only by the possibility of physical suffering, which for Mark's readers was a real possibility, but by the equally real possibility of mental and spiritual suffering. In responding to his call he has left behind everything and everyone and at the end of the road there may stand only a lonely cross. The picture we have sketched so far of Mark's view might suggest that this is his view but Mark has much more to say. The way of Jesus does not end at the cross but continues beyond it into the way of mission: Jesus goes at the head of the disciples and they go together, and not individually, in their activity as fishers of men. We consider this aspect in Part III, though of course many inklings of it have already been perceived.

Note
1   Pp.135ff. One significant exception is provided by 3.35. This is a verse which together with almost all of its pericope Mark has taken over from the tradition (see Best, 'Mark III, 20,21,31-35'). At the point where it appears in the Gospel it is impossible to read any specific content into the clause 'whoever does the will of God'; it is elucidated only in what follows,

Chapter 17: Conclusion to Part I

especially in 8.27-10.45.

PART II
THE DISCIPLE AND THE WORLD

Chapter 18
INTRODUCTION

The disciple cannot be wholly taken up with his own discipleship in isolation; he is a disciple who lives among men, bearing a relation to them. What does Mark indicate that relation to be? If disciples have a concern for others, do all disciples have the same concern, or are there groups among them on whom this concern is specially laid or who are called to exercise it in special ways?

Before we discuss in detail the passages which may offer answers to these questions we recall that we have already detected within 8.27-10.45 an implicit answer to part of the question about the concern of the disciples. Mark's addition καὶ τοῦ εὐαγγελίου in 8.35 suggests an outward look in so far as 'gospel' carries the sense of a message which is proclaimed to unbelievers; the instruction in 9.29 to those who wish to exorcise indicates an interest in the demon-possessed and these would presumably be non-Christian; 9.36f (cf. 10.42b-45a) implies the Christian's care for the outsider even if he is as unimportant as a child; 10.21 suggests that wealthier Christians have responsibilities towards the poor, and there is no implication that the poor must be Christian; this may also be the significance of 14.7 in that Jesus' anointing was once-for-all but the care of the poor is a continuing activity; some of the 'salt' metaphors of 9.49f may also be outward looking; when Peter's mother-in-law is healed she ministers to others /1/.

Within a section devoted to the disciple and the world it may seem odd to deal with the 'call' of disciples but as we shall see the call is a call to a task and therefore may involve action towards the world. Further, though in Mark the 'calls' precede the main discussion of discipleship in 8.27-10.45, this is not surprising since Mark's order is occasioned here by the historical facts of Jesus' life. The disciple's attitude to the world cannot be viewed apart from his attitude to the cross; so in thought, if not in history, a consideration of the disciple's attitude to the world properly follows a consideration of his attitude to the cross.

Chapter 18: The Disciple and the World

Note
1   Schenke, p.124, believes Mark added the reference to her ministry.

Chapter 19
MARK 1.16-20

This passage contains two parallel incidents, and there is yet another in 2.14. In each of the three we find a participle describing the movement of Jesus combined with a verb in which he is said to see someone; that person (or persons) is then briefly described; Jesus speaks to him summoning him to be his disciple; he leaves what he is at and follows Jesus. Given that Mark knew one such incident in the tradition has he created two more of similar pattern? Did all three come to him in the tradition already constructed according to this pattern? Did all three come in the tradition but the pattern has been imposed by him? There are other possibilities but these three questions set out the kind of problems involved. At this stage we confine ourselves to the two incidents in 1.16-20 and ask if Mark composed either in the light of the other /1/?

It is improbable that Mark constructed 1.16-18 in the light of an existing unit 1.19f belonging to the tradition for: (a) 1.16-18 contains a typical Markan parenthetical γάρ clause /2/; he regularly employs these in order to comment on existing material. (b) If Mark introduced the motif 'fishers of men' it is strange that he should have made no use of it later. (c) Apart from the γάρ clause there is nothing of an essentially redactional nature within the body of the incident. (d) While it is possible to believe that Mark might construct an incident narrating a 'call' to Peter who is prominent in the Gospel there is no similar reason for the introduction of Andrew /3/ and Lk. 5.1-11 shows that a call to Peter could exist without reference to his brother Andrew. (e) Lk. 5.1-11 also shows that a tradition about the call of Peter existed independently of Mark's account /4/. We thus conclude that Mark received the main part of 1.16-18 in the tradition.

If alternatively we ask whether Mark constructed 1.19f in the light of 1.16-18, the answer is by no means so clear-cut. There is nothing in 1.19f which could not be Markan and there is nothing which clearly indicates his hand at work on existing tradition. But it is difficult to imagine the circumstances which would have led him to create 1.19f. He might have done so had he wished to stress the importance of James and John over against Peter and Andrew; there is no evidence in the Gospel that he desired to do this; 9.38f implies that he was not

166

elevating John to a special position and 10.35-40 can be read as a rebuke to any pretensions on the part of James and John. Support for a James and John faction in the early church might have led to the production of the incident at an earlier stage in the tradition but Mark would not then be responsible for its construction. Again we conclude that 1.19f came in its essentials to Mark in the tradition.

If then the two incidents existed in the tradition, were they united in it or did Mark bring them together? Various reasons have been offered to suggest that these two incidents could not have happened at the same time: Jesus would have recruited his disciples over a period; nets were mended at a different time of day than that when fishing was done. Such reasons may apply to the origin of the incidents but do not help us in determining their relative position in the tradition. Twin incidents are a common feature of folk-lore; the parables of the mustard seed and the leaven in the Q tradition, the lost coin and lost sheep in the L tradition, the cloth and the bottles in Mk 2.21f. Though Mark does like double statements /5/ we think it is more probable that he found these incidents already united than that he brought them together. There are certainly no clear signs of his hand in their linkage other than the simple καί at the beginning of v.19. If Mark had been creating a section on 'the call of disciples' it would have been logical for him to add in 2.14 after 1.20, for since it was not a part of the underlying complex of chap. 2 /6/ he had to place it somewhere. Conversely it is unlikely that if 2.14 had belonged with 1.16-20 in the tradition /7/ Mark would have split it off in order to use it elsewhere. In any case there would have been less to bind it to the two incidents of 1.16-20 than serves to bind them to one another; for, apart from the theme of discipleship and the common pattern in each, they are united by the double reference to fishing.

If then 1.16-20 was an existing unit of tradition /8/ what signs are there of Mark's hand within it? (a) The use of a compound verb followed by the preposition of the compound is frequent in Mark (cf. 1.21,26,29,42, etc.), παράγων παρά ; a word indicating motion on the part of Jesus appears regularly in discipleship sections in Mark /9/; while clearly the incident must have taken place at the sea of Galilee yet since Galilee has theological significance for Mark /10/ he may have introduced the reference at this point /11/; it may then be that we should attribute the form of the whole initial clause to Mark /12/; καὶ παράγων παρὰ τὴν θάλασσαν τῆς Γαλιλαίας.(b) As we have already noted the principal verb in the first sentence of each of the calls in 1.16-20; 2.14 is εἶδεν. All through the Gospel Mark draws attention to the way in which Jesus looks at people: cf. 3.34; 6.34; 8.33; 9.25; 10.21,23,27; 12.34 (many of these are redactional passages). (c) We have already suggested ἦσαν γὰρ ἁλιεῖς is a typical Markan parenthetical clause /13/; here it serves to define more precisely ἀμφιβάλλειν which has a wide range of meanings and might not have been easily understood by Mark's urban community. (d) καὶ εὐθύς (v.18) is employed frequently by Mark to join together incidents or sentences within incidents; it is found not only in seams but also within pericopae as here; the use of εὐθύς is so predominantly Markan /14/ that it must derive from him. The great majority of instances are found prior to 8.22; it serves to give a sense of urgency to the action; from 8.22 the Gospel is more occupied with instruction and so the phrase disappears until the incidents of the passion. Apart from these redactional details we may assume that the remainder of the passage is from the tradition /15/.

In the second incident we can at best detect Mark's hand only in the participle expressing motion, προβάς, in εἶδεν and in the phrase καὶ εὐθύς. Again we may conclude that the remainder of the incident is pre-Markan /16/.

We have suggested that there is a common pattern in the three incidents of 1.16-18, 1.19f; 2.14 /17/. Schulz /18/ argues that this pattern is based on 3 Kgdms 19.19-21. He detects three stages in each of the Markan stories: (i) Situation data; Jesus meets men who are going about their daily work. (ii) Jesus challenges them to come after him and serve. (iii) Obediently they leave their work and follow him. Clearly both the call by Elijah of Elisha and the Markan incidents fall within this pattern, but there are also differences: (i) The account in 3 Kgdms 19.19-21 is much more expansive in detail than the Markan accounts. (ii) It lacks a parallel to the reference to Jesus looking at those whom he calls. (iii) The word describing the movement of Elijah as he calls Elisha is not expressed nearly as clearly as in the Markan incident. (iv) Elijah performs a symbolic action; Jesus issues a call which is also a commission 'I will make you become fishers of men'. (v) It is doubtful if the three features to which Schulz points are anything other than three general features which would appear naturally in any call of disciples. We cannot therefore accept any argument that the call of Elisha affected the Markan calls through Mark himself but it may have left an impression on the way they were shaped during their passage through the tradition /19/; Lk. 9.59 shows that Elisha's call was creatively active in the primitive church.

If Elisha's call affected the tradition prior to Mark then the differences we detect between it and the Markan accounts (e.g. the reference to Jesus as in motion and as looking at potential disciples) are more likely to be due to Mark himself.

So far we have discussed the internal redactional details of 1.16-20, but its position is clearly also redactional. To us it would appear better if Mark had narrated some of the activity of Jesus and supplied some of his major teaching before he told us of the response of men to him (cf. Lk. 4.14 - 5.11) but we need to realise that all this would already be known to the members of Mark's community. 1.14f, in which the gospel is expressed partly in terms originating with Jesus and partly in those used by the early church, would recall to them the content of the preaching: true preaching should be followed by the appearance of new disciples; similarly 2.13, preceding 2.14, introduces the crowd to which Jesus preaches (to teach and to preach are almost equivalent in Mark). In this way the positioning of 1.16-20 may serve as a lesson for the preachers of the community but it also will remind all members of the community of the total commitment (abandonment of home and possessions) which is involved in their response to the gospel. The paucity of detail in the two calls combined with the absence of preparation for them provided by a narrative of Jesus' work centres attention on the fact of the calls themselves. Within Christian history many have felt the compelling nature of the call which they would not have wished to explain in purely psychological terms; at the same time they have seen others refuse the call. Mark only tells us of one call that is refused /20/, that of the rich man (10.17-22); there, as we have seen, he added the explanation (v.22b) of the man's wealth (cf. the explanations in 4.14-20). Acceptance of the call arises out of its compelling nature (at least to the man who accepts) and needs no explanation; rejection however must be explained.

There are a number of variations in the way in which the same idea is expressed in the two incidents but none appears to be significant /21/. Of apparently greater importance is the absence from the second of the saying about 'fishers' in the first. But this omission can hardly be significant /22/, for in the second it is still emphasised that James and John are fishermen and unless we were told otherwise we should therefore expect the saying to apply to them; its repetition would be tiresome. Of much greater interest is the appearance of what is clearly a variant of this logion in the tradition of Lk. 5.1-11; on this occasion it is addressed to Peter alone and he is called to be a 'catcher of men' /23/. For our purposes it is unnecessary to trace back both accounts to their point of divergence /24/ but a comparison of the two forms of the logion will assist us in elucidating the meaning of the Markan form. ζωγρεῖν means 'to take alive (instead of killing), preserve alive' /25/, but when a fish is caught it is killed. The Lukan form thus appears to be an amelioration of the Markan which could carry an unfortunate implication if the metaphor were pushed to its logical conclusion. The metaphor of catching men is found regularly in the OT (Jer. 16.16; Ezek. 29.4f; Amos 4.2; Hab. 1.14-17); normally it is used in a bad sense, i.e. to catch men is to catch them for punishment and not for salvation. It continued to be used in ths way in most strands of Judaism /26/. It may be that originally on the lips of Jesus it suggested that he and his disciples were the agents of eschatological judgement /27/. Wuellner /28/ has however argued that the 'evil' sense does not necessarily belong to the metaphor but that in each case its significance is to be gleaned from its context; consequently it could carry a redemptive meaning. If this is not so, then prior to its apearance in Mark the metaphor must have changed its meaning; if it is, then its meaning for Mark must be read out of the rest of the Gospel, and, since the task of the disciples in relation to men as described later (3.16f; 6.13-19) is redemptive, this must be its meaning in 1.17 /29/. Such a transition in the understanding of the metaphor could take place more easily in the Hellenistic church because of its use in Hellenistic culture to describe the activity of philosophers, teachers and wise men /30/. But whatever its original meaning and development in the tradition, Mark clearly recognises it as a description of the part disciples play in God's salvation.

A second difference in the Lukan form of the saying is the qualification ἀπὸ τοῦ νῦν ; the fishing for men ought to commence at once /31/. In Mark the fishing is placed in the future, ποιήσω, and when the period of fishing is to begin is not indicated in the text; it may be the moment when the disciples are sent out (6.7ff) /32/ or it could be understood as a reference to the mission of the church in Mark's own day. It would also be possible to take the tense as a logical future, 'Come after me, and if you do I will make you fishers of men'. Certainly in Mark there is no suggestion that the disciples at once begin to fish for men, and only if Mark were primarily interested in writing a history of Jesus and the disciples would we expect to see the future given a historical sense and fulfilled in 6.7ff. Relevant here also is the absence of any formal commission to the disciples in the resurrection period; 14.28; 16.7 may function in this way /33/ or there may have been an actual commission (cf. Mt. 28.16-20) in a supposed lost ending of the Gospel.

A third difference between Mark and Luke relates to the recipients of the saying: in Luke it is addressed to Peter only but in Mark to Peter and Andrew. Since in the latter the incident with James and John is tied so closely to that with Peter and Andrew it is reasonable to assume that Mark understood the saying as addressed to all four fishermen. Is the commission given only to these four, with three of them forming an inner group, or in receiving the commission do they represent the Twelve, either with the implication that the commission was given to the Twelve as a fixed group and was not transferable beyond them, or that the Twelve represent either all the ministry of the future church or some part of it, or in receiving the commission do these four represent the whole Christian community, so that all Christians are sent to fish for men? Clearly this question cannot be answered from this passage alone but only in the light of the way we see the disciples functioning throughout the whole of the Gospel /34/.

Before we leave 1.16-20 there are some other features of the passage to which we need to allude briefly. (i) Jesus summons the disciples; they do not associate themselves with him as a pupil might associate himself with a rabbi or teacher of philosophy; he chooses them and they do not choose him. (ii) In line with that Jesus is the principal character in the scene /35/; although we may be examining it for the light it throws on discipleship we must not forget that it indicates Jesus' commanding position; it is only in the light of that position that discipleship can be understood; discipleship implies obedience; obedience means to follow Jesus and to fish; this the Four do. (iii) Those who respond to the call leave their possessions and their homes; the importance Mark attributes to this can be seen from the way he further elucidates it in 10.28-31. (iv) At the beginning of each incident Jesus is in motion and he says to those whom he calls 'come after me', i.e. get into motion. Thus from the beginning of the Gospel discipleship is depicted as movement after Jesus. (v) From the beginning also mission activity is necessarily involved and it may be implied that this activity is to be directed towards the Gentiles: Galilee, where the commission is given, is Galilee of the Gentiles /36/ and the Sea of Galilee is the bridge to the Gentile world (5.1,13,21; 6.47,48,49; 7.31) /37/.

The metaphor of fishing never became important as a description of the activity of the ministry or of the whole church; we may contrast the pastor/shepherd imagery. The attitude of a fisherman to fish is quite different from that of a shepherd toward sheep. Although both fish and sheep may be designed to end as food there is a long period in which the shepherd cares for his sheep; the fisherman's first encounter with his fish is when he kills it for food for himself or for others.

Notes

1   We do not need to discuss the historicity of the calls to the four disciples; still less do we need to consider their relative wealth as fishermen in the economic conditions of Galilee in the first century; for the latter see W.H. Wuellner, The Meaning of "Fishers of Men", pp. 26ff.

2   C.H. Turner, JTS 26 (1925) 145-56; Pryke, p. 126.

3   Andrew occupies no special niche in the Gospel; at 3.18 he is even dissociated from Peter and his name placed after those of James and John in fourth place in the list of the Twelve.

4   Jn 21 may also reflect independent tradition. On Lk. 5.1-11 and the inter-relationship of the accounts see G. Klein, 'Die Berufung des Petrus'.

5   Neirynck, passim.

6   See below ch.20.

7   So G. Schille, Die urchristliche Kollegialmission, pp.26f. The parallels which Schille provides from the Gospel of Peter 14.59f and the Ebionite Gospel 2 are not convincing; the reference to the 'sea' at 2.13 probably comes from Mark and not the tradition since 2.13 is Markan (see below p.175).

8   In view of this conclusion it is unnecessary for us to discuss the origin of the pericope, either as historical event or as a frame for the saying about 'fishing'.

9   Cf. 2.14; 10.17 and the use of ὁδός.

10   See below pp.200f.

11   Admittedly Mark normally uses the simple ἡ θάλασσα (2.13; 3.7; 4.1; 5.1; 13.21). Only at 7.31 do we find the full phrase as here. 1.16 is the first time the lake is mentioned and Mark is thus identifying it as the lake which will feature later in his story; at 7.31 Jesus is returning from a journey outside Galilee and re-identification is necessary. In 1.16 its use may also serve to unite the incident to 1.14 (cf. Reploh, pp.29f).

12   Cf. Lohmeyer, Taylor, Nineham, Reploh, p.29f.

13   See above p.51 n.81.

14   Used as an adverb 7-42-1-3.

15   Mark consistently uses ἀκολουθεῖν in discipleship pass-

ages; but since the concept of 'following' Jesus certainly goes back to Jesus himself and the actual word probably to Hellenistic Jewish Christianity it would be wrong to attribute its use here to him. On the word see pp.33f.

16 In the two incidents the fishing is described in different ways; 1.16-18 implies a casting net and 1.19f the use of a boat. These details, and the ownership of the boat by Zebedee, certainly represent pre-Markan material.

17 See also B.M.F. van Iersel, 'La vocation de Lévi', pp.212-32; Schille, (as n.7), pp.26f.

18 Pp.98f. Cf. Pesch, ad loc.

19. In particular it may have led to the use of ἀκολουθεῖν and ὀπίσω as Greek terms to describe Christian discipleship.

20 He also uses for other purposes material (10.46-52) which may originally have functioned as a 'call' - narrative.

21 The words of Jesus are different in the two incidents. In 1.16-18 he says δεῦτε ὀπίσω μου; in 1.19f we have ἐκάλεσεν, without content given to his words. δεῦτε (δεῦρο) recurs in a summons to a disciple at 10.21, as does ὀπίσω at 8.34, but, more interestingly, it re-appears in 1.20 of the response of James and John. καλεῖν is used of the call of disciples in 2.17 and was widely used for this purpose in the early church. The response of Peter and Andrew is given with ἀκολουθεῖν, a discipleship word in Mark with a close relationship to ὀπίσω as we see from 8.34.

22 O. Betz, 'Donnersöhne, Menschenfischer und der davidische Messias', argues that Peter represents Judah among the sons of Jacob and that Judah was traditionally a hunter; thus the saying is appropriate in his case. He also argues for parallels between James and John on the one hand and Simeon and Levi on the other; as Levi left his father so James and John leave theirs. It is very doubtful if Mark was aware of these parallels whatever influence they may have had on the earlier tradition. It is Mark who introduces the reference to Levi at 2.14, which he would clearly have omitted if he had been conscious of the parallel suggested by Betz.

23 The reading of D in Lk. 5.10f must be rejected as a harmonisation.

24 There are a number of other differences: Peter is not called to follow Jesus but Jesus says to him 'Do not fear'; there is no fishing miracle in Mark. In considering the origin of the narrative we also need to take account of the story in Jn 21. On the evolution of the tradition see Klein, as n.4.

25 See Wuellner (as n.1), pp.237f, for references.

26   For the evidence see Wuellner (as n.1), pp.88ff.

27   In Mt. 13.47-50 the image is used in relation to eschatological judgement and C.W.F. Smith, 'Fishers of Men', contends that Jesus originally conceived of his mission as one of eschatological judgement in which the disciples would play a part and that the saying must be considered in this light. The Lukan and Johannine ·forms of the tradition would certainly conflict with this interpretation. Cf. Wuellner (as n.1), pp.138f.

28   Pp. 93ff, 113ff.

29   J. Mánek, 'Fishers of Men', draws attention to the place which 'the waters' occupy in Semitic thought where they represent evil, the underworld, the place of sin and death; there are traces of this in Mark (e.g. 4.35-41; 6.47-52); it may then be the task of the disciples to rescue men from 'the waters' and bring them to salvation.

30   Cf. Wuellner (as n.1), pp.67ff, for the evidence. It is unnecessary to argue for the origin of the saying in Hellenistic Christianity.

31   The difficulties this creates within the Lukan structure need not detain us. Klein (as n.4), thinks that it is a survival from the period in which the story had a post-resurrection setting.

32   Pesch says that they can only become fishers of men after they have been with Jesus (3.14f).

33   Cf. C.F. Evans, 'I will go before you into Galilee'.

34   See pp.204-6 and Best, 'The Role of the Disciples in Mark', for further discussion. Certainly we find great difficulty in seeing with Schille (as n.7), pp.28f, ordination terminology as present here.

35   Cf. Reploh, p.36f. Within each incident the first important word is a verb with Jesus as subject and the last a personal pronoun relating to him.

36   Cf. pp.200-2.

37   Cf. Pesch.

As we find it in Mark the story of the call of Levi is part of a paragraph (2.13-17) which is itself part of a larger unity (2.1-3.6) /1/, the complex of controversy stories. 2.15-17 is the only part of 2.13-17 which partakes of the nature of controversy. The very difficult grammar caused by the insertion of the γάρ clause, typically Markan /2/, in v.15 and possibly also by the next clause, confirms that Mark has been at work on an existing pre-Markan pericope /3/. If some, even if not all of vv.15-17 is pre-Markan, it is unlikely that v.13 goes back behind him. It reads like one of his summaries /4/; πάλιν is a Markan favourite /5/; the sea is mentioned but does not re-appear in the immediately succeeding material; Jesus is said to teach though little of his teaching is given, a characteristic found frequently in Markan seams; the imperfect tense is used.

As we have already suggested 2.14 is different from the rest of the material in the complex in that it is not a controversy story. 'Sins', 'sinners' forms a catch-word link /6/ between vv.1-12 and vv.15-17 suggesting that these passages were connected in the oral tradition. As it stands it is not clear grammatically whose house is intended in v.15; since there is no evidence that Jesus possessed a house and since he is regularly found in the houses of others we must assume that the house is Levi's; yet in v.14 Levi set out to follow Jesus /7/! Verse 14 cannot then have belonged originally to this context. The Markan characteristics to which we have referred imply that he himself inserted it.

If he did so, did he take it from the tradition or did he compose it? A strong argument can be put up for the latter /8/. As we have already seen it follows the same pattern as 1.16-18 and 1.19f/9/. There is nothing in it which is non-Markan and almost all of it accords with his compositional habits: (i) καὶ παράγων εἶδεν followed by a participle repeats 1.16. (ii) A participle followed by the aorist of ἀκολουθεῖν and αὐτῷ concludes this pericope as it did that of 1.16-18 /10/. (iii) While ἀκολουθεῖν appears in the tradition as a term of discipleship /11/ it is also used redactionally /12/; ὀπίσω never seems to be used redactionally by Mark /13/; we find the first term used twice in this passage and the second not at all. (iv) καὶ λέγει αὐτῷ is used redactionally at times by Mark (1.44; 5.19; 7.18).

Pesch /14/ supposes that the tradition contained the account of the meal in vv.15ff which was said to take place in the house of Levi the tax-collector; using 1.16-20 as model Mark then composed v.14 to explain the appearance of Levi and to provide a positive example of the fulfilment of the invitation of Jesus as given in v.17b. It is also admittedly difficult to conceive of such a small pericope as v.14 circulating by itself. There is, however, another possibility. The tradition may have contained a more detailed story of Levi which Mark streamlined into the pattern he had used in 1.16-20; in doing this he would naturally have re-cast it in his own language, altering its terminology to bring it into line with 1.16-20 and his normal words for the expression of discipleship; he would then have inserted it in its present position because of the existing references to 'tax-collectors'. There is much to be said in favour of this solution since we lack convincing evidence that Mark invented incidents. But in either case Mark is responsible both for the pattern of the incident and for its position.

So far we have used the name 'Levi' but there is both a textual uncertainty in 2.14 and Levi does not appear in any of the lists of the Twelve. The cross identification of names within the lists is difficult; by the time they appeared in writing many of the original Twelve had probably turned out to be unimportant and in consequence their names varied in the tradition. What are the facts about Levi? (a) In Mk 2.14 D θ fam 13 it a,b,c,d,e ff(2) n(1), Orig read 'Ιάκωβον; the remainder of the evidence is unanimous in referring to Levi /15/. (b) In 2.14 the disciple is described as the son of Alphaeus. (c) In 3.18; Mt. 10.3; Lk. 6.15; Acts 1.13 James is described as the son of Alphaeus. (d) In Mk 3.18 e fam 13 add τὸν τελώνην after Matthew's name. (e) In Mt. 10.3 Matthew is termed the tax-collector. (f) In Lk. 6.15; Acts 1.13 Matthew's name is unqualified and James is described as the son of Alphaeus. (g) In Mt. 9.9, the parallel to Mk 2.14, the tax-collector is named Matthew. (h) In the Lukan parallel (5.27) he is named Levi. The simplest solution to this complex situation is to suppose that attempts have been made in the transmission of the Markan text either to bring 2.14 into line with the list of the Twelve in 3.18 by changing the name Levi to James, who in 3.18 is described as the son of Alphaeus, so that we do not have two sons of Alphaeus (or sons of two Alphaeuses), or, under the influence of the Matthean text, by describing Matthew in 3.18 as the tax-collector to imply that Matthew and Levi are the same person /16/.

If, then, Levi is the original reading in 2.14, does Mark take him to be one of the Twelve, i.e. did he in his own mind equate Levi with James or Matthew or some other name in the list of 3.18? If he did so, it must surely have been with James because of the identity of their fathers' names. Peter and Simon are the same person; up to the appointment of the Twelve he is always called Simon but in the list of the Twelve the two names are expressly identified and after that he is regularly called Peter (8.32). We would expect the same care to be taken if Levi and James were to be identified. Identifications are given in the list of the Twelve but they are either names which Jesus has given to particular disciples (Peter, Boanerges) or qualifications where there might be confusion in the list itself (Simon the zealot is so termed to distinguish him from Peter; James the son of Alphaeus to distinguish him from James the son of Zebedee). We must conclude that for Mark Levi was not one of the Twelve.

Looking now at the incident as a whole we can see that 2.14 is as bare of unnecessary detail as 1.16-20. Even though the mission of Jesus had been in progress for some time there is no psychological preparation of Levi for Jesus' call. 'There is the same authoritative command, the same prompt obedience, the same break with ordered existence /17/; only the disciple called and the details are different' /18/. As in the earlier calls Jesus is in motion when he summons Levi, Jesus is said to look at him and the disciple is said to leave his normal occupation. There is perhaps one difference in that the context of vv.15-17 implies that Levi is a sinner /19/; Jesus' call is not only for those who are outwardly respectable but also for moral outcasts; he draws his disciples from all types of people. The association of v.13 with v.14 implies that before he responded to the call Levi was a member of the crowd, i.e. the unevangelised /20/.

If Mark has added 2.14 to the complex of controversy stories what, in addition to the implication that Jesus calls all men, does he hope to achieve by this insertion? We saw that 1.16-20 followed the proclamation of the Gospel in 1.14f. In our present context we have the claim of Jesus to forgive sins (2.6f,10) /21/ which serves as a proclamation of the Markan gospel /22/. In 2.13 Jesus is said to teach; Mark probably does not distinguish between teaching and preaching (cf. 6.12 with 6.30) /23/. 2.17b is again a declaration of the Gospel to which Levi has responded. Thus preaching and response are associated here as in the earlier calls. When the gospel is preached men are won to the community.

As in 1.19f no commission is given to Levi. It would have been easy to coin a similar saying to that of 1.17 along the lines

177

'I will make you to become a gatherer of men (and not of money)', but the nature of Levi's occupation was despised in the Roman world almost as much as in the Jewish. However while Levi is not given a specific commission he is seen at once to exercise the commission given to Peter and Andrew: he holds a feast in his house and invites to it those who need the gospel; the gospel is proclaimed to them (2.17b) and so Levi has in fact become a fisher of men.

Notes

1 We do not need to discuss the exact extent of this complex. Kuhn, p.86, argues that it did not contain the second sabbath pericope.

2 C.H. Turner, JTS 26 (1925) 145-56. The insertion is clumsy and it is not clear to whom it refers. It can hardly be the tax-collectors and sinners because they have just been described as 'many'; it can hardly relate forward to the scribes of the Pharisees for Mark uses ἀκολουθεῖν almost always of disciples, and never of opponents of Jesus; it must therefore refer to the disciples; this is confirmed by Mark's general use of γάρ parentheses to relate to what has just been dealt with (Meye, pp.142-5, reaches a different conclusion). Although the call of only five disciples has been described Mark is not writing like a modern historian to give an exact and detailed account; the existence of many disciples is implied by 3.13.

3 The exact analysis of vv.15-17 need not detain us. Kuhn, pp.58ff, and van Iersel, 'La vocation de Lévi', give a full discussion of its development, van Iersel opting for vv.16,17a as the original unit, and Kuhn for vv.15f.

4 Kuhn, p.82; Schmidt, p.82; Egger, pp.151-3.

5 17-28-3-43.

6 Kuhn, p.86.

7 Cf. Wellhausen, pp.18f.

8 So R. Pesch, 'Levi-Matthäus'.

9 See ch. 19.

10 The pleonastic use of ἀναστάς may also be Markan, cf. 1.35; 2.14; 10.1; see Doudna, pp.55f.

11 E.g. 8.34; 9.38.

12 2.15; 6.1; 10.28,32,52.

13 1.7,17,20; 8.33,34; 13.16.

14 As n.8.

15 Cf. Pesch (as n.8); B. Lindars, 'Matthew, Levi, Lebbaeus'.

16 Pesch's analysis (as n.8) leads him to conclude that the alterations in Matthew are redactional.

17   Luke says that Levi leaves everything (5.28); he thus stresses the element of renunciation more than Mark does (cf. Lk. 5.11 and Mk 1.18). We do not know if Levi was as wealthy as Zachaeus; there is nothing in Mark's story to suggest it. In Mark Levi certainly abandons his occupation; that he brings Jesus back to his home is not an indication that he did not give this up (Peter still has his at 1.29-31) but derives from the way Mark has united 2.14 with 2.15-17.

18   Bundy, ad loc.

19   Cf. Schulz, pp.99f. H. Simsonsen, 'Zur Frage der grund-legenden Problematik in form- und redaktionsgeschichtlicher Evangelienforschung', pp.7f, argues that the reference to Levi as sitting at his office is not intended to emphasise his abandonment of his work but to draw out the 'unworthiness' of the one called.

20   Cf. pp.28f.

21   Schweizer, ad loc.

22   See Best, pp.69-71.

23   Best, pp.71f.

Chapter 21
MARK 3.13-19

The problem of determining the Markan contribution to this pericope, already difficult enough in other passages, is here compounded by textual uncertainties. It can be safely assumed that the list of the twelve names in vv.16-19 is traditional /1/ and not a post-Markan addition, but the grammar is unclear in respect of the clauses explaining the 'nicknames' of Simon, James and John for they break the construction. The list must be understood as standing in apposition to δώδεκα in v.14 (or v.16, if it is to be read there), for all the names after the first are accusatives; yet the initial 'Simon' is a dative. Andrew is also unexpectedly (in the light of 1.16-18) separated from his brother (contrast Lk. 6.16). It looks as if Mark either received the list in this awkward form in which Peter, James and John appeared as a separate group at the head linked already to nicknames or, more probably, altered the order of the names, pushing Andrew back, and added from a separate source the clauses giving the nicknames /2/. In the latter case Peter, James and John were probably already isolated as a unit. The solution to this problem does not affect our present study and we can leave it.

At first sight v.13a would appear to be Mark's editorial introduction to the pericope since it is cast in the historic present and employs his favourite προσκαλεῖσθαι but Reploh /3/ argues correctly that it comes from the tradition. The historic present is used regularly by Mark within pericopae as well as in redactional passages and is therefore no certain guide to redaction. More importantly προσκαλεῖσθαι is used here differently from its other occurrences in Mark /4/ except 6.7 where it is again the Twelve who are summoned; this verse, as we shall see, is closely related to 3.13; they have either influenced each other or both have come from the same segment of tradition. In 3.13 the verb, over and above its normal meaning 'summon', seems also to carry the nuance of selection. Reploh also argues that the introduction of the mountain (v.13) /5/ is unexpected since there has just been a reference to a boat in v.9 which is taken up again in 4.1; the 'mountain' thus comes from the tradition and the use of the article suggests that it may at some stage have been identified /6/.

If v.13a implies some kind of selection it would be natural for οὕς ἤθελεν αὐτός to be followed directly by a statement either identifying those who are chosen or supplying the purpose of their choice. The passage does indeed go on to provide statements answering both these implicit questions but before it does so there are two brief clauses linked paratactically καὶ ἀπῆλθον ... καὶ ἐποίησεν ...The second of these clauses is not a proper answer to the implicit question about choice; this comes only with the identification of those chosen in vv.16-19. Thus we assume that in the tradition the relative clause was followed either by vv.14b,15 or by the list of the Twelve. (Because of the grammatical difficulties of the passage it is most unlikely that the tradition used by Mark had already united the list of names and the purpose of their choice.) The former of these is more probable for: (i) ἵνα ὦσιν ..could not have existed by itself in the tradition but must have had some introduction and v.13a would fulfil the need. (We assume now, but shall argue later, that vv.14b,15 is not entirely a Markan construction.) (ii) The list of the Twelve could have existed independently more easily in the tradition. (iii) The connection of call and commission, which we find in v.13a and vv.14,15, was pre-Markan in 1.16-18 and probably therefore is so also here. (iv) The greatest obstacle to this solution appears to be the paratactic clauses in vv.13b,14a; did Mark insert them? The first clause conveys the sense of motion which is found in almost all of his discipleship references and which would otherwise be lacking in this passage. The second clause /7/ could have been the original introduction to the list of the Twelve. We note that it re-appears in some Markan texts in v.16 at the head of the list /8/. If it is the correct reading at this point Mark may have taken it forward to make an immediate reference to the Twelve and then used again at its original position. If it is incorrect to read in it v.16 then some MSS may read it because it was known to be the introduction to the list of the Twelve in the tradition; their scribes in fact re-introduced an omission or, more precisely, a transference which Mark had made. Alternatively δώδεκα may have appeared in Mark's source linked to οὕς ἤθελεν and Mark have derived it therefrom /9/. The first of the two clauses may be accounted for in a different way if we note that Mark normally uses ἀπέρχεσθαι εἰς (1.35; 6.32,46; 7.24,30; 8.13 etc. - all in redactional clauses) but that here we have the verb with πρός (only also at 14.10) /10/. The introduction to vv.14b,15 may then have read '... and they went away to him that they might be with him and ...'; 'went away to' and 'be with' then balance one another. The second of the clauses would then have come from the original introduction to the list of names of the Twelve.

Verses 14b,15 have two difficulties: (i) that the disciples should be 'with him' and that he should send them away appear to be inconsistent; (ii) it is unclear what it means to send someone to have power /11/. We begin with the latter. Either (a) the sentence came to Mark in the tradition and already contained the difficulty or (b) the sentence originally read 'that he might send them to preach and to cast out demons' into which he inserted ἔχειν ἐξουσίαν, or (c) he composed the whole of vv.14b,15 /12/. The last is unlikely for apart from the reference to having power over demons there is little which is Markan in the sentence; while he does use μέτα more regularly than σύν much of this usage is found in traditional material /13/. The reference to the sending of the Twelve and their equipment with power over demons is also found in 6.7b where it is expressed clearly. If Mark were composing v.15 there is no reason why he should not have written as in 6.7. Therefore we must reject (c) and choose between (a) and (b). Because of Mark's interest in demons /14/ it is probable that he inserted ἔχειν ἐξουσίαν, /15/ into a piece of existing tradition and created the difficult construction. He may have taken the idea from 6.7b but it is more likely that he himself wrote 6.7b where he expressed himself clearly and that here he adapted tradition. We conclude that v.15 lacked ἔχειν ἐξουσίαν in its pre-Markan form. But did Mark also add ἵνα ὦσιν μετ' αὐτοῦ or did it belong to the tradition? E. Meyer /16/ took this difficulty (i above) as indicative of two sources: ἵνα ἀποστέλλῃ comes from his Twelve-source and the other phrase from his disciples source /17/. But is the difficulty as great as it is made out to be? We already find the implicit marriage of the two ideas in 1.16-18 where Jesus' call and commission of Peter and Andrew is both an invitation for them to be with him as they follow after him and a demand to go out from him as fishers of men. While the combination of ideas might have seemed difficult to a contemporary of the original statement of 3.14b,15 in the life of Jesus (supposing that it is genuine Jesus-tradition) it would not be so for Mark, his readers or the earlier church; they would naturally think of the ideas of 'being with him' and of 'being sent to preach etc.,' not as simultaneous but as successive, since that was what had actually taken place: the disciples had been with Jesus during his earthly life and had gone on to preach and exorcise after his resurrection /18/; it was also what happened in their own experience.

An element of choice is inherent in προσκαλεῖται οὕς ..., but from what group is this choice made /19/? Are the Twelve selected from a wider group of disciples /20/ or directly from the crowd? Are those signified by οὕς identical with the Twelve or are the Twelve chosen from them? As we have seen the pre-Markan tradition ran 'He went up to the mountain and summoned those he wished (and they went away to him) so that they ...' We cannot recover the larger context of this portion of the tradition and so do not know whether in it Jesus summoned men from the crowd or from a larger group of disciples, and we are indeed uncertain whether it referred to the Twelve or more generally to disciples as those who were summoned. In Mark the larger context is that of the crowd (cf. vv.7-12) but we cannot be sure if Mark was always aware of such larger contexts. However his insertion καὶ ἐποίησεν δώδεκα confirms and suggests that he envisaged a two stage choice: Jesus chooses /21/ disciples from the crowd and then when they have gone up the mountain with him he appoints twelve from their number so that they might be with him and go out to preach and exorcise /22/. This interpretation is supported by indications in Mark that a group of disciples larger than the Twelve was already in existence; Levi (2.14) was not one of the Twelve and 2.15 speaks of many disciples /23/. The first of Mark's two stages is thus a generalisation of the calls of 1.16-20 and 2.14 and as in them there is a movement towards Jesus (ἀπῆλθον); the second stage, the appointment of the Twelve, is something new. There may appear to be a certain inconsistency here in that there is a 'commission' in 1.16-18 equivalent to that of 3.14b,15. But the commission of 1.17 is much more vague: preaching and exorcism are specific ways of fishing for men; fishing itself can be carried out in many other ways. Consequently every disciple may fish for men but not every disciple is necessarily chosen to preach and exorcise /24/. We should note also that neither in 3.14f nor in 6.7 is any limitation placed on the people to whom they are sent (contrast Mt. 10.5).

What then is the function of the Twelve in Mark's Gospel /25/? In the tradition there would have been pericopae in which they were featured and pericopae in which the disciples were featured. As we have seen throughout 8.27-10.45 Mark was directing the minds of his readers to discipleship and wherever the Twelve or the disciples appeared in the tradition he used them as examples of what discipleship is, or is not. But here, and in 6.6b-13, the Twelve are given a special position. What this position was must be learnt from these two particular pericopae, modified by what we may learn from the rest of the

Gospel. Long before Mark wrote the Twelve were a recognised group. They appear as a unit in the early tradition of 1 Cor. 15.3-5 (cf. Mt. 19.28; Lk. 22.30) and the list of their names in Mark 3.16-19 pre-dates him. In Mark they are not given the apocalyptic role they possess in Mt. 19.28; Lk. 22.30; this means they are not presented as the core of the New Israel. Nor are they the cell or kernel from which the community grew /26/, for the community began with the call of Peter and the other fishermen (1.16-20) and was increased by the addition of Levi (2.14) before the Twelve were selected; and in 8.34 and 10.17-22 Jesus is still calling disciples; there is no picture of the Twelve as a centre from which growth takes place; it is always Jesus who calls; new disciples are not added to an original core; they join Jesus and follow him. In 3.13-19 certain disciples are chosen from a larger number, appointed as a group /27/ and given a commission to preach and exorcise. As distinct from the missionary activity of every Christian we find here the consecration of a group as full-time missionaries. Missionary activity at first took place haphazardly as Christians went from one area to another, either driven away from the old area by persecution or attracted to a new area by the needs of business or commerce, or when within a household one member of the family won another or one slave gained another. Most could never be full-time missionaries; slaves could not leave their 'employment'; wives could not desert their husbands. But there were those whose whole time for at least a period (at 6.30 they return) was given to mission work; Mark's church will have sent out some of its members to this task and some solemn act will have celebrated their choice and commission /28/. This pericope supplied the community with its authority and its pattern for such an action /29/. In it the 'missionaries' are given 'authority' but it is an authority over 'demons' outwith the community and not an authority over the community. Acts 13.1-3 functioned in a similar way; in that passage Luke suggests not only how full-time mission began but also provides a model for its continuance in any community /30/. Understood in this way 3.13-19 not only coheres with 6.6b-13 but supplies a basis for it.

It may be objected that while it is possible to conceive of preaching and exorcism limited to a small group in the community this restriction cannot apply to μετ' αὐτοῦ /31/. Does not every Christian need to be 'with Christ'? While this is true it is arguable that Mark sees it as true in a special way for missionaries. He has shown already how Jesus after a day's preaching and exorcism withdrew to pray to his Father (1.35).

Later he tells of an occasion when the disciples, or some of them, are separated from Jesus and they engage in missionary activity (exorcism - cf. 3.15) and the result is failure (9.18). Unless missionaries are 'with their exalted Lord' they will also fail /32/. That εἶναι μετά is used elsewhere in Mark of physical presence (1.13 /33/; 2.19; 4.36; 5.18; 14.67) /34/ does not mean that it cannot here refer to presence with the exalted Lord, though this was not its original reference. The 'spiritualisation' of physical statements is common in religion.

The function of 'missionaries' in exorcism is emphasised by the context Mark has given 3.13-19 /35/ for it is immediately preceded by the homage of the demons (3.11f) and followed by Jesus' rebuttal of the claim of an alliance with them (3.22-30). Nothing however is said about the content of the missionaries' preaching, unless 3.11f with its confession of Jesus as Son of God is intended to indicate this; such a confession as a summary of the content of the gospel would not be out of harmony with the 'gospel' which the Gospel itself proclaims.

Notes

1   This is confirmed by the omission of Levi's name (2.14) and the preservation of the nickname 'Boanerges', though its meaning has been lost. For more detailed discussion and literary references see G. Schmahl, pp.46-49 and 'Die Berufung der Zwölf im Markusevangelium'.

2   Cf. E. Hirsch, Frühgeschichte, I, pp.19ff (I owe this reference to Grundmann). Since the nicknames are non-Greek in character they clearly come from the tradition. The clauses containing them are parenthetical and have not been properly worked into the text; this suggests that Mark is not just inserting occasional information but introducing another piece of tradition which gave the list of nicknames (cf. S. Freyne, The Twelve, pp.87-9; see also J. Roloff, Apostolat - Verkündigung - Kirche, p.147). Mark has not previously used the name Peter but from now on, apart from 14.37, he invariably employs it.

3   Pp.43f; cf. Freyne (as n.2), pp.84f.

4   See p.130 n.8. Cf. Meye, p.147.

5   The 'mountain' was regularly used to denote a place of revelation in the early church and in Judaism (cf. 9.2). Here, however, it may indicate either separation from the crowd or the adoption of a position from which Jesus can select (cf. Stock, p.10), perhaps imparting some transcendental nature to that action (cf. W. Burgers, 'De instelling van de Twaalf'). There is no emphasis in Mark on Jesus as the new Moses so the

mountain is not Sinai. Even if the mountain indicates the transcendental nature of what takes place that is no reason for attributing its presence to Mark; both the mountain of the transfiguration and the Mount of Olives are pre-Markan.

6   ἀναβαίνει εἰς is not necessarily Markan as Schmahl, p.52, argues. At 6.51 and 10.33 it is from the tradition and at 10.32 it is derived from 10.33.

7   There is nothing in ἐποίησεν δώδεκα itself to help us determine if it is Markan in origin. The parallels usually adduced (1 Macc. 1.51; 3 Kgdms 12.31; 13.33; 2 Chron. 2.18) refer to someone being appointed to an already recognised post or function. 1 Kgdms 12.6 is an exception and is presumably the most satisfactory parallel; in it the function is spelt out in the ἵνα clause (cf. Stock, pp.15ff). Is it then a septuagintalism or an aramaism in Mark? Heb. 3.2, where it cannot be the latter, indicates the former as a real possibility. It could also be a latinism (cf. the use of facio). A much less satisfactory solution gives it the sense 'create' (Lohmeyer, Schniewind, Schmahl, pp.54f); with this meaning we would expect τοὺς δώδεκα; since elsewhere Mark always uses the article with δώδεκα its omission here is significant; even if we adopted this solution it goes too far to see in it also the creation of the New Israel, for Levi is already a member of the latter.

8   א B C Δ 565. Schmahl (as n.1) denies that it could have been the introduction to the list arguing that the introduction in Mt. 10.2 would be more suitable; the Matthean introduction, however, divorces what happened from the direct action of Jesus. In his book (pp.49f) Schmahl argues correctly for its traditional nature.

9   Freyne (as n.2), p.85, argues that if we read 'he appointed the Twelve' in v.16a and if this originally headed the list, Mark has duplicated the expression when he inserted 3,14b,15. In this case also the Twelve belongs to the pre-Markan tradition.

10   Cf. L. Schenke, Studien zur Passionsgeschichte des Markus, p.127.

11   D W itb c f ff i r vg remove the difficulty using 6.7.

12   Cf. Reploh, p.46; Freyne (as n.2), pp.84-6; Stock, pp.17ff; Schmahl, pp.56ff. That κηρύσσειν appears elsewhere in Mark in redactional passages does nothing to indicate its redactional nature here as Schmahl, p.58, alleges; it was too commonly used in the primitive church for any exclusively Markan claim to be sustained.

13   Pesch, ad loc., argues that δαιμόνιον is Markan. Yet in 3.22; 7.26,29,30; 9.38 it is pre-Markan and 'unclean spirits' is Markan in 1.27 and 3.11,30, and probably also in 7.25 (otherwise

why is there a change in word here?). That ἐκβάλλειν τὰ δαιμόνια was part of the tradition in 3.22-30 (so Stock, pp.22f) does not prove Mark derived it from there to use here.

14   Cf. Best, pp.1-27, 187-9.

15   The verb and noun come together in 1.22, a redactional passage, and 2.10. Mark also uses ἐξουσία redactionally at 1.27; 6.7 (see ch. 22) and 13.34 (see p.152).

16   Meyer, I, pp.135-8. His theory is criticised by C.H. Turner, JTS 28 (1927) 22-30.

17   Knox, I, pp.17f, has a different analysis of the sources and regards all of vv.14f as deriving from the Twelve-source.

18   We assume that in v.14a the clause οὓς καὶ ἀποστόλους ὠνόμασεν was not original but came from Lk. 6.13 (cf. Taylor, ad loc.; W. Schmithals, The Office of Apostle in the Early Church, p.72; Stock, p.17; etc.); it was possibly inserted to create an 'office' after ἐποίησεν. The concept of the office of the apostle is not important in Mark, though as we shall see the function of 'missionary' is.

Schmithals, in a more recent article, 'Der Markusschluss, die Verklärungsgeschichte und die Aussendung der Zwölf', has argued that 3.13,16-19 was part of the resurrection narrative in Mark's source where it followed 9.2-8 and preceded 16.15-20. In 'The Markan Redaction of the Transfiguration' we have given reasons for believing that Schmithals is wrong in this matter in respect of the transfiguration; his argument in respect of 3.13,16-19 depends in part on the appearance of the mountain in both 3.13 and 9.2. So far as 3.13-19 goes he fails to account adequately for Mark's insertion of 3.14b-15 with its very peculiar grammatical form in comparison with the simpler 6.7; he appears to believe Mark composed both and inserted 3.14b-15 into the tradition. In its supposed position in the source the call of the Twelve was linked to the worldwide preaching of the gospel (16.15f); this is lost in 3.14b,15 and 6.7. He also assumes that the Twelve were originally anchored in the post-resurrection situation; there are good reasons for believing that their choice goes back to the pre-resurrection Jesus. He fails to provide an adequate explanation why Mark should move the account from a seemingly more appropriate position (cf. Mt. 28.16-20); to attribute this to the Messianic secret is only to make the secret more difficult to understand. Finally Schmithals fails to produce a single instance of Mark's redactional activity in stylistic matters.

19   There is as little interest here in the psychological motivation of the disciples as there was in 1.16-20; 2.14; Jesus summons and they come; cf. Schulz, p.104.

20 As in Lk. 6.13 (cf. Jn 6.66f).

21 οὓς ἤθελεν αὐτός emphasises the sovereignty of Jesus' choice (Stock, pp.13f).

22 Matthew apparently understood Mark to imply that the Twelve were chosen from the crowd and not out of a larger group of disciples whereas Luke understood it in the latter way.

23 3.7,9 mention disciples but give no clue to their number; 4.10; 10.32; 15.40f all imply that in Mark's eyes the group of disciples was larger than the Twelve. Pace Burgers (as n.5) the Twelve and the disciples are not the same for Mark.

24 Schmahl (as n.1) views 1 Kings 19.19-21 as the model Mark used in 3.13-16; we have rejected this solution for 1.16-20 (see ch. 19) and there is even less reason for accepting it here, and still less for attributing the whole of 3.13-15 to Mark because its structure resembles 1.16-18; 1.19f; 2.14; the resemblance is less clear than Schmahl, p.63, supposes and could easily be pre-Markan.

25 On the wider issues see Best, 'The Twelve'.

26 Cf. Reploh, p.48.

27 Mark's omission of the article implies that he realises that his reference to the Twelve differs from other references in that here he deals with their appointment. The use of the article in the later references is normal; it does not prove Mark introduced the Twelve into the material. They would already have been 'The Twelve' in tradition (cf. 1 Cor. 15.5) if they existed as a group in it.

28 There is nothing in the passage to suggest that they are guarantors of the tradition (so Burgers, as n.5) and so of the reliability of Mark's own report. Their presence with Jesus is so often related in his presentation to their lack of understanding that they would have been poor guarantors - which is not, of course, to say that in fact Jesus' disciples did not hand on tradition reliably.

29 Schille, Der urchristliche Kollegialmission, p.121, appears to see the origin of the concept of the Twelve in mission but this goes beyond the evidence.

30 See Best, 'Acts XIII. 1-3'.

31 It is hardly a technical term as alleged by J.M. Robinson, The Problem of History in Mark, pp.79f.

32 It is also possible that Mark, receiving the μετ' αὐτοῦ in the tradition, retained it because it was there, although he was only interested in the reference to missionary activity. Taylor's view (ad v.14) that, since the Twelve are not actually sent to preach and exorcise until 6.13, it is Mark's intention to suggest a period of prior intimate companionship, fails because the

companionship depicted in 3.21-6.6a differs in no way in intimacy from that in 1.16-3.12 and 6.14ff. Meye, p.113, is much nearer the truth when he argues that the apostles are shown all through the Gospel as in a period of learning or training.
33   Were, in fact, the 'beasts' of the temptation beings who were physically present?
34   So Stock, pp.17ff.
35   3.7-12, 3.13-19 and 3.20-35 did not form a pre-Markan complex. Mark brought them together.

Chapter 22
MARK 6.6b-13,30

This paragraph has within it a large section of traditional material, viz. vv.8-11, for: (a) there is an independent parallel in Q (cf. also Lk. 10.1ff); (b) there are signs of Markan editorial activity in the linkages between the sayings, in particular καὶ ἔλεγεν αὐτοῖς (v.10) /1/; (c) there are variations in the structure of the sayings; we begin in v.8 with παραγγέλλειν ἵνα but this changes in v.9 to a participle and an infinitive; in vv.10f we have direct speech /2/. The differences in content between Mark and the other Gospels over the sandals, the staff and the non-possession or non-wearing of the χιτών are almost certainly pre-Markan; they represent a change due to the conditions of a new geographical area (Italy rather than the Middle East) or to the duration of the journey in mind (a longer journey requires more adequate equipment) or, if Mark rather than Q reproduces an earlier stage of the tradition, to a greater degree of asceticism in Q.

Assuming then that Mark has made use of tradition in vv.8-11 we need to examine the material in which it is encased to ascertain what part of it may be his.

Verse 6b is so short that it is impossible to be certain but the introductory καὶ and the use of the imperfect tense and of διδάσκειν in a seam suggests his hand /3/; moreover nothing suggests that this half-verse came from the tradition /4/. Verse 6b lies between sections which there is no reason to believe were previously united in the tradition and commentators are divided whether it should be taken with vv.1-6a /5/ or vv.7-13 /6/. If the former then they depict Jesus after he has been rejected in Nazareth, not as giving up his mission, but as turning to the surrounding country /7/; if the latter they connect the mission of the disciples to the period when Jesus moved around from village to village /8/. Both these explanations seem directed more to an attempt to give v.6b a biographical context than a Markan. Either connection might represent Mark's intention but that with vv.7-13 is more likely for Markan seams normally introduce new pericopae and v.6b then relates the mission of the Twelve to that of Jesus in that both involve movement; v.11 with its clear reference to 'place' and the probability that a disciple on mission will have to move is prepared for by vv.1-6a which speak of Jesus leaving an area and v.6b which describes him as moving into a new one. This idea of movement is also linked as we have seen in 8.27-10.52 to the theme of discipleship as movement 'on the way' after Jesus.

V.7 has been composed at least in part by Mark /9/. We have seen /10/ that in 3.15 he inserted ἔχειν ἐξουσίαν into an existing formula; now in the last clause of v.7 he expresses the same conception but since he is no longer tied by the tradition he is able to express the concept of authority more fluently: καὶ ἐδίδου /11/. This conclusion is re-inforced by the use of 'unclean spirits' which while it could have come from the tradition (cf. 1.23,26; 5.8) is more probably Markan since he alone of the evangelists uses it redactionally (1.27; 3.11,30, /12/. The connection between ἐξουσία and demonic powers is probably also Markan /13/. The second clause of v.7 clearly contains a Markanism in its use of ἄρχεσθαι as an auxiliary /14/, but the reference to the disciples as sent out two by two comes from the tradition for it is also found in the parallel at Luke 10.1 /15/. Since the directions to missionaries must have had some introduction this probably lay in the reference to 'two by two' which Mark has completely re-written in v.7. But did this original introduction contain the first clause in which Jesus is said to summon the Twelve? προσκαλεῖσθαι although a Markan favourite is not used in his normal fashion (cf. 3.13) /16/. Probably therefore he derived it from the tradition he had used in 3.13. It may well be that 3.13-15, most of which we saw was traditional, was originally followed by 6.8-11 (or some portion of it) /17/; on splitting off the latter Mark had to provide it with an introduction and for this he chose the verb which lay to hand. The reference to the Twelve in v.7 would then also be derived from the tradition /18/. Thus in v.7 Mark has re-written tradition introducing into it the reference to the giving of power over unclean spirits.

If we are correct in the view that 6.8-11, with a suitable connection, was previously linked to 3.13-15 then at least part of 6.12f may have formed the conclusion. We note in it the use of 'demons', the more common term in the tradition /19/, instead of 'unclean spirits' as in v.7. κηρύσσειν is not elsewhere found in Mark with a ἵνα construction /20/; 'repentance' is hardly a regular Markan concept /21/; it derives from the tradition in 1.4 though it may be Markan in 1.15. It is much more difficult to decide about v.13b. Anointing as a Christian method of healing sickness /22/ is found in the N.T. only here and in Jas 5.14; the use of oil for spiritual healing rather than as a medicine was apparently more frequent in Jewish circles than elsewhere and this might suggest that the reference comes from the tradition; the infrequency of allusion to it may imply that it was only in use in a limited number of Christian churches, of which Rome was one. The use of θεραπεύειν tells us nothing; it is not a Markan favourite /23/; he tends to use particular words for particular illnesses /24/ but a general word has to be used here because the reference is general /25/. We conclude that most, if not all, of vv.12f is pre-Markan.

6.30 clearly resumes 6.6b-13 but why did Mark interpolate the incident about the death of John the Baptizer? Normally in Markan sandwiches the two pericopae which have been woven together throw light on each other or are linked in some other way, but there is no obvious connection between the death of John and the mission of Jesus' disciples. To suggest /26/ that Mark introduces Herod at this point because Jesus' disciples made his name more widely known and Herod heard of him (6.14-16), and then to suppose that Herod's name leads on by association to John is extremely flimsy and is a biographical rather than a redactional explanation. Certainly Mark required some incident to indicate the passage of time between the departure of the disciples and their return. But why this incident? It contains nothing which suggests that time is elapsing either in the life of Jesus or in the lives of his disciples. But it may be that it is the very absence in it of reference to Jesus and the disciples which led Mark to choose it. After 3.15 he never portrays Jesus as working apart from his followers until Gethsemane is reached /27/, and at 6.31 he stresses again their presence with him. In most of the tradition which he has used the disciples feature quite naturally (e.g. the feeding accounts, the crossing of the lake, the healing of Jairus's daughter, their instruction in 8.27-10.45) but where they do not Mark introduces them (e.g. in 3.20-35 they appear as those who do the will of God, in the parable chapter they have a role at 4.10-12, in 5.1 the verbs are plural and in any case their presence was essential to the preceding incident /28/). If Mark followed out this policy he could not insert an incident which showed Jesus acting apart from the disciples. So this pericope /29/ about the death of John was suitable. Mark in any case had positive reasons for using it; he viewed it as a 'minor passion' /30/.

6.30 is probably Markan /31/. It may well be that the tradition of the sending out of the Twelve possessed an ending in the pre-Markan material for the parallel in Luke 10 did (10.17-24). If there was such an ending Mark has re-shaped it. Whereas the earlier traditional material (3.14; 6.12) uses

Chapter 22: Mark 6.6b-13,30

κηρύσσειν v.30 has Mark's favourite διδάσκειν; συνάγειν, while not appearing frequently in Mark, occurs elsewhere only in redactional seams (2.2; 4.1; 5.21; 7.1); ὅσος is a Markan favourite /32/ and the particular use of it with ἀπαγγέλλειν and ποιεῖν /33/ is found also in 5.19 which is itself probably redactional.

In 6.30, however, Mark has employed one word, ἀπόστολος which he does not use elsewhere /34/ but which belongs to church usage; if Mark rewrote the ending of this section of the tradition it probably belonged to the original form /35/. The word appears only once in Matthew (10.2), six times in Luke and once in John. In the primitive church it possessed a variety of meanings, or, more precisely, the name was applied to people who exercised, or were supposed to have exercised, a variety of functions /36/. Its meaning in any instance of its use can only be determined from its immediate context, or if it is widely used by a particular author, from his total context. Some scholars would deny that it has any technical meaning in v.30 and would take it 'simply as a verbal noun' /37/. While this is possible it seems unlikely in view of the widespread use of the word in Paul's letters which predate the Gospel; indeed in 1 Cor. 15.7; Gal. 1.17 it is pre-Pauline. Paul may not always have used it with the same meaning but Mark and his readers would have been aware of some of the possible meanings and would not therefore have been able to accept a wholly non-technical usage of the word. In 6.30 it is set in the context of mission (cf. 1 Th. 2.7); those who return to Jesus from their mission are not envisaged as occupying a position of government (as in Acts) or as related to any collection or distribution of money (Phil. 2.25; 2 Cor. 8.23) or as future holders of a special position (Mt. 19.28; Lk. 22.30) or as witnesses of the resurrection (1 Cor. 9.1; 15.7; Acts 1.21) but as concerned to extend the church. For this purpose the English word 'missionary' /38/ seems appropriate; it is a quasi-technical term; it does not give an official status as do 'priest', 'minister of the Word and Sacraments', 'bishop', 'elder', 'deacon', yet it suggests someone with a recognised position in the life of the church /39/ and this position arises out of the function which is carried out and to which the cognate verb is applied in 3.14; 6.7. This picture is not materially altered if we allow the disputed reading in 3.14, for the context of the disputed clause is again that of mission.

If 6.8-13 was the continuation of 3.13-15 in the pre-Markan tradition, why did Mark separate them? Normally when he inserts material into existing tradition and creates a sandwich the intervening material and the original material throw light

193

on one another. It is difficult to discern such a procedure here, not least because so much material has been inserted. It might possibly be argued that 3.14f is expanded in two ways: in 3.20-6.6 we find the μετ' αὐτοῦ element /40/ and in 6.6b-13 the ἵνα ἀποστέλλῃ element. But: (i) The amount of material allotted to the two elements seems disproportionate. (ii) The μετ' αὐτοῦ element appears as clearly after 6.6b as before it, e.g. 6.31f, and as clearly before 3.13 as after it, e.g. 3.7; consequently 3.20-6.6 cannot be said to expand this element any more than any other part of the Gospel, with the exception of the passion story where Jesus' isolation is stressed. (iii) There is little explicit reference to the mission of the disciples after 6.30. Much more probably Mark separated the two pericopae because in a connected narrative it would be strange to say that Jesus called the disciples to be with him and then immediately sent them away. This does not, however, tell us why Mark inserted it where he did. Because of the way the traditional material was grouped there were only a limited number of places where he could have done so, e.g. he could not break into 3.20-35; 4.1-34; 4.35-5.43 or 8.27-10.45, for these are all units, some of them pre-Markan and others carefully constructed by him. It is probably impossible to determine why he chose the spot he did but there were only a very limited number of possibilities.

What function does 6.6b-13 play in Mark's teaching for his church? Whereas in 8.27-10.45 the instruction on discipleship applies to every Christian this can hardly be true of the present passage /41/; here it obviously envisages a journey of some considerable length (sandals, staff, movement from place to place), and by this period of the church the abandonment of all necessities (money, food) can hardly have been demanded of every Christian; already in 1 Th. 5.14; 2 Th. 3.6-12 Paul was insisting on the need of Christians to work for their living and his admission that missionaries could expect to receive help from other Christians (1 Cor. 9.3ff) implies that most Christians continued at their daily work. If the instruction is not then directed at every Christian is it intended specifically for the leaders of the church? If so it envisages them as leaving the church while they go on their journey and no provision is made for the church in their absence; nowhere else in the Gospel is there explicit teaching on the duties of leaders; if this was what was intended here we should expect that somewhere else there would be instruction on the administration of the church (10.41-5 is the only implicit reference) and we should expect that this would have priority over instruction on how to be missionaries. We may therefore conclude that this pericope offers an example of behaviour for missionaries who are sent out on mission from the community /42/. The demands which are made on them are not primarily ascetic but relate to their missionary activity /43/. These demands are balanced by the requirement that they should be alone with Jesus (v.31 takes up the 'with him' of 3.14). The missionary needs his time of privacy with Jesus, though he may not always get it because of the crowds /44/.

What was said at the close of the discussion of 3.13-19 about the function of the Twelve in that pericope applies equally to their role in this section and coheres with what we have just said about the Apostles. They are full-time missionaries. As such they are not repeatedly sent out but once-for-all /45/, though the Church will repeatedly send out new missionaries. The Twelve may thus be a link between the missionary activity of the early church and that of Jesus but not a link between Jesus and the ministry of the church /46/.

Notes

1   For the redactional nature of the phrase see p.31. The use of the phrase does not necessarily imply that Mark has brought two portions of tradition together at this point. In 4.24 he has used it to re-connect previously united tradition; cf. Best, 'Mark's Preservation of the Tradition'. He would be all the more likely to do this if, as here, the various sayings differed in grammatical structure. In the independent Q parallel (cf. Lk. 10.4ff) the sayings are also attached to one another; thus their connection, if not its form, is pre-Markan. Schmahl, pp.71f suggests Mark is abbreviating the tradition and after an omission uses this phrase as his link.

2   On these changes cf. Taylor, Lohmeyer, ad loc.

3   κύκλῳ (0-3-1-0) could also be Markan, but the total number of occurrences is too small to draw any certain conclusion. Lohmeyer, ad loc., claims that περιάγειν belongs to the missionary language of the church (cf. 1 Cor. 9.5); a single additional text is hardly sufficient to sustain this view.

4   Reploh, pp.51f, takes v.6b to be a Markan summary: cf. Stock, p.83; Egger, pp.153-155.

5   So Schmidt, pp.158ff: Lagrange, ad loc.

6   So Taylor, Lohmeyer, and the vast majority of commentators.

7   Cf. Grundmann.

8   In depicting Jesus as moving from place to place, Mark is dependent on the tradition. In how far and in what areas the

historical Jesus moved is another matter; cf. F.H. Borsch, 'Jesus, the Wandering Preacher'.

9   The reading προσκαλεσάμενος (D fam 1) accommodates the text both to Mark's usual phrase (cf. p.130 n.8) and to Mt. 10.1 (cf. Schmahl, p.68).

10 Ch. 21.

11 The imperfect could refer to the repeated despatch of the pairs but it more probably refers to the continuance of the authority (cf. Stock, p88), still applicable to the missionaries of Mark's own time.

12 2-10-6-0 (cf. δαιμόνιον 10-12-10-4).

13 Cf. 1.22-28; 3.14f. See Best, pp.1-27,187-9.

14 See p.25 n.8.

15 For our purposes it is unnecessary to determine whether the idea originated with Jesus or with the practice of the primitive community. Cf. J. Jeremias, 'Paarweise Sendung'. Stock (p.86f) argues that it is to be understood in the light of the O.T. concept of truth as sustained at the mouth of two or three witnesses.

16 See n.9 above.

17 Meyer, I, p.137, takes 6.7ff as the direct continuation of his Twelve-source after 3.14; Knox, I, pp.22f, argues that 6.7 followed directly after 3.15 in his Twelve-source.

In Mt. 10.1ff we find the list of the disciples and the statement of their call joined to the instructions given to them as they are sent out. This may appear to be evidence for the original linking of these two sections. Has Matthew, knowing Mark's source, restored the union of 3.13-19 and 6.6b-13, or did he have another source in which they were united, or has he by choice brought them together ignorant of their earlier union. In Mt. 9.35-10.42 we find linked successively Mk 6.6,34; 3.14b,15 and/or 6.7, followed by a set of instructions to missionaries which combines the Q and Markan forms of the instructions with other material peculiar to Matthew. There are many signs of Matthew's hand in this passage; the commission of 10.1 significantly alters both Mk 3.14b,15 and Mk 6.7 by adding references to sickness in such a way as to play down Mark's interest in exorcism; the list of the Twelve varies their order and implicitly identifies Matthew and Levi. Matthew is probably therefore of little help in ascertaining the earlier tradition at this point, in particular in indicating an earlier union of Mk 3.13-19 and 6.6b-13.

18 After 3.15 the tradition would have continued: ἀπέστειλεν αὐτοὺς δύο δύο καὶ παρήγγειλεν .... παραγγέλλειν is not a Markan word (2-2-4-0; in Acts and the Pauline corpus it is found

22 times).
19 Mark may use δαίμων redactionally twice at 1.34 and almost certainly does once at 1.39; both passages are probably Markan summaries, cf. Egger, pp.65-77.
20 It is difficult to determine whether ἵνα should be taken as final or with its verb as equivalent to an infinitive; cf. Stock, pp.93f. On the tense difference with v.13 see Swete, ad loc.
21 The verb 5-2-9-0; the noun 2-1-5-0.
22 Cf. H. Schlier, TDNT II, pp.470-3; F. Mussner, Der Jakobusbrief, ad Jas 5.14f.
23 16-5-14-1.
24 Lepers are cleansed, sight is restored; in 5.21ff he uses σῴζειν but this may be for soteriological reasons.
25 The verb appears to be used redactionally with a general reference at 1.34; 3.10.
26 Wohlenberg, Markus, ad 6.14; Haenchen, p.223; Reploh, p.56. Contra Taylor ad 6.14.
27 Cf. Trocmé, pp.160f; Burgers, 'De instellung van de Twaalf'.
28 If our interpretations of 8.22-26; 10.46-52 are correct, even though Jesus appears to act alone in them, they are primarily passages about discipleship.
29 We cannot say if it was the only suitable pericope for we do not know the total tradition available to Mark.
30 Cf. Best, pp.76, 101f, 119f.
31 Cf. Egger, pp.124-6.
32 15-14-10-9.
33 ποιεῖν probably belongs to the mission vocabulary of the early church; cf. Acts 14.27; 15.4; it appears with διδάσκειν at Acts 1.1.
34 See discussion in ch. 21 of the text of 3.14.
35 Cf. Roloff, Apostolat - Verkündigung - Kirche, pp.141f.
36 See for example, C.K. Barrett, The Signs of an Apostle; W. Schmithals, The Office of Apostle; R. Schnackenburg, 'Apostles Before and During Paul's Time'; T.W. Manson, The Church's Ministry; K.H. Rengstorf, TDNT, I, pp.407-445; Roloff (as n.35).
37 Barrett (as n.36), p.29.
38 Cf. Haenchen, pp.242ff; Taylor, ad loc.
39 Barrett's term 'envoy', (as n.36), p.29, is too neutral since it lacks any ecclesiastical significance. It is interesting that Barrett acknowledges (p.70) that for Paul the term 'meant not "agent" simply, but "missionary agent"'.
40 Taylor, ad 3.14f.
41 Kee, p.89, applies the demands of 6.8-11 to all believers.
42 In so far as it does do this it is in line with the general discipleship teaching given in 1.17 which implies the need to

carry out a mission and with 1.18,20; 8.34; 10.28-30 which imply
the need to abandon earthly possessions.
43   Cf. Schulz, pp.92f.
44   Verse 31 is probably redactional; cf. Stock, pp.102ff; Egger,
pp.126-128; the latter however thinks the saying of v.31a may
have come from the tradition.
45   This may be the significance of the aorist ἤρξατο; at any
rate no idea of iteration is contained in it as if the same
missionaries were sent off on a number of occasions. One
commissioning and one despatch correspond (cf. Stock, p.85).
46   On the passage see also Best, 'The Twelve'.

Chapter 23
MARK 14.28; 16.7

Discipleship is a journey and on it the disciple is given tasks to execute. These are the themes of Parts I and II; in 14.28; 16.7 they are united. After the resurrection Jesus continues at the head of his disciples as they go on his work; he is with them as he was with them before his death /1/.

It is now almost unanimously agreed that 14.28 and 16.7 represent a detached logion which Mark has employed /2/ at two different points; therefore it is appropriate to consider these two verses together. While some scholars still continue to follow Lohmeyer /3/ in seeing in them a reference to the parousia we find no reason to alter our previous conclusion that they refer to the resurrection /4/. But are they intended to refer primarily to an actual historical resurrection appearance in Galilee? Stein limits them in this way pointing to the change in tense in the use of προάγειν from the future in 14.28 to the present in 16.7. While the verses certainly include a belief in the actual resurrection we have to ask whether this is the sole reason Mark employs them. If we assume that he finished his Gospel at 16.8 and did not go on to record an appearance of Jesus in Galilee then it can be easily argued that he has little interest in recounting an actual appearance in Galilee, though by stopping his Gospel at 16.8 he may not be intending to deny such an appearance. The fact of appearances of the risen Jesus would have been known to his community; Mark has indicated his belief in the resurrection and probably therefore his knowledge of appearances in the three predictions of 8.31; 9.31; 10.32f; when the obvious is known to his community he often fails to state it, e.g. he does not ever clearly say that Jesus defeated Satan (cf. 1.12f) /5/. 14.28; 16.7 would then indicate a belief in the actual resurrection but would point beyond this to some other meaning; to what that is we shall come shortly.

Though we think it more probable that the Gospel was intended to end at 16.8 we cannot glibly assume that it did so. If Mark originally went on to record an appearance in Galilee which fulfilled the prophecy of 14.28, must not the reference of 14.28 and 16.7 be restricted to this physical sense alone? Against this we would argue that while Mark generally accepts the pericopae of the tradition as historically true he almost invariably moves beyond this to draw from the reported events a lesson for the life of his own community. Historical events are thus always more than historical events. Consequently we would expect Mark to be saying something to his own congregation in 14.28; 16.7 which went beyond establishing the mere fact of the resurrection.

When we go on to examine 14.28; 16.7 we find that in fact this is so. (i) The interpretation of 14.28; 16.7 which sees in it a journey in which Jesus goes at the head of his followers appropriately follows the account of the journey to Jerusalem on which his followers have accompanied him (8.27-10.52). (ii) προάγειν more probably means 'go at the head of' than 'go ahead of, precede' /6/, i.e. it suggests a movement of disciples behind Jesus rather than their movement from where they are to a place to which he has already gone, viz. Galilee. Statistically Mark's use of the verb reveals nothing; the first meaning appears at 10.32 and 11.9 and the second at 6.45, but it is the context of its appearance at 10.32 which suggests that the first meaning is important for him. This meaning also fits the context of 14.28. Mark has almost certainly joined the O.T. citation of Zech. 13.7 with its shepherd image (v.27b) to the logion of 14.28 /7/; it was an obvious thing to do since in the ancient world the shepherd went at the head of his flock and did not precede it to a place where he waited for it to catch up with him eventually /8/. The verb then serves to link the journey prior to the cross to the journey after it. (iii) If Mark intended 16.7 to relate entirely to an actual event then we should have expected an aorist at 16.7, 'Jesus is risen; he has gone on already to Galilee'; the use of the present tense suggests an action which is in process; Jesus is in motion towards Galilee and they are to be in motion after him. The use of the present also encourages the application of the logion to Mark's own congregation: Jesus is at their head. (iv) The failure of the women at the tomb to take action in accord with the message they received militates against understanding the message as a reference to the actual resurrection.

If then these verses are intended to have meaning beyond a historical reference to the place of resurrection, what is this meaning? It is generally agreed that the use of Galilee is largely redactional in Mark's Gospel /9/. This accepted, it is still difficult to determine its precise significance in these two verses. As the place of salvation it has been contrasted with Jerusalem the place of crucifixion and rejection, but Jesus was partially rejected in Galilee (6.1-6) and his final rejection was foreshadowed there (3.6) /10/. It can be argued more accurately that while the achievement of salvation was acted out in

200

Jerusalem (11.1 onwards) the proclamation of the meaning of salvation (Christology, discipleship) took place in the earlier part of the Gospel (prior to 10.52) and that Galilee and the earlier part of the Gospel are related /11/. Galilee itself can be understood as Galilee of the Gentiles; Mark has a special interest in the Gentiles; his congregation are Gentiles, and their mission must be exercised among Gentiles. The message to be given the disciples (16.7) says that they will see Jesus in Galilee; as we argued 'see' does not relate to the Parousia but to the resurrection. But it does not relate to seeing a physical Jesus in an appearance (though this may have been its meaning as a logion in an earlier stage of the tradition) but to the spiritual sight which understands. In the earlier parts of the Gospel the eyes of the disciples were closed (8.14-21), half open (8.22-33), burdened with sleep (14.40); now they will see fully and they will see the risen Jesus. This will also be true for Mark's community; they will see, understand, the risen Jesus as they follow out their commission to fish for men (1.17), or, at least for some of them, as they preach and exorcise (3.14f), and as they experience suffering and rejection (the disciple can expect no better than his master and so can expect to be rejected by his family and friends, 6.1-6). If Galilee is the place of mission /12/ it is this because it is the place where their lives are lived; it is then also the place of suffering. The suffering of Jesus in Jerusalem is unique for Mark; the disciple suffers as he responds to the call which comes from the cross to him. And as he responds he is not left alone; he sees Jesus; Jesus is with him and he with Jesus. But Jesus is still at the head; the disciple can never be in front; he must always follow /13/.

It is interesting that there may be a foreshadowing of 14.28 and 16.7 in 1.39 /14/. This verse is generally recognised as Markan /15/ and in it Jesus is said to go preaching and exorcising /16/ in Galilee. These are the activities given to the Twelve in 3.14f; 6.7,12f, and implied as in some part relating to all the disciples (1.17; 9.28f); Galilee is the area in which Jesus is to go at the head of the disciples (14.28; 16.7). Moreover, whatever the nature of the greater part of 1.35-8, v.35a appears to be Markan in its double temporal data /17/ and its use of an aorist participle (ἀναστάς) followed by a finite verb (cf. 1.16,19,29; 2.1,14, etc.). The temporal data indicate the completion of the 'first' or 'ideal' day in the life of Jesus which began at 1.21 but also imply activity (ἀναστάς) on the first day of the week, i.e. the risen Jesus goes out to preach and exorcise on the first, or resurrection day of the week. He is sought by Peter (cf. 16.6) and the other disciples; in 14.27; 16.7

Following Jesus: Discipleship in Mark

we again have attention drawn to Peter, who is singled out, and the other disciples. Then at 1.39 the risen Jesus goes out into Galilee at their head (ἄγωμεν) as he finally goes to the cross (14.42, ἄγωμεν). From 1.39 onwards, except where he specifically sends the disciples to it, Jesus does the preaching and exorcising. After the resurrection they do it. Preaching is the future task of the church (13.10; 14.9).

Notes

1. In the discussion which follows we depend on our earlier treatment, Best, pp.157f,173-7 and on the references given there. See more recently, R.H. Stein, 'A Short Note on Mark xiv.28 and xvi.7', and the literature quoted there. To it we may add, J.-M. van Cangh, 'La Galilée dans l'Evangile de Marc'; G. Stemberger, 'Galilee--Land of Salvation?'.

2 Despite the arguments of J.D. Crossan, 'Redaction and Citation in Mark 11:9-10.17 and 14:27', and Schenke, Studien zur Passionsgeschichte der Markus, pp.406f, there is insufficient evidence to suggest that Mark created the logion; its origin is obscure, as would be its original meaning if it is a genuine saying of Jesus. At some stage in its history it probably functioned as a guide to a resurrection appearance in Galilee; cf. T. Lorenzen, 'Ist der Auferstandene in Galiläa erschienen?'. If Turner, JTS 26 (1924/5) 19f, is correct in regarding ἐκεῖ αὐτὸν ὄψεσθε as a Markan insertion then the remainder of the logion is pre-Markan. Dormeyer, Die Passion Jesu, pp.221-235, and Pesch, II, pp.381f, are among the few who take 16.7 to have belonged to its pericope prior to Mark. On the redactional nature of the framework of 16.7 see Best, 'Peter'.

3 Lohmeyer, Galiläa und Jerusalem, pp.10ff.

4 The evidence has been thoroughly re-examined by Stein (as n.1), and G. Stemberger (as n.1) who come down in favour of a reference to the resurrection.

5 Nothing is ever said about the fulfilment of 1.8b or that Jesus carried out his Father's will (14.36).

6 R.H. Fuller, Resurrection Narratives, p.61, argues for 'precede' since 'go at the head of' would 'entail the picture of the Risen One as an earthly wanderer'; this is only true if Mark is regarded as emphasising the actual resurrection of Jesus rather than the relationship of the risen Jesus to the community.

7 Cf. Best, p.173.

8 Cf. Jeremias, Parables, p.222 n.56, who says that the verb is 'a technical term belonging to the shepherd's calling'.

9 On its redactional nature see now (cf. Best, pp.174f, for

earlier references), Schreiber, pp.170ff; van Cangh (as n.1); this view has been criticised in part by Stemberger (as n.1).

10   Cf. T.A. Burkill, Mysterious Revelation, pp.252ff.

11   The precise geographical meaning and extent of Galilee for Mark is uncertain.

12   The acceptance of Fuller's view (as n.6), p.62, that for Mark Galilee is not itself in 14.28; 16.7 the place of mission but the place from which the mission commences would not affect our conclusion.

13   Stemberger (as n.1), p.438, 'the task of the past, begun in Galilee, has to be carried on until Christ's return'. Cf. Schenke, Studien zur Passionsgeschichte, pp.442-460.

14   Cf. M. Wichelhaus, 'Am ersten Tage der Woche'.

15   Best,   p.69;   Wichelhaus   (as   n.14),   p.58;   Pryke, pp.67f,103f,119f; Egger, pp.73-79.

16   We assume that the reference to exorcism was part of the original text; cf. Best, p.69.

17   πρωΐ 3-5-0-2; λίαν 4-4-1-0; the two words occur together at 16.2. ἔννυχα is only found here in the NT.

Chapter 24
CONCLUSION

What is the relation to one another of the passages we have studied in Part II? In 1.16-20; 2.14 we had the 'calls' of individual disciples; in 3.13-19; 6.6b-13,30 we had the 'commissioning' of the Twelve to a special function as 'missionaries' and their instruction in the way they should exercise their mission; in 14.28; 16.7 Jesus says that he goes ahead of the disciples in mission and suffering. This suggests at least that there is a special mission for some and a general mission for all.

For Mark the Twelve and the disciples are not necessarily the same group; he can distinguish between them though he can also use in similar ways the tradition in which either group appears /1/. The disciples are the larger group containing the Twelve. Levi was not one of the Twelve; in 3.13 the Twelve are selected out of a larger group; 2.15 speaks of many disciples. In 1.16-20 do Peter, Andrew, James and John function as 'disciples' or as members of the Twelve /2/? The former solution is preferable, for: (i) Mark uses his normal discipleship words ἀκολουθεῖν, ὀπίσω, καλεῖν (cf. 2.17); (ii) Levi is not one of the Twelve but he is called in the same way as are the Four; (iii) 1.16-20 must differ in some way in its function for Mark from 3.13-19; (iv) Levi certainly advances the cause of mission by bringing Jesus into contact with other tax-collectors and sinners (2.15-17) and so may be said to 'fish' for men, which is the commission of 1.16-20; (v) Bartimaeus (10.52) becomes a disciple but is not one of the Twelve; (vi) all the disciples have some duty towards the outside world /3/. Thus there is a general mission for all disciples and a special mission within that general mission for the Twelve (who for Mark represent a limited group of 'missionaries' which his own community sends out). Because of this distinction we cannot argue /4/ that the Twelve alone continue the activity of Jesus. It is true that they preach and exorcise as Jesus did but others also preach (1.45; 5.20 /5/; 7.36; all of these passages are probably redactional) and in the general statements of 13.10 and 14.9 there is no implication that preaching is restricted to the Twelve. The strange exorcist whose activity earns Jesus' approval (9.38f) is not one of the Twelve. Apart from this there is the more general point that much of Jesus' activity, in particular in its soteriological aspects, is peculiar to him and not continued by anyone.

Chapter 24: Conclusion to Part II

What now of 14.28 and 16.7? The twelve are present in the context because of the tradition which restricted the Last Supper to them, yet the Eucharist is not restricted to the Twelve or those whom Mark views as their successors, the 'missionaries', but is for all Christians, and in 14.27 the sheep who are scattered and of whom Jesus is the Shepherd, while according to the context they are the Twelve, they represent for Mark the whole community. Thus we take whatever commission lies in 14.28; 16.7 to be a commission to the whole church. No details are given in it as to the nature of the mission. Not all will exercise it in the same way; some like the Twelve in special ways, preaching, healing, exorcising; others as they carry out their daily lives. Confirmation of this is found in occasional references to those who are clearly not the Twelve but who heal and preach (1.45; 5.20; 7.36; 9.38f).

A little more of the nature of the commission of every disciple towards the outside world can be gleaned from 8.27-10.45. It is emphasised that the disciple is to accept the humblest member of society and serve him or her (9.36f; cf. 10.42b-45a). This is not put in evangelical terms, i.e. that he is to preach the word (the evangelical emphasis is part of 1.17), but in 'caring' terms, i.e. he is to love his neighbour /6/. This is expressed explicitly in 12.28. But we can hardly argue that this commission is expanded in detail, and we cannot indeed expect it to be; care for others which is not expressed in deliberate full-time ministry must be offered in so many different ways that it would be impossible to detail them /7/; any detailing would itself be a limitation in so far as it might imply that what was suggested was the only way or ways. Looking at all aspects of it we must conclude that the commission to disciples is both 'evangelical' (1.17) and 'caring' (9.36f) /8/.

In 3.13-19 the 'missionaries' are given their commission and in 6.6b-13 they are instructed how to fulfil it; in 6.30 it is implied /9/ they have fulfilled it; yet the main emphasis on the failure of the disciples to understand lies in the material that follows (e.g. 6.52; 8.14-21; 9.33-7; 10.24,38) rather than in what precedes (4.11f); in particular at 9.18 they are unable to exorcise, i.e. they are unable to use a power given to them in 3.15 and 6.7, and which according to 6.30 they had already successfully exercised. The problem which seems to lie here is artificial, created because Mark wishes to use the tradition for different purposes. For him the role of the Twelve is that of example: either their goodness can inspire his community to follow its pattern or their failure, as when they are ignorant, serves to open up the discussion towards positive teaching on

205

the nature of Christ's mission and the discipleship of the community.

Mark unlike Matthew (28.16-20) and Luke (24.47f) has no post-resurrection commissioning of the disciples (or the Twelve). If the ending of Mark has been lost it may have contained such a commission. If 16.8 was the intended ending the absence of a commission may seem a problem. Yet before we conclude that Mark did not intend a commission for believers we should note that the Christian community has never had any difficulty in seeing the applicability of the instructions of 6.8-11 to its missionaries (sometimes it has sought arguments why these instructions should be evaded!); they have functioned as guides for the post-resurrection church. May not Mark have intended them, and 3.14f, to function in this way and not to serve merely as historical accounts?

Finally we may observe that 14.28; 16.7 form a fitting conclusion to both Parts I and II in so far as they indicate the continuance of the way of discipleship (following Jesus with him at the head) and the fact of mission (into Galilee). They are also a fitting introduction to Part III to which 14.28 with its conception of the community as Christ's flock points forward. Jesus does not move forward at the head of some vague mass of individuals but as the shepherd whose sheep (to change the metaphor) are brothers and sisters of one another /10/.

Notes
1.   See Best 'The Role of the Disciples' and 'The Twelve'.
2   Stock, pp.42ff, draws attention to certain important vocabulary differences between 1.16-20; 2.14 and 3.13-19, though in his attempt to distinguish the passages and emphasise the uniqueness of ἐποίησεν in 3.14 he apparently does not observe the ποιήσω of 1.17.
3   Cf. 1.31; 9.29,36f; 10.21; 12.31. See below.
4   So Stock, pp.24ff.
5   The healed demoniac from a Gentile area who returns to preach in that area perhaps indicates a disciple engaged in mission to the Gentiles. On 5.1-20 see F. Annen, Heil für die Heiden.
6   Nothing is said directly about the political activity of disciples but 12.13-17 implies they must be aware of their duty towards the state.
7   The context may suggest that the paying of taxes is to be included as part of the responsibility of the disciple towards all men.

Chapter 24: Conclusion to Part II

8   When Kee, p.163, understands 4.3,14 as an instruction to Christians to sow the word he is only giving a new and (to Mark) unauthorised twist to the allegorisation of the parable.
9   Mark does not always make implications explicit; cf. p.199.
10   Because Kelber takes little account of 14.28; 16.7 he can write of the way of the disciples as 'the road to ruin', The Kingdom in Mark, p.69.

Part III
THE DISCIPLE IN THE COMMUNITY

Chapter 25
INTRODUCTION

We have discussed the central meaning of discipleship as it appears in 8.27-10.45 (Part I) and seen that it entails a general responsibility towards the outside world for every Christian and for some Christians a special (Part II). If disciples have such a responsibility towards those who are not disciples will they not also have some responsibility towards those who are their fellow disciples? In saying this it is not intended to imply that the responsibility towards fellow disciples and towards non-disciples will necessarily be the same. It is perhaps better to speak of the relation of disciples to one another rather than of their responsibility for one another.

Jesus called disciples to follow him and thus brought them into a relationship with himself; throughout the rest of the New Testament the relationship of believers to Christ results in their mutual relationship: does the same hold for Mark's Gospel? Already we have seen indications of this in the way disciples are to avoid making claims of superiority (9.35; 10.42b-45) over against other disciples and avoid putting stumbling blocks in their way (9.42); the direction to receive the strange exorcist (9.38f) implies the existence of a community into which he will be received; in so far as entering the kingdom (10.15,23-25) refers to a realised present Kingdom it refers not to a place but to a community /1/.

We cannot expect to find the element of corporate life prominent in Mark for he makes his case through the use of material from the tradition about the life of Jesus and not through straightforward theological instruction. He is not wholly master of his material; as well as controlling it in the way he arranges and modifies it he is also controlled by it. At least he can work from the base that Jesus led about a group of disciples who formed a company around him. How then does he use the tradition to show the nature of that company? As we examine what he has to say we shall see that he takes up and employs some of the metaphors for the church common among the early Christians.

Chapter 25: Introduction

Note
1   Cf. Kee, pp.108f Kelber, The Kingdom in Mark, p.91, writes of 'the way into the true fellowship of the hidden Kingdom'.

We ended our discussion of the nature and task of the disciple (Parts I and II) with two passages (14.28; 16.7) where the disciple is seen as following Jesus the shepherd on the way which he goes to the cross and beyond, and it is not inappropriate that we should pick up that aspect of the same concept which serves to show the disciples as a community. If Jesus is shepherd then disciples are the flock. This image serves both to set the flock in relation to Jesus and to suggest the relationship of the various members of the flock to one another: if the disciple follows his risen Lord on the way he is accompanied on his journey by his fellow disciples. The historical disciples were scattered at the death of Jesus (14.27b) but in the resurrection they were reconstituted as God's flock /1/ and continue as his flock; of this flock Mark's community is a part.

Mark had already previously used the imagery of the flock at 6.34. The final clause of that verse is certainly redactional /2/. It is replaced in both the Matthean and Lukan parallels with a clause telling of the healing of the sick. The clause ὅτι ἦσαν .. ποιμένα is omitted by Matthew and Luke but the former has an equivalent at 9.36 (an editorial passage) where it again relates to the compassion of Jesus. It was probably an isolated logion dependent in some way on the O.T. /3/. The reference to the compassion of Jesus reappears in Mark at 8.2 where it leads on directly to the feeding of the four thousand. Since the first clause of the verse also reveals Markan characteristics /4/ we may conclude that Mark composed the verse using both a logion from the tradition and the concept of the compassion of Jesus drawn either from the same source or more directly from the second feeding account (8.2) /5/. Mark has thus related the activity of the shepherd to the teaching given the flock. Jesus is envisaged as fulfilling his role of shepherd by teaching /6/.

Who are the 'crowd' whom Jesus teaches? The image of sheep is always used in the O.T. of Israel and not of the Gentiles /7/. In the N.T. apart from 6.34 it is always used either of Israel or the church. It is extremely unlikely that Mark intends a reference to Israel; normally in his Gospel the crowd signifies the unevangelised mass /8/ which could certainly be said to be without a shepherd and untaught. Yet it is more probable that

Mark intends his reference on this occasion to denote the church, for: (i) He is not wholly consistent in his use of the crowd as the unevangelised mass /9/. (ii) The appropriateness of the unfed, i.e. untaught, nature of the crowd to the Markan theme of the incomprehension of the disciples (not just of the historical Twelve) who normally stand for Christians is immediately apparent. (iii) In 14.27b it is the disciples, i.e. the community, who are scattered and to whom Jesus is shepherd. (iv) Since the crowd here acts as a symbol for the instruction of Mark's church rather than as a historical reality Mark is free to vary its symbolic meaning so long as the symbolic meaning can easily be understood: given the context of the feeding of the crowd it would not have been possible for him to take the disciples in it as the symbol of the whole community. Mark then has picked up and is playing on an image of the church well-known to the early Christians.

The shepherd nourishes the church with his teaching /10/; this accords with a stress we have detected elsewhere (8.35,38; 9.7) on the importance of the teaching of Jesus for Mark's community. If the feeding of the five thousand had been related to the Eucharist in the earlier tradition then Mark has altered this interpretation. The raised Jesus gathers the scattered flock and thenceforward feeds it with his Word. Christ as shepherd both leads and feeds the flock, and he does the latter in desert places (v.32) where the church might not expect to be fed.

Notes

1   'The imagery of "scattering" and "gathering"...is very widespread in the Old Testament, where it describes the dispersion of Israel, usually understood as an act of God's judgement, and his merciful gathering of them, which is anticipated and prayed for.' W.A. Meeks, The Prophet King, p.97. On 'scattering' cf. Deut. 30.1-10; Jer. 10.21; Ezek. 20.34; etc. On the imagery of the 'Flock' in the NT see 1 Pet. 2.25; 5.4; Jn. 10.1ff; Heb. 13.20; Rev. 7.11; Lk. 12.32 (?). On its use in the Gospels, see A.Tooley, 'The Shepherd and Sheep Image'.

2   Note the use of ἄρχεσθαι as an auxiliary, the introduction of the reference to teaching though no teaching is given, the adverbial πολλά (1.45; 3.2; 4.2; 5.43; 8.31; etc.), all found regularly in Markan redactional passages. See I. de la Potterie, 'Le sens primitif de la multiplication des pains'; Egger, pp.130f.

3   It is not the exact reproduction of any one particular OT text but is related to such passages as Num. 27.17; 1 Kings 22.17; 2 Chron. 18.16; Ezek. 34.8; Zech. 10.2.

4   καί + introductory participle; πολὺς ὄχλος appears usually in Markan seams (5.24; 8.1; 9.14; 12.37).
5   Cf. Best, p.76.
6   On food as a metaphor for teaching see Best, p.77; cf. Tooley, as n.1.
7   Cf. Tagawa, p.143.
8   Cf. pp.28f.
9   As n.8.
10   See Best, pp.77f; Egger, pp.130f.

Chapter 27
THE CHURCH AS TEMPLE

At two points (14.58; 15.29) in the passion account we have a possible reference to the church as temple. The analysis of that account is very difficult; is Mark combining material from two or more different earlier accounts, adding additional material to an account he has received in the tradition, modifying a received account or accounts without the use of tradition, or is he at times freely composing, creating incidents of which he has little or no detail or record in the tradition? In particular, did Mark receive both 14.58 and 15.29 in the tradition as parts of an existing account, or did he receive one of them and insert its logion a second time, or was there a basic logion which he received in isolation from the passion story and which he inserted at both points, or did he himself create the logion and insert it twice? An examination of the contexts of the saying in its two positions will show the complexity of the problem: 14.56b and 14.59 are clearly doublets and 15.29f and 15.31f /1/ may be also; 14.57-9 may have been deliberately created by Mark using 15.29f /2/; 14.57f may have been pre-Markan and 15.29f created out of it /3/. The redactional analysis at both points is exceptionally difficult and for our purposes it is unnecessary to work through it. If Mark received the logion about the temple twice in the tradition he had ample opportunity to drop one occurrence; he must therefore have thought it important. If he received it once and inserted it a second time he obviously thought the same. This is even more true if he received the logion in isolation from the passion story and inserted it twice or if he created the logion. With this in mind we shall concentrate our attention on the meaning of the logion for Mark /4/.

The basic vocabulary of the two forms of the logion in 14.58; 15.29 is the same. In 14.58 it is expressed in the first person; in 15.29 in the third person as part of a 'Woe'. In 14.58 false witnesses allege Jesus spoke it and their testimony is said not to be consistent among themselves; in 15.29 passers-by speak it and clearly do not believe that Jesus is capable of fulfilling what it sets out. In 14.58 two temples are contrasted - one built with hands and one built without - but this explicit contrast does not appear in 15.29 /5/. In 14.58 the event is said to take place διὰ τριῶν ἡμερῶν/6/ but in 15.29 ἐν τρισὶν ἡμέραις.

We commence with the variation in the temporal phrase. In the NT the normal temporal expression for the resurrection of Jesus is τῇ τρίτῃ ἡμέρᾳ but in Mark we also find μετὰ τρεῖς ἡμέρας (8.31; 9.31; 10.34). The forms of 14.58 and 15.29 do not correspond to either of these /7/. This suggests that in neither instance has Mark formulated the logion and that, additionally, both forms come from the tradition /8/. 15.29b assumes that those who mock Jesus believe that he spoke the logion, but leaves open the question whether he actually did so or not; however 15.30 could hardly have much meaning unless he had used the saying. 14.58 puts the accusation that Jesus said it on the lips of 'false' witnesses and so seems to imply that he did not say it. Did Mark consider what the false witnesses said to be untrue? Explanations of the appearance and role of the false witnesses have usually been related to their possible historical reality /9/ rather than to their place in Mark. False witnesses who afflict the righteous appear in the Psalms (27.12; 35.11) and since the OT, in particular the Psalms, has at other points affected the development of the passion account it is not surprising to find false witnesses in it. Their role is not so very different from that of the 'taunters' of 15.29-32; what the taunters say in 15.30f is true, not at the surface level but at a deeper /10/. The taunts of the soldiers (15.16-20) are also true. Looking more widely into the Gospel the demons who confess Jesus (1.24; 3.11f; etc.) speak the truth and the scribes who complain (2.7) that Jesus forgives sins say what the church accepts as true. Mark then often allows positive statements with which he agrees to appear on the lips of Jesus' enemies. More particularly we find an anti-temple polemic in 11.12ff; 13.2; 15.38 /11/; in 13.2 Jesus explicitly teaches the negative side of the logion of 14.58. The members of Mark's community would have been used to mockers who spoke the truth in ignorance and false witnesses who might accuse them of saying that Jesus was Lord were certainly speaking the truth. Consequently within the total Markan context it is not surprising to find true words on the lips of false witnesses /12/. It is quite probable that no content was given to the testimony of the false witnesses when they first entered the passion story.

What now of the contrast 'made with hands'/'not made with hands'? It is most unlikely that these two adjectives belong to the earliest strain of the tradition; they are present neither in 15.29 nor in Jn 2.19 /13/. If they have been added was Mark responsible /14/? It is almost impossible to determine at what stage they were inserted but since χειροποίητος is a term drawn from Hellenistic /15/ rather than Palestinian Judaism this suggests they came either from Hellenistic Jewish Christian or Hellenistic Gentile Christian circles /16/. Donahue believes that not only did Mark introduce the logion at 14.58 and add the two adjectives but that he actually brought together the two halves of the logion, the threat and the promise, which had previously existed separately in the tradition /17/. While there are grounds for arguing the original distinctness of the two parts (e.g. Mk 13.2 and Acts 6.14 contain only the threat) it is much more difficult to demonstrate that it was Mark who united them. In fact Donahue provides no effective redactional evidence for his claim /18/. On the contrary there are good grounds for doubting it: if Mark did it why did he use different temporal formulae in 14.58 and 15.29? Why did he use the contrast 'made with hands'/'not made with hands' at 14.58 alone? That the second half of the saying shows greater variation, as Donahue points out, may indicate development in different oral traditions of the whole saying or of the bringing of the two halves together in different Christian communities.

Of the two adjectives the first, χειροποίητος, is found fairly frequently in Jewish writings; apart from its literal use it appears in Jewish apologetic in a derogatory sense in relation to idols (Lev. 26.1; Isa. 46.6; cf. Philo, Mos. 2.168) and heathen temples (Isa. 16.12). It is probable that the early Christians took it over with this derogatory sense and extended its use in a way the Jews would never have done, for we find it applied to the Jerusalem temple (Acts 7.48; Heb. 9.24), to circumcision (Eph. 2.11) and negatively to the temple in the heavens (Heb. 9.11). ἀχειροποίητος is applied to a non-literal circumcision and to resurrection existence (2 Cor. 5.1); the latter is a natural extension in its context since there the 'body' is depicted under the image of a building (οἰκία). How then is it used in Mk 14.58? The temple which belongs to Christian existence can only be the church /19/.

This conclusion is disputed by Linnemann who argues: (i) ἀχειροποίητος really adds nothing to the logion; a temple which is built in three days can only be built supernaturally and therefore necessarily without hands /20/. (ii) The metaphor of the church as temple is not used frequently enough in the NT to necessitate understanding 14.58 of the church /21/. (iii) The word does not carry the idea 'spiritual' which regularly adheres in the NT to the metaphor of the church as temple /22/. Linnemann's first point may be allowed, but that an added word need not introduce a fresh idea does not mean it may not give a fresh nuance to an existing idea; this is what happens here because the particular words which have been added serve to contrast a physical with a non-physical temple. As for her second point we can only assert that she has completely underrated the extent of the NT evidence for the temple-metaphor in respect of the church /23/ and by omitting to consider its background in the Qumran material /24/ she sets the NT evidence by itself without allowing for the soil in which it grew. Her third point is more difficult to evaluate. It is true that in 1 Cor. 3.16f; Eph. 2.20-22; 1 Pet. 2.4f, the temple is in some way related to the Spirit /25/ but it is not in 2 Cor. 6.16 and the omission of a reference in a brief passage like our logion is not surprising. In the context of Christian apologetic against Judaism χειροποίητος is a suitable word to use of the Jerusalem temple and the natural word with which to balance it is ἀχειροποίητος denoting something belonging to the sphere of Christian existence, i.e. the domain of the Spirit. Moreover in the Qumran material the metaphor is found without relation to the Spirit (1 QS 5.5f; 8.4-10. 4QFlor. 1.1-13 and 4QpIsa^d are relevant if, as is probable, they are also instances of the Temple metaphor) /26/. Accordingly we conclude that in Mk 14.58 the 'temple not made with hands' indicates the church /27/.

Since the 'three days' in 14.58; 15.29 cannot have suggested to the early Christians anything other than the period from the cruficixion to the resurrection we have to draw the further conclusion that the new community comes into existence with the risen Jesus. This accords with what we found in 14.28; 16.7: the new community has been constituted by the risen Jesus and he is at its head /28/. To this the temple metaphor adds a further strand of meaning for in ancient thought the ναός was the place where the god was believed to live /29/. Jesus therefore lives in, as well as being at the head of, his people. Believers are not individuals but part of the community of Christ.

There is evidence of an anti-temple polemic in the last few chapters of Mark (11.1ff) /30/. In 14.58 this anti-temple polemic is balanced by a promise about the new community expressed in terms of a new temple; do we find this latter concept associated elsewhere with the anti-temple polemic? While it is by no means as clear as in 14.58 it re-appears at least once and possibly on a second occasion.

(i) 11.15-19 /31/. Mark has set the account of the cleansing of the temple within that of the cursing of the fig-tree. He thus indicates that Jesus' action in the temple constitutes judgement on it and through it on Israel /32/. If, then, the placing of the incident of the cleansing is redactional is there also redaction within it? The geographical datum of v.15a clearly falls into this category but almost all the remainder of that verse and all of v.16 /33/ come from the tradition. The introduction to v.17 is Markan: he regularly introduces references to the teaching of Jesus without supplying much content to the references /34/; καὶ ἔλεγεν αὐτοῖς /35/ is a Markan phrase; the duplicate expression 'taught and said' is Markan (cf. 4.2; 9.31, passages which are generally recognised as redactional); the use of the imperfect tense in both verbs accords with Mark's practice. γέγραπται is the normal word with which he introduces citations from the OT (cf. 1.2; 7.6; 9.12,13; 14.21,27) and implies that the citation here is in some way due to him; this conclusion is reinforced when we observe that at the equivalent point in the Johannine account (2.17) a different passage from the OT is used /36/. Crossan /37/ however argues that Jer. 7.11 lay in the tradition and that Mark only added Isa. 56.7. He suggests that the present format of the quotation as a question derives from Jer. 7.11 and was present in the tradition /38/, and that since there are common words to Jer. 7.11 and Isa. 56.7 that part of Jer. 7.11 in which they appeared was suppressed by Mark and Isa. 56.7 inserted. To this suggestion of Crossan we would add that the use of Isa. 56.7 with its reference to the Gentiles could only have become part of the pericope after the beginning of the Gentile mission /39/ whereas the accusation 'den of robbers' could have been part of Christian anti-Jewish polemic from the time of Stephen onwards. Whether Mark inserted the quotations from both Isaiah and Jeremiah or that from Isaiah alone or neither /40/ we can be certain that by providing the introduction to the quotations he wishes us to view them as significant. Before we discuss this significance we should note that v.18, while it would appear to incorporate tradition, may also have been shaped by Mark since a number of his characteristics are present: (i) the reference to the teaching of Jesus; (ii) ζητεῖν appears elsewhere in redactional passages relating to the attempted arrest of Jesus (12.12; 14.1,11; cf. 14.55); (iii) ἐκπλήσσεσθαι likewise appears in redactional passages (1.22; 7.37; 10.26a; cf. 6.2) and the theme of astonishment is Markan /41/; (iv) the γάρ clauses /42/. The reference to the crowd may be traditional but Mark may have introduced the high priests and scribes for he generally attributes the death of Jesus to them /43/.

Within v.17 we note the contrast between 'my house' and 'den of robbers' and the reference to 'my house' as 'a house of prayer for all nations'. The description of the temple as a den of robbers together with Jesus' action in cleansing it corresponds to the first half of the logion of 14.58. We suggest that the reference to the house of prayer for all nations as promise corresponds to the second half of the logion. Both Matthew and Luke omit the phrase 'all nations' from the quotation /44/; this does not necessarily imply that the words were significant for Mark but suggests they may have been /45/. That this is indeed so can be supported from the emphasis Mark lays on the gospel as a gospel for Gentiles. The first human to confess Jesus as son of God is the Gentile centurion at the cross (15.39); Jesus goes at the head of his community in a mission to Galilee of the Gentiles (14.28; 16.7); by yielding to the entreaties of the Syro-Phoenician woman (7.24-30) Jesus is pictured as agreeing that the gospel is for Gentiles as well as Jews; 13.10 /46/ explicitly refers to the necessity of taking the gospel to the Gentiles and 14.9 implies the same in its present form, whatever its original meaning /47/; both these verses have at least been shaped by Mark as their use of the absolute τὸ εὐαγγέλιον shows /48/. The union of Jew and Gentile in the new community may be part of the reason Mark has two feedings, that of the five thousand is for Jews and that of the four thousand for Gentiles; the two are then unified in the one loaf (8.14-21) which alone is necessary and is sufficient for both.

In Isa. 56.7 the μου of 'my house' refers to God but in the Christian context which Mark provides and in the context of Jesus as speaker it probably refers to Jesus. The new community belongs to Jesus; it is not just any 'new community' but his community, 'his house'.

(ii) It is possible also, but with less certainty, to see in 12.1-12 a reference to the new temple which is the Christian community. Whatever we say about its origin few would deny that within the Gospels this parable has taken on the nature of an allegory /49/ in which Israel is the vineyard, God is its owner, those who tend it are Israel or its rulers, and the son is God's son. Many scholars /50/ argue that Mark gave it its present setting between 11.27-33 and the controversy stories of 12.13ff. Whether this is so or not we can certainly attribute 12.1a to Mark as we can see from the use of ἄρχεσθαι as an auxiliary verb and of the plural παραβολαῖς (cf. 4.10,33) when there is only one parable in the context /51/. In 12.1a αὐτοῖς would appear to refer to the high priests, scribes and elders (11.27) who have just been questioning Jesus about his authority. But Mark is not always exact in his references back; those who bring children to Jesus (10.15) are not the owners of the house of

218

10.10; those who forgot to take bread (8.14) are hardly the Pharisees of 8.11. If the servants of 12.2ff signify the prophets /52/ then these were sent to the people of Israel as a whole and not to its leaders only /53/. The matter is not clear. 12.12 has probably also been formed by Mark for it bears a close resemblance to 11.18 where we have seen his hand /54/; in addition there is the use of κρατεῖν /55/ and the appearance again of the theme of fear. Here, however, leaders and crowd are distinguished. This would seem to make it certain that Mark views the parable, whatever its earlier significance, as spoken against the Jewish leaders /56/.

According to the conclusion of the parable (v.9c) /57/ their authority is given to 'others'. Who are these? Consistency would suggest that as the vineyard was given new tenants so Israel will be given new leaders. At this point vv.10f must be drawn in. We find it difficult to believe that Mark added them /58/: the introductory formula to the OT citation is non-Markan; nowhere else does he use the singular γραφή /59/, and though he uses the plural twice (12.24; 14.49) on neither occasion does it introduce a citation; he could easily have employed his normal γέγραπται without needing to alter the citation. To say, however, that the addition of these verses to the parable is pre-Markan does not imply that he thought them of no importance; quite clearly they form the climax to the pericope. The son /60/ who was killed /61/ has now become 'the head of the corner', and this through his resurrection /62/. Ps. 118, from which the quotation is derived, is also related to the temple (cf. vv.19,26ff); thus if the rejected stone is given a new position it is in the temple, the new community /63/. The imagery of the stone at the corner is not fully clear /64/ but whatever it denotes it is a stone which is essential to the building. Jesus is essential to the new community: its existence depends on his rejection, acceptance and allotment to a new position in the building. Thus we have the same thought as in 14.28 and 16.7 but linked now in some way to the Christian community as the new temple; through the death and resurrection of Jesus the new community has come into being and Jesus is its centre. Jesus must then be one of the 'others' of v.9c or, much more probably, the 'others', unlike the original tenants, will be those who recognise his position. If the allegory up to v.9 were strictly carried out old Israel /65/ would be given new rulers; but this could not be intended in a Christian context; Mark continually emphasises judgement on old Israel; new Israel replaces it and we have seen that this is implied by vv.10f. The underlying logic is therefore clearer if we take the 'others' of v.9c to be the new Israel /66/ rather than either new rulers for old Israel or rulers for the new Israel. The new Israel has a responsibility to the whole world to bring to it the gospel. As we saw in Part II it is a duty laid on all members but also in a special way on 'missionaries'. This double statement of the church's duty is in line with the ambiguity we have seen in 'others' (v.9c) if we understand the 'others' not of church officials but of those to whom the task of evangelism has been specially committed. All have a responsibility as tenants of the vineyard of the world.

The teaching on the church as the new temple is only incidental to this pericope; its stress lies rather on the failure of old Israel and the possible failure of the new Israel and its leaders /67/. What God has done once he can do again. Neither church nor missionaries should feel themselves secure. The duty of evangelism must not be neglected.

Notes

1   Many commentators hold that 15.29f and 15.31f come from different accounts which Mark has combined, e.g. Taylor, p.657; Nineham, ad loc.; Bultmann, p.273. Schweizer, ad loc., regards vv.29b-32a as an insertion into the tradition but allows the possibility that vv.29b-30 and vv.31-32a are doublets. Schreiber, pp.41-4, considers v.29 and vv.30-32 to be Markan insertions. J.R. Donahue, Are You the Christ?, pp.53-102, sees Mark as playing a much more creative role than merely that of uniting tradition in 14.55-65; in particular he argues that all of vv.56-59 come from Mark though he has used tradition for the logion of v.58. P. Winter, On the Trial of Jesus, pp.20ff, and many others believe Mark created the whole of 14.55-64. The most recent study is that of D. Juel, Messiah and Temple.
2   So Bultmann, p.270; he is followed in this by many others. E. Linnemann, pp.109-35, analyses the Markan passion account in a very different way and takes vv.57f to have belonged to one part of the tradition and v.56 to another; v.59 was added when they were combined. In the crucifixion narrative she regards vv.29b-30 and vv.31a-32a as Markan insertions (p.158).
3   Cf. Linnemann's analysis (as n.2), pp.136-70.
4   The historical origin of the saying does not concern us; the most recent and full discussion will be found in Lloyd Gaston, No Stone On Another, pp.65ff.
5   Matthew drops these contrasting words, thus bringing his equivalent (26.61) of 14.58 more closely into line with his

equivalent (27.40) of 15.29, though he does not make the temporal qualifications verbally identical. There is no reason to suppose that they are a post-Markan addition to Mark. Their omission in Matthew may indicate that he knew the logion in connection with the trial but in a form lacking the adjectives, which in turn would indicate that Mark probably added them, or their omission by Matthew may come from the different emphasis he places on ecclesiology. Matthew also changes Mark's καταλύσω into δύναμαι καταλῦσαι, perhaps because he realised that the temple had been destroyed but not by Jesus; it is not a weakening of the statement. Luke, who employed other sources as well as Mark for his passion account, drops both 14.58 and 15.29. In Acts 6.14 he uses another form of the logion; this transference is in line with other parallels which he draws between the deaths of Jesus and Stephen.

6   Classical usage would suggest this meant 'after three days', but in Hellenistic Greek διά was used as equivalent to ἐν 'within three days' (Bl-Deb. § 223.1); N. Turner, p.267.

7   To make this comparison implies we see a connection with the resurrection; this will be clearer as we proceed.

8   That neither has been brought into line with the normal 'on the third day' suggests they represent a tradition formed relatively early. That Mark has brought neither into line with his own regular form 'after three days' suggests his respect for the tradition.

9   R.J. McKelvey, The New Temple, pp.68ff, outlines and discusses some of the explanations. Nineham, pp.406f, does attempt to find a meaning in Mark, viz., his desire to concentrate all attention on 14.62 as the cause of Jesus' death; this explanation, however, does not account for the double reference to the false witnesses of which at least one is Markan (see below n.10).

10   Cf. Best, pp.96f; Juel (as n.1), pp.207-8.

11   Cf. Burkill, Mysterious Revelation, pp.285-7.

12   Donahue (as n.1), pp.74ff, seeks to argue that Mark's use of ἴσος in vv.56,59 weakens the attribution of v.58 to 'false witnesses'. By his introduction of this word Mark implies that their testimony is 'not in agreement' or 'inadequate' rather than 'false'. Donahue supports his case with a claim that it is possible to detect a series of Markan insertions which begin and end with similar phrases both of which, he seems to suggest, are due to Mark (see pp.241-3 of his book for a list of these insertions). Initially it would appear much more probable that either the introductory or the terminal phrase was traditional and that in inserting his material Mark rounded it off at either the end or

the beginning with a similar phrase; why, for instance, at 3.7 and 3.8 should Mark introduce the word πλῆθος which he never uses elsewhere instead of his customary ὄχλος? We believe Mark found ἴσος in the tradition and used it a second time; it does not therefore represent an attempt to weaken the 'false witness' concept. Indeed v.56a is a typical Markan γάρ clause which he normally inserts into existing material, i.e. here between v.55b and v.56b; but v.56a refers to the 'false witness' of those who spoke; Mark therefore intensifies the reference rather than weakens it.

13   This is important evidence since it is improbable that John knew the Synoptics; Acts 6.14 is not in the same category since its author knew Mark.

14   So Bultmann, p.120; Gaston (as n.4), p.69; Donahue (as n.1), p.106. Linnemann, p.131, wisely leaves the matter undecided.

15   See the evidence for its use as given in Bauer, s.v. and E. Lohse, TDNT, IX, p.436. If however the contrast in the adjectives can be traced back to Palestinian Judaism, as Juel (as n.1) suggests (pp.143-158), the argument against their Markan insertion is strengthened.

16   The confidence with which some scholars attribute the two adjectives to Mark without producing any redactional evidence is amazing.

17   (As n.1), pp.108f.

18   That Mark contains an anti-temple polemic is not evidence for the assumption that he united the two halves of the saying.

19   In Jn 2.19 the reference is different but this comes about through the deliberate qualification of 2.21. On the NT use of the words see Juel (as n.1), pp.147ff.

20   P.121.

21   Pp.123ff.

22   P.122. Pesch, II, pp.433-5, understands the rebuilt temple as the temple of the last days.

23   For the evidence see McKelvey (as n.9), passim; B. Gärtner, The Temple and the Community in Qumran and the New Testament, pp.47ff; Gaston (as n.4), pp.176-205. See also Best, 'Spiritual Sacrifice' and 'I Peter 2:4-10'.

24   See Gärtner (as n.23), pp.1-46; Gaston (as n.4), pp.163-76; Juel (as n.1), pp.159ff. In the light of this evidence the claim that it is difficult to discover traces of a Jewish concept of an eschatological temple prior to 70 A.D. is hardly relevant.

25   The phrase 'spiritual temple' is probably drawn from I Pet. 2.4f; it is misleading in English where 'spiritual' often means 'non-material' or indicates something which belongs to the world of religion; in either of those senses ἀχειροποίητος is

certainly spiritual.

26   In 1QS 9.3-6 the Spirit is mentioned, but somewhat remotely.

27   Cf. Gaston (as n.4), pp.242f; Donahue (as n.1), pp.108f; Schreiber, pp.114-6; Juel (as n.1), pp.144ff, 168. Contrast T.J. Weeden, 'The Cross as Power and Weakness'. For a more detailed refutation of Linnemann see Juel (as n.1), pp.146ff.

28   Since Matthew does not accept this Markan understanding of Mk 14.28; 16.7, he is consistent in his omission of 'made with hands'/'not made with hands' in his parallel to Mk 14.58.

29   Apart from 14.58; 15.29,38 Mark elsewhere uses τὸ ἱερόν for the temple.

30   Cf. Donahue (as n.1), pp.113ff; Gaston (as n.4), pp.75f.

31   Most writing on this passage is taken up with historical questions. References to recent views will be found in the very comprehensive article of E. Trocmé, 'L'expulsion des marchands du Temple'; cf. also G.W. Buchanan, 'Mark 11.15-19'; R.W. Hiers, 'Purification of the Temple'; V. Eppstein, 'The Cleansing of the Temple'. Schenk, Der Passionsbericht nach Markus, pp.158-66, deals with the redaction.

32   Cf. Best, pp.83f. Juel (as n.1), p.131, believes that it is only the official representatives of Israel who are rejected, but surely the fig-tree represents all Israel and not a part of it.

33   The difficulty of explaining this verse in its Markan context implies it belonged to the tradition.

34   Verse 17, while presented as the teaching of Jesus, summarises the significance of that teaching in relation to the Temple, rather than giving actual historical content to the teaching.

35   See p.31.

36   The suggestion of Bultmann, p.20, developed by Sundwall, pp.71f, that 11.27-33 was originally linked to 11.15f has often been refuted; e.g. see Trocmé (as n.31).

37   'Redaction and Citation'.

38   In view of its use in 14.48; 15.27 λῃσταί is an inappropriate word to describe the dealers in the temple (cf. Juel, as n.1, pp.132f) and it does not illuminate in any way the Markan view of the cleansing; it probably therefore lay in the pre-Markan tradition.

39   Gaston (as n.4), p.87, avers that the rights of the Gentiles in respect of the outer court of the temple were much less clearly understood than the term 'court of the Gentiles' would suggest; he claims that the term was unknown to the ancient world.

40   Trocmé (as n.31) would retain the essential content of the

verse as pre-Markan.

41   Cf. Tagawa, pp.99ff; Minette de Tillesse, pp.264ff.

42   Schenk (as n.31), pp.146-8, argues that 14.1 is Markan on the assumption that 11.18 is traditional, but he has not fully examined 11.18.

43   Trocmé (as n.31).

44   Crossan (as n.37), says: 'Matt. 21:13 would have decided to omit this because the period of universalism had not yet begun. The period of the earthly Jesus was the time of Matt. 10:5-6 (εἰς ὁδὸν ἐθνῶν μὴ ἀπέλθητε); only after the resurrection was it that of Matt. 28:19 (μαθητεύσατε πάντα τὰ ἔθνη). So also with Luke. He had drastically abbreviated the manifesto of Mark 7:1-23 to his own 11:37-41 because the time was not yet ready for the great revelation of Acts 10 which is his own manifesto on the same point' (p.34).

45   Gaston (as n.4), pp.84f, suggests that the reference to the Gentiles represents a survival of tradition which interferes with the contrast between 'den of robbers' and 'house of prayer' in Mark. He supports his theory by arguing that at the time when Mark wrote the temple was in the hands of the Zealots whom Mark regards as robbers. If this was so then there was no need for Mark to have written v.18 in its present form in which blame is thrown on the high priests and scribes. Gaston also erroneously assumes that Matthew and Luke did not know the pre-Markan tradition; so he argues that their omission of the reference to the Gentiles is intended to ease the difficulty of the reference in Mark. But the tradition did not cease to exist in oral form once Mark wrote it down and they may have known and restored its pre-Markan form.

46   We cannot accept the suggestion of G.D. Kilpatrick, 'The Gentile Mission in Mark and Mk 13:9-11', in relation to the punctuation of this passage.

47   Cf. J. Jeremias, Jesus' Promise to the Nations, pp.22f; despite his elimination of any reference in the original saying to the Gentiles he allows that the reference is present in Mark.

48   Juel (as n.1), pp.134-6, suggests that Mark may have intended the phrase 'the house of prayer' to imply opposition to a physical sacrificial cult; he observes that our passage is followed by sayings on prayer (11.24f). But the latter sayings may have already been attached to the story of the fig-tree and Mark have preserved them because they were in the tradition; 'house of prayer', as we have seen, is more probably to be contrasted with 'den of robbers' than linked to the sayings on prayer; Mark does not show Jesus as doing anything to disturb or interfere with the sacrificial cultus in the temple.

49 We are not concerned to discover the original form of the pericope: see recently, J.D. Crossan, 'The Parable of the Wicked Husbandmen'; J. Blank, 'Die Sendung des Sohnes'; J.A.T. Robinson, 'The Parable of the Wicked Husbandmen'.

50 E.g. Gaston (as n.4), p.32; Donahue (as n.1), p.122.

51 Both Matthew and Luke change the plural to a singular.

52 See A Weiser, Die Knechtsgleichnisse, pp.49-57, for the most recent discussion. Pesch, II, pp.213ff, believes the parable was joined to 11.27-33 and 12.13-17 in the pre-Markan passion account.

53 Cf. Blank (as n.49) who suggests this as a possibility.

54 Pesch, II, p.223, also sees a connection with 11.18 which, he holds, belonged with 12.12 in the pre-Markan passion narrative.

55 12-15-2-1.

56 So the majority of commentators.

57 There is nothing in v.9c to assist us in deciding whether Mark wrote it. Jeremias, Parables, p.76, argues that it is original and refers to 'the poor', i.e. the pious (cf. Mt. 5.5). J.A.T. Robinson (as n.49) disputes its originality saying that it is not in the form found in the Gospel of Thomas and that it is unusual for Jesus to answer his own questions, but he does not argue that it is Markan.

58 Donahue (as n.1), p.122, assumes, without examination, that Mark added these verses. If we say that Mark did not add them this does not mean they were originally linked to the parable, though if the whole parable is a post-Easter creation that might be true.

59 15.28 is a gloss.

60 The 'son' is pre-Markan though his description as ἀγαπητός may come from Mark.

61 Note the use of ἀποδοκιμάζειν in the passion prediction of 8.31.

62 Cf. B. Lindars, New Testament Apologetic, pp.169ff.

63 Cf. Donahue (as n.1), pp.124ff.

64 Jeremias has argued strongly on a number of occasions for the meaning 'key-stone, cap-stone', e.g. in TDNT I, pp.791-3; his conclusions are disputed by McKelvey (as n.9), pp.194-204, and 'Christ the Cornerstone', who prefers to think of a stone at the base of the building.

65 Cf. Best, pp.97-102.

66 Cf. Pesch, II, pp.220f.

67 Cf. Schweizer, ad loc.

Chapter 28

THE CHURCH AS HOUSE AND HOUSEHOLD

The Temple can be described as 'house of God' but 'house' has another significance in Mark. Trocmé /1/ has suggested that there is a certain link between the frequent references in the Gospel to 'house' and the house-churches of early Christianity (Rom. 16.5; 1 Cor. 16.19; Col. 4.15; Philm. 2; Acts 2.2,46; 5.42; 8.3; etc.). If we examine the occurrences of 'house' in Mark then it is at once clear some of them can initially be dismissed from consideration because the reference tp 'house' or 'at (to) home' is an essential part of the story or saying in which it is found; these are: (οἰκία) 1.29; 6.4,10; 10.29; 12.40; 13.15; 14.3; (οἶκος) 2.1,11; 5.19,38; 7.30; 8.26; of these only 2.1 appears in a redactional passage /2/ but it is clearly required by the story which follows. Having set these aside there still remain a sufficient number to justify our attention, and we shall examine them individually considering first those in which οἰκία is used.

(i) 2.15; although 2.15a may be redactional the reference to the house is necessary in order to set the scene for a meal.
(ii) 3.25,27; the two little parables here are from the tradition; in any case there is no reference in them to the use of 'house' for the church.
(iii) 7.24 /3/; this verse is largely Markan; the house plays no part in the succeeding story; the reference to it is therefore Markan. The house functions as a place of withdrawal /4/.
(iv) 9.33; a redactional /5/ verse; the reference to the house is Markan and is not required by the succeeding story; the house functions as a place of instruction /6/.
(v) 10.10; a redactional verse /7/ and the reference to the house is Markan; the house functions first as a means of separating the disciples from the crowd and then as a place of instruction /8/.
(vi) 13.34f; Mark received the basic parable in the tradition and 'house' is essential to the imagery but in v.35 which is redactional /9/ ὁ κύριος τῆς οἰκίας ἔρχεται reflects Christian expectancy about the parousia of Jesus and 'house' probably denotes the community itself to which Jesus comes /10/.

We examine now the occurrences of οἶκος:
(i) 3.20: the verse is Markan /11/; the house serves to separate

the disciples from the crowd (v.21) and instruction is given in the house /12/.

(ii) 7.17: the verse is Markan /13/; the house serves to separate the disciples from the crowd and as a place of instruction /14/.

(iii) 9.28: the verse is Markan /15/; the house serves to separate the disciples from the crowd and as a place of instruction /16/.

(iv) 11.17: here the word is found in an OT citation which may well be due to Mark /17/; it denotes the church but obtains this meaning not from itself but from the temple metaphor which underlies it.

Summing up we see that the house /18/ appears as a place of withdrawal (7.24), a place which serves to separate the disciples from the crowd (10.10; 3.20; 7.17; 9.28) /19/ and a place of instruction for the disciples (9.33; 10.10; 3.20; 7.17; 9.28) /20/; it also denotes the community as such (11.17; 13.35). Obviously all these uses cohere. The three emphases on withdrawal, separation from the unconverted and teaching represent in large part what the house-church would have provided for the early Christian. As they met in their house-churches and as Mark's Gospel was read they would have been instructed in the true meaning of discipleship; as Jesus, in Mark's presentation, once took his disciples aside into houses to teach them, so now his words as they are read and discussed continue to teach Christians in their house-churches.

All this has an allied aspect. The church is not 'house' in the sense that any or all of its members are the stones with which the house is built (cf. Eph. 2.20) but in the sense of 'household'. The community is house and as house is separate and instructed - and within the 'house' the disciple is with his brothers and sisters. At 3.31-5 Jesus is clearly depicted as 'within', and this implies a house (it was last mentioned at 3.20). Here he teaches both crowd and disciples /21/ on the nature of discipleship: to be a disciple is to do the will of God. But, more than this, he calls those within his brothers, sisters and mothers. It is implicit at this point that disciples are brothers, sisters and mothers to one another; it becomes explicit in 10.28f /22/. The disciple who has had the experience of Jesus in finding that he is scorned or rejected by his family (3.20f; 6.1-6) finds within the church a new family or household, many more brothers, sisters, mothers, fathers than ever he had before (10.28f) /23/. The position of Jesus in relation to this household is not clarified but since he is the one who with authority enunciates the logion of 3.34f, is the one in whose name instruction is given in the house-church and is the one about the meaning of whose life the members of the community are instructed his position must be central within it and he cannot be on the same plane as others within the community. Those who belong are his 'kinsfolk' and 'kinsfolk' of one another, yet he is never just 'kinsman'. They are only kinsfolk of one another because he has called them his kinsfolk. He lives at the centre of their community and nourishes them with his teaching (6.34; 8.38; 9.7) mediated through the Gospel /24/.

Notes

1   Pp.162f. 'House' could mean 'community' in pre-Christian Judaism; see S. Aalen '"Reign" and "house"'.
2   Cf. Best, pp.69f.
3   Tagawa, p.119; T.A. Burkill, New Light on the Earliest Gospel, pp.48-120.
4   The pericope does not appear in Luke; Matthew omits the reference to the house.
5   Cf. pp.75f.
6   Both Matthew and Luke omit the reference to the house.
7   Cf. p.100.
8   Luke omits the pericope; Matthew omits the reference to the house.
9   Cf. p.152.
10   In what appears to be Matthew's equivalent (24.42) the reference to the house disappears; in Luke the whole section (vv.33-7) disappears from the apocalyptic discourse.
11   See Best, 'Mark III. 20,21,31-35'.
12   Luke is very different at this point; Matthew omits the reference.
13   E.g. the use of ἐπερωτᾶν and παραβολή. See Pryke, p.16, for references.
14   Luke does not have the pericope; the house disappears in Matthew.
15   See p.66.
16   Both Matthew and Luke omit the house. Their regular omission of the word shows that they do not regard it as integral to the sections in which it appears and confirms its redactional nature.
17   See p.217.
18   There is no discernible difference in the way Mark uses οἶκος and οἰκία.
19   Cf. Wrede, p.134, 'Das Haus bedeutet die Isolierung'.
20   Schreiber, p.164, quotes with approval G. Strecker's reference (at p.63) to the house as the place of revelation in 'Das Geschichtsverständnis des Matthäus'. Though it may be at

times difficult to distinguish between revelation and teaching Mark always uses λέγειν of what Jesus says in the house and the content of 9.29; 10.11f can hardly be described as 'revelation'. For these reasons we prefer the term 'instruction'. Behind this idea may lie the Jewish concept of the Beth Din, but this would hardly have been significant for Mark's Roman readers. Burkill (as n.3), p.65, sees the house only as a place of retreat.

21 Both crowd and disciples are also present in 8.34 (see above, pp.29-32); for a full discussion of 3.31-35 with a listing of relevant literature, see Best, 'Mark III. 20,21,31-5'.

22 'House' is not used here in the sense of 'church', but relates either to physical houses or to those who inhabit them.

23 10.28f also speaks of a fellowship in houses and fields. This can hardly be taken as indicating a sharing in, or joint ownership of these possessions, or indeed anything similar to what is depicted in the early chapters of Acts; it probably is similar to the kind of sharing which we see today in many small sects who take care of their members, either finding them work or maintaining them when unfit to work.

24 Kee, pp.109f, stresses the necessary disruption of the disciple's original biological family relationships.

Chapter 29
THE CHURCH AS SHIP /1/

As in the case of the 'house', references to the ship come both
from the tradition and from Mark's redaction /2/; he knew that
Jesus was associated with a boat in the tradition and takes this
up and develops it for his own purposes.

In 4.35-41 and 6.45-62, to both of which we shall return, the
ship is intrinsic to the story; in 1.19 it belonged to the pre-
Markan tradition /3/. At 5.2, although the reference may be
editorial, it is necessary in order that Jesus may be on land at
the time he heals the demoniac /4/; the same applies to 5.18
where he embarks to return to the other side of the lake; if ἐν
τῷ πλοίῳ is read in 5.21 it too is part of the mechanism of
moving Jesus from one place to another and little happens in
the ship; the same is true of 8.10.

3.7-12 is a Markan compilation and no use is made of the ship
at this point (3.9); we may conclude that Mark introduced it /5/;
the ship is to serve as a means of separating Jesus from the
crowd. 4.1f is a Markan seam and Mark has again introduced the
ship for its presence is not essential to the teaching which
follows; it both separates Jesus from the crowd and provides
him with a place from which he may address it. While the crowd
is said to be on the shore it is not said where the disciples are;
but the context implies that they are in the ship with Jesus, for
at 3.9 they prepared the ship and at 4.10ff they are alone with
Jesus. It may be that in 6.32 Mark is continuing to use the
means of linking the miracle stories which existed in the
pre-Markan collection, if such existed, but 6.30-4 is a Markan
construction and 6.32 shows particular signs of his hand /6/; the
ship here, however, is only a means of conveyance and nothing
is told of what happens in it; it is not in the ship but in the
wilderness that Jesus seeks to be alone with his disciples. 6.53-6
is a Markan summary and in it Jesus leaves the ship in order to
heal; the ship is again the means of conveyance to the place
where Jesus may heal. In 8.14 the ship appears for the final
time; 8.14-21 is a Markan passage; the reference to the ship is
strictly unnecessary; the conversation between Jesus and his
disciples could have taken place anywhere provided they were
alone and it would not have been surprising to have found the
house mentioned in place of the ship; perhaps the relation to
miracles has led to the choice of the latter.

Chapter 29: The Church as Ship

If we put together the references from the redaction and from the tradition we see: (i) the ship is a means of conveyance. (ii) It appears regularly in miracle contexts, moving Jesus to and from them and providing the place where they are discussed (8.14); only at 4.1 is there no direct or indirect relation to miracles. (iii) The occupants of the ship whenever they are explicitly named are always Jesus and the disciples, and usually where they are not named this is implied in the context; neither the crowd nor Jesus' enemies are ever in the ship. In addition to these general points there are two clearly redactional passages in which the ship is related to teaching: in 4.1 it is the pulpit from which Jesus addresses the crowd; in 8.14 it is the setting for private instruction of the disciples. In 8.14 and 3.9 its purpose is to separate Jesus from the crowd; this is probably also its significance in 4.10-12.

We must now look at the two passages in which the ship plays a major role: 4.35-41; 6.46-52. The former of these probably belonged to a chain of miracle stories (4.35-5.43) which Mark took over /7/ and at least in the case of this miracle preserved it almost in the form he received it. Thus it was not originally attached to the parable complex (4.1-34), in particular to 4.1 with its reference to the ship /8/. The story, really an exorcism in which the storm is regarded as demonic, serves to demonstrate the power of Jesus /9/. At the same time the disciples' lack of understanding and fear is brought out, and this may have been the reason for Mark's choice of the incident; in the minor way he edits the incident he may draw more attention to this aspect. In v.36 ἀφέντες τὸν ὄχλον does not harmonise with the reference to other ships being with Jesus' ship /10/; it serves to emphasise the separation of Jesus and the disciples from the crowd. It is a miracle for the community of disciples and not for the unevangelised crowd /11/. Kertelge /12/ argues correctly that prior to Mark the story was related to the situation of the church and Mark's readers will easily have seen its relation to themselves. They are fearful of persecution (whether they thought of it as apocalyptic or not is irrelevant); Jesus is superior to danger and can still manifest his power for the benefit of the community. The disciples, and the church of Mark's time, are fearful and without faith (v.41) yet they have enough faith to call on Jesus for help (v.38) /13/; in this they are like the father of the demon possessed child (9.24).

In the second story, 6.46-52, the epiphanic element is more pronounced /14/, and again Mark's redactional work is fairly minimal. Whether or not the story was attached to the feeding miracle /15/ in the pre-Markan tradition Mark has re-written the introduction (v.45) and thereby stressed the separation of the disciples from the crowd /16/. He has also added v.52 which again drives home his emphasis on the failure of the disciples to understand. As well as these two themes, an epiphany of Jesus and the lack of understanding by the disciples /17/, there is a third: the presence of Jesus. By walking on the water Jesus manifests his power; his entrance into the ship goes beyond this; indeed 'he wished to pass by' (v.48) /18/. It is only when he climbs into the boat that they are freed from their hard task of rowing against the wind.

Jesus' presence can be understood in either of two ways: (a) he will come at the End and deliver his people, or (b) as their risen Lord he comes continually to them when they are in need. We prefer the latter, for: (i) 6.30-44 refers to the risen Jesus feeding his people and Mark has tied the feeding closely to the walking on the water (see v.52). (ii) When Jesus comes at the End the day has arrived; here he comes and it is still the fourth watch of the night; the End is near but it is not yet /19/. (iii) In Jn 6.21 once Jesus has entered the ship they are suddenly at their destination; here only the wind falls; the journey is not yet finished.

The disciples failed to understand the story of the feeding (v.52); Mark introduced v.52 because they have equally failed to understand how the presence of Jesus can bring calm. It is therefore the 'presence' rather than the 'epiphany' which is uppermost in his mind. In the earlier story (4.35-42) Jesus was of course present in the ship all the time.

In both these sea miracles we have the emphasis on the separation of the disciples from the crowd. These are the only two miracles from which the disciples benefit; in every other case it is members of the crowd who are helped or healed, though probably in the case of the two feedings the crowd represents the church and not the unevangelised mass. These four miracles, for us distinct from the others as nature miracles, were distinct for Mark because in them Christ comes to the assistance of the community /20/. We see their connection not only in 6.52 but also in 8.14-21 where Jesus discusses the feeding stories when alone with the disciples in a boat. Jesus then delivers the church from its trials and continuously nourishes it. In respect of the sea miracles this leads on easily to the development within the later church of the ship as a symbol for the Christian community. Indeed this may already underlie Mark's use for the image may be pre-Christian and Jewish and have been taken over. In T. Naph. 6.1ff there is a ship which is termed 'The ship of Jacob' and in which Jacob and his sons sail /21/.

Notes

1   Cf. Schreiber, pp.169f. E. Hilgert, The Ship and Related Symbols, was unavailable to me.

2   Weeden, p.156, denies that the ship motif has any special theological importance for Mark but he does not pause to examine the evidence.

3   Even if the saying about fishers of men led to the formulation of a setting for it in the call of the disciples this setting was already in being when Mark received the tradition.

4   The tradition may have contained a 'complex' or 'catena' of miracles in which they were linked together by means of the ship. On the existence of the complex see Kuhn, pp.191-213; Koch, pp.17-22; L.E. Keck, 'Mark 3.7-12 and Mark's Christology'; P.J. Achtemeier, 'Towards the Isolation of Pre-Markan Miracle Catenae' and 'The Origin and Function of the Pre-Markan Miracle Catenae'. T.A. Burkill, 'Mark 3.7-12 and the Alleged Dualism in the Evangelist's Miracle Material', disputes the existence of the complex and argues that Mark himself is responsible for the references to the boat at 5.2,21; 6.32,45,54.

5   Keck (as n.4) disputes this, but see Burkill (as n.4). Even if the reference to the ship is pre-Markan so much of 3.7-12 is allowed by Keck to be Markan that Mark must have been aware of his use of the ship.

6   Cf. Egger, pp.127f. κατ' ἰδίαν and ἔρημος τόπος are Markan.

7   See n.4 above.

8   Cf. Schenke, pp.3-16. Kertelge, p.91, argues for the connection.

9   Kertelge, p.92; Burkill, Mysterious Revelation, p.54; Schreiber, pp.208f.

10   Cf. Schenke, p.82.

11   Cf. Schenke, p.82; Koch, p.95.

12   P.98.

13   Cf. Koch, pp.93-98.

14   Cf. Kertelge, p.147; A.R.C. Leaney, 'Theophany, Resurrection and History'; T. Snoy, 'La rédaction marcienne de la marche sur les eaux'.

15   This is assumed by the majority of commentators because of the similar attachment in John 6. Achtemeier (as n.4) disputes this arguing that the feeding story concluded the original catena.

16   Verse 52 is certainly Markan and probably parts of v.45; cf.

233

Koch, p.107; Schenke, pp.239f. Snoy (as n.14) also argues for parts of vv.50,51.

17 Lohmeyer, ad loc., suspects that two separate narratives are present in our pericope. If so their union was pre-Markan; cf.Koch, pp.105-7.

18 For a discussion of this difficult verse see T. Snoy, 'Marc 6,48: "... et il voulait les dépasser." Proposition pour la solution d'une énigme'.

19 This accords with a belief in an early parousia but not with an understanding of the miracle as a representation of the parousia.

20 For the positive significance to Mark of the miracles which occupy over a quarter of his Gospel see Best, 'Miracles'.

21 The ship metaphor is found in a more developed form in the Hebrew fragment of the same writing; cf. R.H. Charles, Pseudepigrapha, pp.361-3.

Chapter 30
THE COMMUNITY AS THE COMMUNITY OF KNOWLEDGE

Mark's awareness of the disciples as a community comes out in another way. While it is generally recognised that he depicts the disciples as lacking in spiritual insight and hard of understanding it is necessary also to remember that he shows them as recipients of special knowledge. In this aspect again they represent the community which Mark is instructing with Jesus' words and actions. Both the historical disciples and the members of Mark's community receive instruction or revelation which is not normally communicated to the crowd, still less to the opponents of Jesus or the persecutors of the church. Our present concern is not the content of that instruction, which relates to the nature of Jesus, his mission and discipleship, but the fact that given it the disciples become a group sharing special knowledge.

There are a number of occasions, as we have seen, when Jesus goes apart with his disciples (3.7; 6.31), often into a house or a boat, and instructs them (e.g. 4.10-12,34b; 7.17ff; 8.14-21,31;9.2ff,30f;10.10-12; etc.) /1/. The most significant passage is 4.10-12; here a clear distinction is drawn between teaching given to the group around Jesus, i.e. the Christian community, and those outside, the crowd, the unconverted, who are kept in ignorance. The community thus possesses special knowledge and this separates it from those who do not belong to it. It should be noted that this special knowledge is never given to individual disciples but always to a group described sometimes as the disciples, sometimes as the Twelve, and sometimes identified as a sub-group of one or other of these larger groups. The knowledge therefore belongs to the community as such and not to individuals within it. That smaller groups within the number of the disciples are sometimes instructed does not imply that there is an inner group in the Christian community who for their own benefit receive special revelations /2/. Peter, James and John are the only disciples present with Jesus at 5.37-43; 9.2-13; 14.32-42, but 9.9 implies that they are not to keep to themselves what they have heard. If Mark has widened an original reference to Peter into one to these three in 9.2; 14.33 /3/, then he is also probably indicating once again that instruction or revelation is not to be restricted to a few within the church. In chap. 13 apocalyptic teaching is given only to four disciples but the final verse (13.36) indicates that it is intended for all. At 10.42 Jesus after dealing with the request of James and John turns from them to teach all the disciples the nature of true authority. The very centre of Mark's instruction on discipleship (8.34-9.1) is not confined to disciples alone but is also offered to the crowd. Mark, then, does not envisage a group within the church possessing esoteric knowledge.

Sociologically we know that shared knowledge unifies a group, serves to differentiate it from those who do not have the knowledge and makes it more conscious of itself as a group, but it also creates the danger that the group will harden and, retaining its knowledge to itself, will refuse to expand and will seek a privileged position for itself. It is against such dangers that Mark warns his readers in the story of the strange exorcist (9.38-40) /4/: a rigid definition of membership may exclude those whom God views as true followers of Jesus. The knowledge of Christ which the group has is always a knowledge which can only grow by being given away (4.24). As well as rebuking those who would seek isolation Mark attacks the danger positively by emphasising the duty of the community to expand (1.17) and to see that there are those who are engaged in preaching the gospel and exorcising and healing (3.14f; 6.7); the community can only exist as long as it continues to enlarge the circle of those who share its special knowledge.

Notes
1   Kee, p.165, points to the use of προσκαλεῖν in many of these passages.
2   Cf. Kee, pp.166f.
3   See the discussion of those passages.
4   See the discussion of the passage.

Chapter 31
A NOTE ON THE RISEN JESUS IN THE COMMUNITY

In all of Part III we have explicitly or implicitly assumed that Jesus was alive in the community either as the centre of its life or as the one who is at its head as it goes in his way. T.J. Weeden in his book, Mark: Traditions in Conflict /1/, would deny this for he argues that 'after the crucifixion Jesus is not only absent from the disciples but from all members of the Christian community' (p. 114). If this is so Mark cannot be expressing the kind of theology of the church which we have been uncovering. In Weeden's view the Christian community in Mark would be a society of like-minded individuals with no relationship to Christ other than that to a dead teacher whose return they awaited with eager expectancy. Allied to Weeden's theory of an absent Jesus and supportive of it is his belief that in Mark the historical disciples either represent a Christological heresy which Mark refutes or were themselves exponents of this heresy in the Jerusalem church /2/. To sustain his argument about the absence of the Lord he uses evidence drawn from chap. 13 and from 2.18-20, 14.25 and 14.28; we shall examine in turn how he uses these passages.

According to Weeden Mark is contending against opponents who claim to be theoi andres and who in their spiritual enthusiasm identify themselves with Christ (13.6,22) /3/; the evangelist therefore denies the presence of the risen Christ in the midst of the community /4/. This does not mean that the true disciple is left alone through the period of persecution in which the Gospel was written for he has the Spirit as his guide (13.11) /5/. The 'community finds itself in much the same predicament as the servants in the parable about the absent master (13.34-36). Like the master of that story the resurrected Jesus is absent from his community' (p. 89). Mark takes up and uses the traditional apocalyptic material in 13.7f,14-20 because persecution shows no sign of slackening and will continue to the End itself: the quandary of Christians is aggravated by the Lord's absence from his community (p. 95). In relation to this we must note that if Mark intended to represent the Spirit in place of Christ as the guide of the community he has given singularly little teaching about the Spirit's activity in the community; 1.10,12 relate the Spirit to Jesus /6/; in 12.36 it is David who is said to speak by the Spirit; 3.29 refers to blasphemy against the Spirit. Thus only 13.11 relates the Spirit to the community. Mark can hardly be regarded as meeting the needs of the community with an adequate doctrine of the Spirit! The absence of positive instruction is even more striking when we recollect how much there is in the remainder of the NT, where also there is no attempt to deny the presence of Christ with his community. Moreover· if Mark is countering the claim of opponents to be theoi andres it is surprising that he should stress (!) the Spirit for such opponents usually claimed to be enthused by the Spirit and this emphasis would suit their case. Weeden's explanation of the false Christs and prophets of 13.6,22 as theoi andres is only one among a number of competing interpretations none of which is fully satisfactory. Even if his view were correct it would not necessarily follow that Christ was absent from his church; Mark denies the correctness of the identification of the one who identifies himself as Christ; if someone wrongly identifies himself as the President or Prime Minister that does not mean that the President or Prime Minister is not somewhere else in the world. Nor does the parable of 13.34-6, with its expectation of Christ's return, lead to a necessary rejection of a belief in his existence and presence in fellowship; Paul makes the same point as that of the parable in 1 Th. 5.2f but he believed that already prior to the parousia he was 'in Christ' and a member of the body of Christ: indeed in most of the NT we find both the expectancy of the parousia of Christ and a belief in his real presence.

From 2.18-20 Weeden deduces that the community had its Lord taken from it at the crucifixion and is now without him /7/. We have already looked at these verses and seen how difficult they are to interpret, especially when vv.21-22 are associated with them /8/. 2.18-20 is the only occasion in the Gospel where 'mourning' for Jesus is mentioned; if the Lord were absent we should expect this element to appear more often. Mourning the death of Christ and celebrating his risen presence have never been regarded as contradictory in Christianity. The crucial words 'when the bridegroom is taken away' are also found in Matthew (9.15) yet he shows the risen Christ speaking of his continual presence with the community (28.20).

In relation to 14.25, where Jesus says that he will not drink again of the fruit of the vine until he drinks it new in the Kingdom of God, Weeden argues that 'the implication is that he will not be with the disciples or the company of believers in any real sense until the kingdom has come, an event still awaited at the time of Mark' (p.114). Weeden dismisses the view that Mark

believed that in the Eucharist there was a mystical togetherness with Christ on the grounds that a mystical experience of
Christ cannot be found elsewhere in Mark. Against this it can
be argued: (i)Weeden is using here a desired conclusion to reject
evidence which would upset that conclusion. (ii) Elsewhere in
Mark there is a considerable amount of evidence for a
'togetherness' with Christ - though 'mystical' may not be the
best adjective with which to describe this experience. (iii)
Unless there is a strong reason to accept the contrary, and
Weeden does not provide this, it would be wrong to interpret
14.25 apart from what we know of other early Christian
thinking on the Eucharist. If Paul provides any clue to this then
Christians believed that they partook of Christ in the Eucharist
(1 Cor. 10.16f), i.e. they had some kind of real fellowship with
him. 14.25 would then have led them to think not of an absent
Jesus but of a future Messianic banquet. It is possible that 14.25
might be held to conflict with Lk. 24.30 where Jesus may
possibly be envisaged as participating in a post-resurrection
Eucharist, but this is not really what is at issue. None of those
who hold to a continuing presence of Jesus within the church
believe that he actively partakes of the cup in each Eucharist.
Robbins /9/ confuses the matter further when he attempts to
support Weeden's conclusion with a reference to 14.7. Both Paul
and John would have been shocked to think that anyone should
construe their concepts of a continuing fellowship with Christ
into a belief that this implied they would be able to anoint
Christ with physical oil.

Finally Weeden draws attention to 14.27f; 16.7f. For Mark
there are no resurrection appearances; therefore Christ is
absent. Weeden accepts the view of Lohmeyer and Marxsen that
14.28 and 16.7 refer to the parousia; we have already argued
that this is wrong and that they refer to the resurrection /10/.
Apart from this it does not follow logically that because Mark
omits resurrection appearances he therefore believes in an
absent Christ. Other solutions are possible; Mark may have
omitted these appearances because he did not wish attention
concentrated on a risen Christ who only appeared on earth for a
day or two and was afterwards absent in heaven but wished
instead to argue for a continued fellowship of Christians with a
risen and ever present Christ. Alternatively Mark may be
arguing that Christ's real presence is to be found by readers and
hearers of his (i.e. Christ's) words when they read the Gospel:
Christ is alive in his teaching.

Crossan /11/, assuming that the Gospel always ended at 16.8,
argues that Mark composed 16.1-8 and created the story of the

empty tomb in order to counter the tradition that the risen Lord had appeared to Peter and other disciples; he believes that Mark had an anti-Jerusalem and anti-disciple bias. By this construction an absent Jesus is presented: 16.6,7 indicate that Jesus will appear again at the parousia but meanwhile he 'is not here'. While we can accept Crossan's view that the Gospel was designed to end at 16.8 Mark's alleged anti-Jerusalem and anti-disciple bias is very questionable /12/; the Markan invention of all of 16.1-8 is difficult to sustain as the many and varied studies of the passage show /13/. Moreover if Mark did create 16.1-8 for the reasons Crossan supposes he did not do it very intelligently. Not only is the meaning Crossan adopts for 16.7 unlikely, but Mark could have made his point with absolute clarity if he had written, 'He is ascended; he is not here'. 16.7 would then have referred quite naturally to the parousia. If however Mark was compelled by the tradition to employ the word 'risen' /14/ he would surely have needed to make it clear that he did not mean by the word what all other strands of early Christian thought meant by it, that it covered not only some particular appearances of Jesus to disciples but also the continued presence of Christ with believers (cf. Mt. 28.20 and the emphasis of Paul on Christ-fellowship); that Mark did not make it clear is borne out by the subsequent history of interpretation of the Gospel. If Mark did construct 16.1-8 then, as we have seen, it is possible to draw an entirely different conclusion: Mark wished to turn attention away from a limited number of appearances in order to stress the continual presence of Christ with believers /15/.

Weeden indicates one general principle of interpretation which has guided his analysis: 'the fact of the matter is that if one read Mark alone, without supplying the consensus of New Testament tradition there would be no reason to assume...' (p.114). Is this a sound hermeneutical principle? It could be opposed by that of the Reformers that the more obscure parts of Scripture are to be interpreted by those which are clear. Neither view taken simply is correct. A balance needs to be struck between the peculiarities of one NT writing and the general characteristics of the whole New Testament. The peculiarities may be real or they may represent our failure to understand. If the aberrant views are to be accepted as valid they require a strong exegetical foundation; Weeden has not supplied the necessary strong exegetical arguments for his views. If the consensus of opinion among Christians of Mark's time believed in a risen and present Jesus, as it did, then Mark, if he did not, would have had to make his point with absolute clarity. He did not do so.

Before we move to the more positive exegetical grounds for the rejection of Weeden's interpretation it is important to point out the all but total absence from his work of redactional evidence: he moves almost entirely in the world of ideas without discussing the, admittedly, more difficult facts of Markan style and vocabulary; but without the control which these supply it is possible to make Mark mean almost anything. Positive exegetical support for the view that Mark believed in a risen and present Jesus can be found in the passages we have discussed which relate the community to Christ (14.28; 16.7; 14.58; 15.29; 11.17; 12.10f; 3.34f; 'the flock', 'the house', 'the ship'); these imply a fellowship with a Christ who cannot then be described as 'absent'. The miracles occupy more than a quarter of the Gospel and Mark introduces them into his summaries: this indicates their importance for him; if he had wished to controvert a false Christology involving their use it would have been sufficient to introduce one or two; the large number indicates the availability of the power of the risen Christ to the community. The disciples are continually depicted as 'with Jesus': a phrase which comes to formal expression at 3.14 /16/; it is true that in this connection our reading of the place of the 'disciples' in the Gospel is entirely different from Weeden's: for him the Gospel has been written to oppose them and their views; for us they function as examples by which Mark's church may be instructed /17/. As we have seen throughout, the call of Jesus, 'Follow me', is much more than a call to an imitation of Christ; it implies a positive relationship with a living Lord. We would point again to the lack of a detailed doctrine of the Spirit in Mark: if Weeden is correct Mark's community is really left without either a living Lord or much knowledge of a present activity of the Spirit and if Weeden were to suggest that such knowledge of the Spirit could be assumed in any Christian congregation then the same assumption could be made about the risen Christ. Finally we would note that right through the NT there is a tension between an expectancy of a return of the Lord, which might be thought logically to imply his absence, and an appreciation of his living presence. Given a belief in the parousia this tension must occur. Weeden has allowed himself to be so carried away by one side of the tension that he has denied the existence of the other.

Notes

1   Weeden was preceded in his views by N.Q. Hamilton,

'Resurrection Tradition and the Composition of Mark'. Weeden has followed up his book with an article 'The Cross as Power in Weakness'. See also V.K. Robbins, 'Last Meal: Preparation, Betrayal and Absence'; J.D. Crossan, 'Empty Tomb and Absent Lord' and 'A Form of Absence'. It is not entirely clear if N. Perrin, The Resurrection Narratives, also adheres to this view (cf. p.35).

2   I have disputed Weeden's views on this point in 'The Role of the Disciples'.

3   Pp.80f,87ff,85f (all the references are to his book and not to his article).

4   'No aid can be given for identifying the authentic presence of the resurrected Lord in the community because he is absent' (p.89).

5   Pp.85ff.

6   2.8 and 8.12 are not references to the Holy Spirit.

7   Pp.114,125,133-5.

8   See pp.88-90.

9   As n.1.

10 See p.199.

11 As n.1.

12 Cf. Best, 'Mark III. 20,21,31-5', 'The Twelve', 'Peter'; J. Lambrecht, 'The Relatives of Jesus'.

13 See the long list of references in Pesch, II, pp.541-3.

14 Perhaps by the existence of one or more of the passion predictions.

15 For further criticism of Crossan see J.E. Alsup, 'John Dominic Crossan, "Empty Tomb and Absent Lord"—A Response'.

16 See Best, 'Miracles'.

17 For a fuller discussion see Best, 'Disciples'.

Chapter 32
CONCLUSION

For Mark the disciple is not a solitary individual but the member of a community. This community was clearly distinct from the world around it and from which it had been recruited; so it can be described as flock, house and ship. To it the members may withdraw for protection and instruction but in using the term 'withdraw' this should not be taken as if it suggested that there were times when the members were physically out of it and times when they were physically in it; rather there are times when they are more concerned with extending it, as they fish for men, and other times when they are more in need of refreshment of spirit or further instruction in the meaning of what they have already begun to believe.

The community functions in different ways. Paul's stress on the interdependence of members, which he expresses above all through his use of the term 'body of Christ', is largely missing. We approach it most closely when we pass from the depiction of the community as house to its depiction as family, in which the members are brothers and sisters and share in one another's possessions. This image puts members on the same level; no one is isolated as 'father' and therefore the bearer of authority within the family; equally no one is picked out as 'pastor' or 'shepherd' in relation to the metaphor of the flock and no one as 'pilot' in relation to the ship.

Presumably Mark's community possessed some form of ministry but we never learn its nature from the Gospel /1/; no one member or group of members is given a special responsibility for others; instead everyone is responsible to avoid putting stumbling-blocks in the way of others (9.42). The only ministry which is clearly recognised is one directed towards the outside world, a ministry of healing and evangelisation (3.13-19; 6.6b-13). When the community, or some part of it, meets for instruction in the house the instructor is not one of its own members but Jesus himself. This emphasis may be inevitable because of the way Mark has chosen to guide his community, for in a Gospel Jesus must be central. And just as Christ is the instructor of the community through his words and actions recorded in the gospel and interpreted by Mark so he is also the protector and encourager of the community. He is within the temple which the community forms and he is at the head of the flock as it moves forward in suffering and mission. He feeds it (6.34-44; 8.1-9) and delivers it (4.35-41; 6.45-52). The community always enjoys his living presence.

Having noted some of the positive elements of the Markan community it is well also to note what is not mentioned. The flock image is used to relate the flock to the shepherd but not to distinguish it from other possible flocks; there is no idea of a heretical or schismatic flock from which Mark's flock needs to be preserved in safety /2/. The house to which Mark's readers come for instruction and the ship in which they are protected are not distinguished from alternative houses or ships where a false community may exist. If Mark does not draw a distinction between the true group for which he writes and other possible heretical or schismatic groups, he equally gives no indications that there are divisions within the community; there are no appeals or prayers for unity (contrast Jn 17) and no real evidence of internal dispute. It is true that there are indications that some members of the community may be unwilling to accept the way of the cross and they may make claims to 'superiority' over other members. Such claims to superiority are unfortunately normal within any community; they can lead to grave division but there are as yet no signs of fissures between groups in Mark's community. The refusal to accept the way of the cross may suggest heresy; if so there is again no sign of a definite heretical group; the peril is one which faces all members of the community, and it is one which continually has beset the church. There is no 'good' group over against which Mark isolates a 'bad' group for which the rejection of the cross is a special danger. Moreover it is not only in respect of the way of the cross that disciples are rebuked but also, and in as strong terms, against a failure to realise the power of Christ in miracle. When we attempt to isolate the views which are attacked in the Gospel they do not form a consistent whole /3/, i.e. there is no one group which is being attacked; the community as a whole is being instructed through the failure of the disciples and the teaching they are given. In this connection we should also note that there are no rules for the expulsion of dissident members and no steps outlined by which the community may guard itself from their presence or their views; indeed 9.38f points entirely in the opposite direction. In line with the attitude outlined in it we cannot detect much indication of a narrow sectarian spirit developing within the community. The command of Jesus to love one's neighbour became rapidly changed in the early church into a command to love one's fellow Christian as we see from Jn 13.34f; 15.12,17; 1

Pet. 1.22; 2.17; 4.8; 1 Jn 3.23; Heb. 13.1 (cf. Rom. 12.10 and 1 Th. 4.9; but Paul is aware of the commandment of Jesus in its original form as we learn from Rom. 13.8-10 and Gal. 5.14); there are no signs of the narrowing of the command in Mark (cf. 12.28-34). This demand of love for all men is not merely in line with the call to 'fish' for them but even more so with that to sell possessions and give to them (10.21) and with the honouring of the unimportant (9.36f).

Notes

1   Kee says that 'the Markan community offers nearly no evidence of organisation' (p.152).

2   There may be a danger from false teachers (13.5f,21f).

3   Cf. Best, 'The Role of the Disciples'.

PART IV

Chapter 33
CONCLUSION

It is unnecessary to restate in detail the conclusions to the three parts of our discussion. The disciples are on a journey, or pilgrimage, on which they travel after Jesus seeking a dedication like his, on which they do not travel alone but know themselves to be with one another and with him, and to which they invite others. All this appeared in germ at the very beginning of the Gospel where 1.16-20 tells the story of the call of disciples rather than of members of the Twelve. Disciples are called in this passage to follow Jesus, more than one /1/ is called so that from the beginning they form a group, and they are given a task to fish for others. In the remainder of the Gospel these points are developed and elaborated, and new points introduced.

While Mark pictures the historical disciples as challenged to journey after Jesus it is not his primary purpose to record how they reacted but to summon his own community to enter more seriously on the same journey. The final words of Jesus' formal teaching are found in 13.37, 'What /2/ I say to you (i.e. the historical disciples), I say to all: Watch.' This verse is not only the conclusion to the apocalyptic discourse but it is also the conclusion to what Mark reports of the systematic teaching of Jesus. Jesus certainly speaks to his disciples again in chap. 14 but there on each occasion his words arise out of an incident and are part of it. 13.37, in its present position, is a fitting termination to all the teaching of Jesus in the Gospel; pictured as addressed to the historical disciples it is actually intended for the members of Mark's own community.

The concept of the Christian life as a journey or pilgrimage has been a regular theme in Christian thought; it undoubtedly drew its original inspiration from the journey of Abraham and from the Exodus though it may also, whether consciously or unconsciously, have drawn on gnostic ideas of the journey of the soul to heaven. The pilgrimage has often been depicted as a kind of ordeal for the soul in which it seeks to pass successfully through an alien world to a better world beyond. Sometimes it is implied that every person is involved in this journey, in other cases it is considered that only Christians are on it and then

Christ is portrayed as their guide to the way and their support in the dangers and difficulties that have to be faced. The classic presentation of this pilgrimage is found in Hebrews where the members of the people of God move forward to their sabbath rest along a path which Christ has pioneered; the goal is clear and the pilgrims are solemnly warned that they must strive to keep to the route already marked out by Christ; since he has already traversed it he is able as a merciful High Priest to help them; the pilgrims as they journey have no abiding city but travel through the wilderness until they reach the heavenly city. Luke provides an alternative picture. In the great travel narrative of 9.51-18.27 Jesus is shown journeying to Jerusalem. As with Mark the journey begins with the first passion prediction but in Luke its goal is deliberately expressed in an addition to the transfiguration account (9.31). The 'exodus' which Jesus accomplishes at Jerusalem is fulfilled in the ascension (cf. ἀνάλημψις, 9.51) when the disciples are sent to be his witnesses (Acts 1.8). The goal of the journey of the disciples is also more firmly outlined in Luke than in Mark; Stephen, whose death is depicted in terms similar to those used of Jesus, takes up, as it were, his cross, and Jesus stands to receive him at the end of his journey (Acts 7.55; cf. 6.13 where Stephen has the appearance of an angel). Luke also emphasises more than Mark the equipment of disciples with the Spirit as their guide and support /3/.

The contrast between the commonly accepted Christian picture of the pilgrimage and that provided by Mark is astonishing. Mark does not depict the world as hostile and alien; the obstacles that pilgrims encounter arise out of persecution and their own inability to understand what Jesus' death means, and of these it is the latter which is more regularly stressed. Persecution is not presented openly and in detail but belongs to the total background as a continual threat; persecutors are not shown up as villains; the form of persecution is never made clear. If Mark does not clearly outline the pilgrim's external trials neither does he draw the picture of a glorious compensatory goal to which the pilgrimage leads. Of course he believes that faithful pilgrims will reach heaven (9.1; 10.30; 12.18-27; 13.13,26f) and that the unfaithful will not (8.38; 9.42-8), and the same is implied by the general eschatological colouring of the whole Gospel. Yet though heaven may be the ultimate destiny of Christians it is not depicted as their goal. The goal, if Mark would ever have used the word or thought in such terms, is Jesus. But as goal Jesus is not a fixed or static goal but is continuously on the move, towards the cross and into mission, and for Mark these two are inseparable. Christ goes at the head of his disciples on this twofold journey (and that is why the term 'goal' is so inadequate). The 'goal' is in fact unattainable. Christians go the same way as their Lord but are always in the position of those who follow, never of those who have arrived. But if they are those who follow they are also those who are accompanied - by their Lord and by their fellow disciples. As long as the journey lasts Christians are never alone; the Lord is there to deliver and feed; they are together in the house, the ship and the temple as brothers and sisters.

This does not imply that for Mark to be a disciple simply means to imitate Christ. Jesus took up his cross, denied himself, served others; the disciple is summoned to do all these. Yet Mark always distinguishes between the disciple and Jesus. In the final passage of the main section on discipleship Christ calls men and women to minister to others as he has done, but immediately sets himself out as their ransom (10.45); when he summons them to lose their lives, as he does, they are bidden to do so for <u>his</u> sake and for the sake of the Gospel (8.35); those who fail are not just those who have not walked in his ways but those who were ashamed of <u>him</u> and of <u>his</u> words (8.38); when he is transfigured God bids the disciples listen to <u>him</u> (9.7). The position of Jesus is unique. But its uniqueness does not lie simply in its 'firstness', as if he were an explorer who marked out a path through an impenetrable jungle to make it easier for others to follow. Through his cross and resurrection, which are their redemption, he creates the very possibility of journey for them; the judgement which should fall on them is taken away and they are freed /4/. The history of Christianity shows that the cross itself can exercise and has exercised a compelling attraction on many, but for Mark there is more than the cross: there is both a theory of atonement with a certainty of acceptance by God and a resurrection of the leader which implies the resurrection of those who follow him.

It is instructive to distinguish the way in which Mark relates the Christian to Christ from two apparently similar relationships in the ancient world, viz. those of the rabbi and his disciple and the philosopher and his pupil /5/. The rabbi turns his disciple toward the Law and his own life ought to provide an example of the living Law; it is better to <u>hear</u> the precepts of the Law from a wise teacher than to read them /6/. The philosopher directs his pupil to the true life but his own life ought to exemplify what he teaches /7/. In Mark the personality of the teacher is not neglected nor is his position as example wholly ignored; Jesus points his disciples to God and himself walks the way of God yet it is not possible to substitute another teacher for him; a pupil may move from one philosopher to another and a disciple from one rabbi to another but Christians cannot go to another leader. The disciple of the rabbi, if all goes well, becomes a rabbi; the pupil of the philosopher may equally become a philosopher and have his own pupils; disciples of Christ, however, never become Christs or have their own disciples.

Mark may have thought that the parousia would come soon and that therefore the journey need not be long, but the way in which he formulates the journey allows of indefinite extension. It would be a dead-end journey if it was a short walk to a martyr's cross, or if only a year or two had to be endured until Christ would appear and all would be over. For Mark the journey is open-ended; the cross is always ahead; it is never reached and some happiness found beyond it. The cross continually calls to the denial of self, to the losing of what the self thinks is most precious to itself, to the search to serve others in the forgetfulness of self. The worst enemies on the pilgrimage are not the external foes who may persecute and kill but the pilgrims' own unwillingness to accept a genuine understanding of the meaning of the cross. Certainly external foes can lead to a hesitation to take up the cross but if such foes threaten and are overcome pilgrims may be deluded into thinking they have taken up the cross when in fact they have failed because they did not see the importance of the child, or because they thought themselves superior to others in the community, or outside it. Their pilgrimage is always threatened through their own inadequacy; should they forget this the story of Judas will remind them that not all who start the journey finish it. On the other hand when they have failed the story of Peter and the other disciples is there to remind them that others who have failed have been able to restart the journey and complete it. The way of the pilgrim may be precarious but it is always full of hope; most of those who begin succeed in finishing (cf. 4.3-20). If the journey is open-ended because the cross is not just something reached and left behind but is ever present, it is also open-ended because it is a journey in mission. It is a journey beyond the cross into the resurrection; it is a journey of expansion in search for others. Though in the life of Jesus the cross and the resurrection were sequential, for the pilgrim they are simultaneous; mission and self-denial cannot ultimately be distinguished; cross-bearing and cross-proclaiming are opposite sides of the same coin. While Mark's view of the pilgrimage leaves the possibility of this totally open-ended expansion we have to acknowledge that he expected the parousia to come soon; so pilgrims on their journey must be watchful for the return of the Lord; the end of the journey may come unexpectedly; let the pilgrim watch and pray.

Notes

1   It would be quite wrong to conclude with Schmahl, pp.115f, that their two-by-two calling in 1.16-20 is intended to be in accordance with the two-by-two sending out of the Twelve (6.7) for there is no reason to doubt that Peter and Andrew, James and John, were pairs of brothers. At 2.14, which has the same structure as 1.16-20, only one person is called.

2   We might have expected ἅ (it appears as a variant in A W fam1 fam13 etc.) which would refer to vv.33-37 if not to all of chap. 13 rather than ὅ which refers forward to γρηγορεῖτε at the end of the verse. But ἅ would not of itself refer back to all Jesus' words throughout the Gospel. It is the position of the verse which suggests this (cf. the programmatic position of 10.45).

3   In the Pauline corpus we regularly find the Christian life described with the verb περιπατεῖν; it is used invariably to describe the manner in which the Christian ought or ought not to 'walk', i.e. behave; only at 2 Cor. 5.7 is there a suggestion of the goal of the Christian's progress.

4   See Best, pp.61ff.

5   Cf. Schulz, pp.21-32; K.H. Rengstorf, TDNT, IV, pp.416-441.

6   Cf. Ep. Aristeas 127 and the references given in Daube, pp.87f; C.H. Talbert, Literary Patterns, Theological Themes, and the Genre of Luke-Acts, pp.92f; B. Gerhardsson, Memory and Manuscript, pp.182f.

7   Cf. Talbert (as n.6), pp.90-92, for references.

ABBREVIATIONS

AnBib	Analecta Biblica
AGSU	Abhandlungen zur Geschichte des Alten und Neuen Testaments
Bü	Bücher
BJRUL	Bulletin von Behalt... University Library of Manchester
BA	Biblical Archeology
BZNW	Beihefte zur Zeitschrift für die neutestamentliche Wissenschaft
CBQ	Catholic Biblical Quarterly
ET	English Translation
EKL	Evangelisches Kirchenlexikon Einwohner...
EvTh	evangelische Theologie
ExpT	Expository Times
FRLANT	Forschungen zur Religion und Literatur des Alten und Neuen Testaments
Int	Interpretation
JBL	Journal of Biblical Literature
JTS	Journal of Theological Studies
NovT	Novum Testamentum
NTA	New Testament Research and Preaching
NTS	New Testament Studies
RB	Revue Biblique
RHPR	Revue de Philosophie et de la Philosophie Littéraire
RThPh	Revue de Théologie et de Philosophie
	povazuje na filozof...
SE	Studia Evangelica
SBT	Studies in Biblical Theology
SJT	S. J. T. Scottish Journal of Theology
SNTS	Studia ... Key Testament Series
SANT	Studien zum Alten und Neuen Testament
StTh	Studia Theologica
SUNT	Studien zur Umwelt des neuen Testaments
TDNT	Theological Dictionary of the New Testament (ET of G.W. Bromiley)

ABBREVIATIONS

AnalBib	Analecta Biblica.
ATANT	Abhandlungen zur Theologie des Alten und Neuen Testaments.
Bib	Biblica.
BJRULM	Bulletin John Rylands University Library of Manchester.
BZ	Biblische Zeitschrift.
BZNW	Beihefte zur Zeitschrift für die neutestamentliche Wissenschaft.
CBQ	Catholic Biblical Quarterly.
ET	English Translation.
ETL	Ephemerides Theologicae Lovanienses.
EvTh	Evangelische Theologie.
ExpT	Expository Times.
FRLANT	Forschungen zur Religion und Literatur des Alten und Neuen Testaments.
Int	Interpretation.
JBL	Journal of Biblical Literature.
JTS	Journal of Theological Studies.
NT	Novum Testamentum.
NTD	Das Neue Testament Deutsch.
NTS	New Testament Studies.
RB	Revue Biblique.
RHPR	Revue de l'Histoire et de Philosophie Religieuses.
RTP	Revue de Théologie et de Philosophie.
SBL	Society for Biblical Literature.
SE	Studia Evangelica.
SBT	Studies in Biblical Theology.
SJT	Scottish Journal of Theology.
SNTS	Studiorum Novi Testamenti Societas.
StANT	Studien zum Alten und Neuen Testament.
StTh	Studia Theologica.
StUNT	Studien zur Umwelt des Neuen Testaments.
TDNT	Theological Dictionary of the New Testament (ET by G.W. Bromiley).

Bibliography

TTZ	Trierer Theologische Zeitschrift.
TU	Texte und Untersuchungen.
TZ	Theologische Zeitschrift.
UBS	United Bible Societies.
WMANT	Wissenschaftliche Monographien zum Alten und Neuen Testament.
ZNW	Zeitschrift für neutestamentliche Wissenschaft.
ZTK	Zeitschrift für Theologie und Kirche.
10-5-7-9	A set of four such numbers refers to the frequency of a word or phrase in the Gospels of Matthew, Mark, Luke and John respectively.

BIBLIOGRAPHY

I. Books referred to by Author's Name

Ambrozic = A.M. Ambrozic, The Hidden Kingdom (CBQ Monograph Series 2; Washington, 1972).

Bauer = W. Bauer, A Greek-English Lexicon of the New Testament (translated and adapted by W.F. Arndt and F.W. Gingrich; Chicago and Cambridge, 1957).

Berger = K. Berger, Die Gesetzesauslegung Jesu, I: Markus und Parallelen (WMANT 40; Neukirchen-Vluyn, 1972).

Best = E. Best, The Temptation and the Passion: The Markan Soteriology (SNTS Monograph Series 2; Cambridge, 1965).

Billerbeck = H.L. Strack and P. Billerbeck, Kommentar zum Neuen Testament aus Talmud und Midrasch (Munich, 1922-8).

Black = M. Black, An Aramaic Approach to the Gospels and Acts (3rd edn., Oxford, 1967).

Bl-Deb = F. Blass and A. Debrunner, A Greek Grammar of the New Testament and other Early Christian Literature (ET by R.W. Funk; Chicago and Cambridge, 1961).

Bultmann = R. Bultmann, The History of the Synoptic Tradition (ET by J. Marsh; Oxford, 1963).

Bundy = W.E. Bundy, Jesus and the First Three Gospels (Cambridge, Mass., 1955).

Cook = M.J. Cook, Mark's Treatment of the Jewish Leaders (Suppl. NT 51; Leiden, 1978).

Daube = D. Daube, The New Testament and Rabbinic Judaism (London, 1956).

Dautzenberg = G. Dautzenberg, Sein Leben Bewahren (StANT 14; München, 1966).

Dibelius = M. Dibelius, From Tradition to Gospel (ET by B.E. Woolf; London, 1934).

Doudna = J.C. Doudna, The Greek of the Gospel of Mark (JBL Monograph Series 12; Philadelphia, 1961).

254

Bibliography

Egger = W. Egger, Frohbotschaft und Lehre: Die Sammelberichte des Wirkens Jesu im Markusevangelium (Frankfurt am Main, 1976).

Fuller = R.H. Fuller, The Foundations of New Testament Christology (London, 1965).

Grundmann = W. Grundmann, Das Evangelium nach Markus (Theologischer Handkommentar zum NT, 3rd edn; Berlin, 1968).

Haenchen = E. Haenchen, Der Weg Jesu (2nd edn; Berlin 1968).

Hahn = F. Hahn, The Titles of Jesus in Christology (ET by Harold Knight and George Ogg; London, 1969).

Hauck = F. Hauck, Das Evangelium des Markus (Theologischer Handkommentar zum N.T., 1st edn; Leipzig, 1931).

Horstmann = M. Horstmann, Studien zur markinischen Christologie (Münster, 1969).

Kee = H.C. Kee, Community of the New Age: Studies in Mark's Gospel (London, 1977).

Kelber = The Passion in Mark (ed. W.H. Kelber; Philadelphia, 1976).

Kertelge = K. Kertelge, Die Wunder Jesu im Markusevangelium (StANT 23; Munich, 1970).

Klostermann = E. Klostermann, Das Markusevangelium (3rd edn; Tübingen, 1936).

Knox = W.L. Knox, The Sources of the Synoptic Gospels, 2 vols (Cambridge, 1953, 1957).

Koch = D.-A. Koch, Die Bedeutung der Wundererzählungen für die Christologie des Markusevangeliums (BZNW 42; Berlin, 1975)

Kuhn = H.W. Kuhn, Ältere Sammlungen im Markusevangelium (StUNT 8; Göttingen, 1971).

Lagrange = M.-J. Lagrange, Evangile selon Saint Marc (Paris, 1947).

Lane = W.L. Lane, The Gospel according to Mark (London, 1974).

Légasse = S. Légasse, Jésus et l'Enfant (Paris, 1969).

Linnemann = E. Linnemann, Studien zur Passionsgeschichte (FRLANT 102; Göttingen, 1970).

Lohmeyer = E. Lohmeyer, Das Evangelium des Markus (Meyers Kommentar, 11th edn; Göttingen, 1951).

Martin = R.P. Martin, Mark - Evangelist and Theologian (Exeter, 1972).

Marxsen = W. Marxsen, Der Evangelist Markus (2nd edn; Göttingen, 1959).

Metzger = B.M. Metzger, A Textual Commentary on the Greek New Testament (London and New York, 1971).

Meye = R.P. Meye, Jesus and the Twelve (Grand Rapids, Mich., 1968).

Meyer = E. Meyer, Ursprung und Anfänge des Christentums, 3 vols (Stuttgart and Berlin, 1921).

Minette de Tillesse = G. Minette de Tillesse, Le secret messianique dans l'évangile de Marc (Lectio Divina 47; Paris, 1968).

Neirynck = F. Neirynck, Duality in Mark: Contributions to the Study of Markan Redaction (Leuven, 1973).

Nineham = D.E. Nineham, Saint Mark (London, 1963).

Nützel = W. Nützel, Die Verklärungserzählung im Markusevangelium (Würzburg, 1973).

Pesch = R. Pesch, Das Markusevangelium, 2 vols, (Herders Theologischer Kommentar zum NT; Freiburg, Basel, Wien, 1976-7).

Pryke = E.J. Pryke, Redactional Style in the Marcan Gospel (SNTS Monograph Series 33; Cambridge, 1978).

Quesnell = Q. Quesnell, The Mind of Mark (AnalBib 38; Rome, 1969).

Reploh = K.-G. Reploh, Markus - Lehrer der Gemeinde (Stuttgarter Biblische Monographien 9; Stuttgart, 1969).

Roloff = J. Roloff, Das Kerygma und der irdische Jesus (Göttingen, 1970).

Sabbe = M. Sabbe (editor), L'Evangile selon Marc: Tradition et rédaction (Gembloux, 1974).

Schenke = L. Schenke, Die Wundererzählungen des Markusevangeliums (Stuttgart, 1974).

Schmahl = G. Schmahl, Die Zwölf im Markusevangelium (Trier, 1974).

Schmidt = K.L. Schmidt, Der Rahmen der Geschichte Jesu (Berlin, 1919).

Schniewind = J. Schniewind, Das Evangelium nach Markus NTD, 6th edn; Göttingen, 1952).

Schreiber = J. Schreiber, Theologie des Vertrauens: eine redaktionsgeschichtliche Untersuchung des Markusevangelium (Hamburg, 1967).

Schulz = A. Schulz, Nachfolgen und Nachahmen (München, 1962).

Schweizer = E. Schweizer, The Good News According to St. Mark (ET by D.H. Madvig of Das Evangelium nach

	= Markus NTD, 12th edn; London, 1971).
Stock	= K. Stock, Boten aus dem Mit-Ihm-Sein (AnalBib 70; Rome, 1975).
Suhl	= A. Suhl, Die Funktion der alttestamentlichen Zitate und Anspielungen im Markusevangelium (Gütersloh, 1965).
Sundwall	= J. Sundwall, Die Zusammensetzung des Markus-evangeliums (Acta Academiae Aboensis Humaniora, ix, 2; Abo, 1934).
Swete	= H.B. Swete, The Gospel According to St. Mark (London, 1908).
Tagawa	= K. Tagawa, Miracles et Evangile (Paris, 1966).
Taylor	= V. Taylor, The Gospel According to St. Mark (London, 1952).
Tödt	= H.E. Tödt, The Son of Man in the Synoptic Tradition (ET by D.M. Barton; London, 1965).
Trocmé	= E. Trocmé, The Formation of the Gospel Tradition According to Mark (ET by P. Gaughan; London, 1975).
Turner,C.H.	= C.H. Turner, A series of articles on the Gospel according to Mark in J.T.S., 1924-9, indicated by volume, year and page.
Turner, N.	= J.H. Moulton and N. Turner, A Grammar of New Testament Greek, Vol III (Edinburgh, 1963).
Weeden	= T.J. Weeden, Mark: Traditions in Conflict (Philadelphia, 1971).
Wellhausen	= J. Wellhausen, Das Evangelium Marci (Berlin, 1910).
Wrede	= W. Wrede, Das Messiasgeheimnis in den Evangelien (2nd edn; Göttingen, 1913).
Zerwick	= M. Zerwick, Untersuchungen zum Markus-Stil (Rome, 1937).

II OTHER BOOKS AND ARTICLES

Aalen, S.
'"Reign" and "House" in the Kingdom of God in the Gospels', NTS 8 (1961/2) 215-240.

Abrahams, I.
Studies in Pharisaism and the Gospels, 2 vols (Cambridge, 1924).

Achtemeier, P.J.
'Towards the Isolation of Pre-Markan Miracle Catenae', JBL 89 (1970) 265-91.
'The Origin and Function of the Pre-Markan Miracle Catenae', JBL 91 (1972) 198-221.
'Miracles and the Historical Jesus in Mark 9:14-29', CBQ 37 (1975) 471-491.
'"And He Followed Him": Miracles and Discipleship in Mark 10:46-52', Semeia, No. 11 (1978) 115-145.

Aerts, Th.
'Suivre Jésus : Evolution d'un thème biblique dans les Evangiles synoptiques', ETL 42 (1966) 476-512.

Aland, K.
Did the early Church Baptize Infants? (ET by G.R. Beasley-Murray; London, 1963).

Albertz, M.
Die synoptischen Streitgespräche (Berlin, 1921).

Alsup, J.E.
'John Dominic Crossan "Empty Tomb and Absent Lord" - A Response', SBL 1976 Seminar Papers (ed G. Macrae; Missoula, Montana, 1976), pp.263-7.

Annen, F.
Heil für die Heiden (Frankfurt am Main, 1976).

Arens, E.
The ΗΛΘΟΝ-Sayings in the Synoptic Tradition (Göttingen, 1976).

Ariès, P.
Centuries of Childhood (ET by R. Baldick; London, 1973).

Baarda, T.J.
'Mark IX.49', NTS 5 (1959) 318-321.

Baird, J.A.
Audience Criticism and the Historical Jesus (Philadelphia, 1969).

Baltensweiler, H.
Die Ehe im Neuen Testament (ATANT 52; Zürich, 1967).

Bammel, E.
'Markus 10.11f und das jüdische Eherecht', ZNW 61 (1970) 95-101.

Barbour, R.S.
'Gethsemane in the Tradition of the

Passion', NTS 16 (1969/70) 231-251.

Barrett, C.K.   'The Background of Mark x.45' in New Testament Essays (ed. A.J.B. Higgins; Manchester, 1959), pp.1-18.

'I am not ashamed of the Gospel' in Foi et Salut selon S. Paul (AnalBib 42; Rome, 1970), pp.19-50.

The Signs of an Apostle (London, 1970).

Beasley-Murray, G.R.   Jesus and the Future (London, 1954).

Baptism in the New Testament (London, 1963).

Beauvery, R.   'La guérison d'un aveugle à Bethsaïde', Nouvelle Revue Théologique 90 (1968) 1083-91.

Behm, J.   'γεύομαι,' TDNT I, pp.675-7.

Bennett, W.J.   'The Herodians of Mark's Gospel', NT 17 (1975) 9-14.

Berger, K.   'Hartherzigkeit und Gottes Gesetz; die Vorgeschichte des antijüdischen Vorwurfs in Mc 10.5', ZNW 61 (1970) 1-47.

'Zu den sogenannten Sätzen Heiligen Rechts', NTS 17 (1970/1) 10-40.

'Die königlichen Messiastraditionen des Neuen Testaments', NTS 20 (1973/4) 1-44.

Bertram, G. et alii   'ψυχή,' TDNT IX, pp.608ff.

Best, E.   One Body in Christ (London, 1955).

'Spiritual Sacrifice', Int 14 (1960) 273-299.

'Acts xiii.1-3', JTS 11 (1960) 344-8.

'Bishops and Deacons: Philippians 1,1', SE IV (TU 102; Berlin, 1968) pp.371-6.

'1 Peter 2.4-10, A Reconsideration', NT 11 (1969) 270-293.

'Discipleship in Mark: Mark 8.22 - 10.52,' SJT 23 (1970) 323-337.

'The Camel and the Needle's Eye (Mark 10.25)', ExpT 82 (1970/71) 83-89.

1 Peter (New Century Bible; London 1971).

'Mark's Preservation of the Tradition' in Sabbe, pp.21-34 = 'Markus als Bewahrer der Überlieferung' in Das Markus-Evangelium (ed. R. Pesch; Darmstadt, 1979), pp. 390-409.

'Mark III. 20,21, 31-35', NTS 22 (1975/6) 309- 319.

'An Early Sayings Collection', NT 18 (1976) 1-16.

'Mark 10:13-16: The Child as Model Recipient' in Biblical Studies - Essays in Honour of William Barclay (ed. J.R. McKay and J.F. Miller; London, 1976), 119-134, 209-214.

'The Role of the Disciples in Mark', NTS 23 (1976/7) 377-401.

'Mark's Use of the Twelve', ZNW 69 (1978) 11-35.

'Peter in the Gospel according to Mark', CBQ 40 (1978) 547-558.

'The Miracles in Mark', Review and Expositor 75 (1978) 539-554.

'The Markan Redaction of the Transfiguration', a paper read at the Oxford Conference of Biblical Studies, 1973; due to appear in SE.

Betz, H.D.   Nachfolge und Nachahmung Jesu Christi im Neuen Testament (Beiträge z. hist. Theol. 37; Tübingen, 1967).

Betz, O.   'Donnersöhne, Menschenfischer und der davidische Messias', Rev Qumran 3 (1961) 41-70.

Beyer, H.W.   'διακονέω, κτλ', TDNT, II, pp. 81ff.

Bird, C.H.   'Some γάρ Clauses in St. Mark's Gospel', JTS 4 (1953) 171-187.

Black, M.   'The Marcan Parable of the Child in the Midst', ExpT 59 (1947/8) 14-16.

Blank, J.   'Die Sendung des Sohnes. Zur christologischen Bedeutung des Gleichnisses von den bösen Winzern, Mk 12,1-12' in Neues Testament und Kirche (Für Rudolf Schnackenburg, ed. J. Gnilka; Freiburg - Basel - Wien, 1974), pp. 11-41.

Blinzler, J.   'Kind und Königreich Gottes (Markus 10,14f)' in his Aus der Welt und Umwelt des Neuen Testaments (Stuttgart, 1969), pp. 41-53.

Boobyer, G.H.   'Ἀπέχει in Mark xiv.41', NTS 2 (1955/6) 44-8.

Bornkamm, G.   'Πνεῦμα ἄλαλον' in his Geschichte und Glaube (München, 1971), II, pp. 21-36.

Borsch, F.H.   The Christian and Gnostic Son of Man

(London, 1970).
'Jesus, the Wandering Preacher' in What about the New Testament? (Festschrift for C.F. Evans, ed M. Hooker and C. Hickling; London, 1975), pp. 45-63.

Brandt, W. Dienst und Dienen im Neuen Testament (Gütersloh, 1931).

Braumann, G. 'Leidenskelch und Todestaufe (Mc 10.38f)', ZNW 66 (1965) 178-183.

Buchanan, G.W. 'Mark 11.15-19: Brigands in the Temple', Hebrew Union College Annual 30 (1959) 169-177.

Burger, C. Jesus als Davidssohn (FRLANT 98; Göttingen, 1970).

Burgers, W. 'De instelling van de Twaalf in het evangelie van Marcus', ETL 36 (1960) 625-654.

Burkill, T.A. Mysterious Revelation (Ithaca, N.Y., 1963).
'Mark 3.7-12 and the Alleged Dualism in the Evangelist's Miracle Material', JBL 87 (1968) 409-417.
New Light on the Earliest Gospel (Ithaca and London, 1972).

Burkitt, F.C. The Gospel History and its Transmission (Edinburgh, 1911).

Bursch, F. Zum Verständnis der synoptischen Eschatologie : Markus 13 neu untersucht (Gütersloh, 1938).

Bussmann, W. Synoptische Studien I - III (Halle, 1925-31).

Cangh, J.-M. van 'La Galilée dans l'Evangile de Marc: un lieu théologique?', RB 79 (1972) 59-75.

Carlston, C.E. The Parables of the Triple Tradition (Philadelphia, 1975).

Catchpole, D.R. 'The Poor on Earth and the Son of Man in Heaven. A Re-Appraisal of Matthew xxv. 31-46', BJRULM 61 (1979) 355-397.

Charles, R.H. (ed.) The Apocrypha and Pseudepigrapha of the Old Testament, 2 vols. (Oxford, 1913).

Clark, K.W. 'The Meaning of (κατα)κυριεύειν' in Studies in New Testament Language and Text (ed. J.K. Elliott; Essays in Honour of G.D. Kilpatrick; Leiden, 1976), pp. 100-5.

Citron, B. 'The Multitude in the Synoptic Gospels', SJT 7 (1954) 408-418.

Combrink, H.J.B. Die Diens van Jesus: 'N Eksegetiese

Beshouing oor Markus 10.45 (Groningen, 1968).

Cremer, F.G. 'Der "Heilstod" Jesu im paulinischen Verständnis von Taufe und Eucharistie', BZ 14 (1970) 227-239.

Crossan, J.D. 'The Parable of the Wicked Husbandman', JBL 90 (1971) 451-465.

'Redaction and Citation in Mark 11:9-10,17 and 14:27', Proceedings SBL, 1972 (ed. L.C. McGaughy), Vol I, pp. 17-61.

'Empty Tomb and Absent Lord (Mark 16:1-8)' in Kelber, pp. 135-152.

'A Form for Absence: The Markan Creation of Gospel', Semeia No. 12, 1978, pp. 41-55.

Cullmann, O. Baptism in the New Testament (ET by J.K.S. Reid; SBT 1, London, 1950).

'Que signifie le sel dans la parabole de Jésus?', RHPR 37 (1957) 36 - 45.

Daube, D. 'Four Types of Question', JTS 2 (1951) 45-8.

Davies, W.D. The Setting of the Sermon on the Mount (Cambridge, 1964).

The Gospel and the Land (Berkeley, Los Angeles, London, 1974).

Déaut, R.le 'Goûter le calice de la mort', Bib 43 (1962) 82-86.

Dehn, G. Der Gottessohn (Hamburg, 1953).

Delling, G. 'Das Logion Mark x.11 (und seine Abwandlungen) im Neuen Testament', NT 1 (1956) 263-274.

de Mause, L. (ed.) The History of Childhood (New York, 1974).

Didericksen, B.K. Den markianske skilsmisseperikope (Gyldendal, 1962).

Diels, H.A. and Kranz, W. Die Fragmente der Vorsokratiker, 3 vols (6th edn; Berlin, 1951-2).

Dinkler, E. 'Zur Geschichte des Kreuzsymbols', ZTK 48 (1951) 148-172.

'Jesu Wort vom Kreuztagen' in Neutestamentlichen Studien für R. Bultmann (BZNW 21; Berlin, 1954), pp. 110-129.

'Peter's Confession and the "Satan" Saying: The Problem of Jesus' Messiahship' in The Future of Our Religious Past (Essays in Honour of Rudolf Bultmann; London, 1971), pp. 169-202.

Bibliography

Donahue, J.R.	Are You the Christ? (SBL Dissertation Series 10; Missoula, Montana, 1973).
Dormeyer, D.	Die Passion Jesu als Verhaltensmodell (Münster, 1974).
Dupont, J.	'La parabole du maître qui rentre dans la nuit (Mc 13,34-36)' in Mélanges Bibliques (en hommage au R.P. Béda Rigaux, ed. A. Descamps et A. de Malleux; Gembloux, 1970), pp. 89-116.
Ebeling, H.J.	Das Messiasgeheimnis und die Botschaft des Marcus-Evangelisten (BZNW 19; Berlin, 1939).
Egger, W.	'Die Verborgenheit Jesu in Mk 3,7-11', Bib 50 (1969) 466-90.
Eppstein, V.	'The historicity of the Gospel account of the Cleansing of the Temple', ZNW 55 (1964) 42-58.
Evans, C.F.	'I will go before you into Galilee', JTS 5 (1954) 3-18.
Feneberg, W.	Der Markusprolog (München, 1974).
Feuillet, A.	'Les perspectives propres à chaque évangélist dans le récit de la Transfiguration', Bib 39 (1958) 281-301.
	'La coupe et le baptême de la Passion (Mc, x,35-40; Mt., xx,20-23; Lc, xii, 50)', RB 74 (1967) 356-391.
Fitzmyer, J.A.	'Jewish Christianity in Acts in the light of the Qumran scrolls' in his Essays on the Semitic Background of the New Testament (London, 1971), pp. 271-303 = Studies in Luke-Acts : Essays Presented in Honor of Paul Schubert (London, 1966), pp. 233-257.
Foerster, W.	'σῴζω κτλ', TDNT VII, pp. 980-1012.
Freyne, S.	The Twelve : Disciples and Apostles (London, 1968).
Fuller, R.H.	The Formation of the Resurrection Narratives (London, 1972).
Gärtner, B.	The Temple and the Community in Qumran and the New Testament (SNTS Monograph Series 1; Cambridge 1965).
Gaston, L.	No Stone on Another (Suppl. NT 23; Leiden, 1970).
Gerhardsson, B.	Memory and Manuscript (Uppsala, 1961).
Goguel, M.	'"Avec les persécutions": Etude exégétique sur Marc 10.29-30', RHPR 8 (1928)

	264-277.
Grant, F.C.	The Earliest Gospel (Nashville, Tenn, 1943).
Griffiths, D.R.	'The Salt Sections in the Gospels', ExpT 59 (1947/8) 81f.
Griffiths, J.G.	'The Disciple's Cross', NTS 16 (1969-70) 358-364.
Haenchen, E.	'Die Komposition von Mk VIII 27 - IX 1 und Par.', NT 6 (1963) 81-109.
Hamilton, N.Q.	'Resurrection Tradition and the Composition of Mark', JBL 84 (1965) 415-421.
Hawkin, D.J.	'The Incomprehension of the Disciples in the Marcan Redaction', JBL 91 (1972) 491-500.
Hedinger, Ù.	'Jesus und die Volksmenge', TZ 32 (1976) 201-6.
Held, H.J.	'Matthew as Interpreter of the Miracle Stories' in G. Bornkamm, G. Barth and H.J. Held, Tradition and Interpretation in Matthew (ET by P. Scott; London, 1960), pp. 165-299.
Hengel, M.	Nachfolge und Charisma: eine exegetisch-religionsgeschichtliche Studie zu Mt 8.21f und Jesu Ruf in die Nachfolge (Berlin, 1968).
Hiers, R.H.	'Purification of the Temple: Preparation for the Kingdom of God', JBL 90 (1971) 82-90.
Higgins, A.J.B.	Jesus and the Son of Man (London, 1964).
Hilgert, E.	The Ship and Related Symbols in the New Testament (Assen: Van Gorcum, 1962).
Hirsch, E.	Frühgeschichte des Evangeliums, vol I (Tübingen, 1940).
Holladay, C.H.	Theios Aner in Hellenistic Judaism (SBL Dissertation Series 40; Missoula, Montana, 1977).
Hooker, M.D.	Jesus and the Servant (London, 1959).
	The Son of Man in Mark (London, 1967).
Howard, W.F.	J.H. Moulton and W.F. Howard, A Grammar of New Testament Greek, Vol II (Edinburgh, 1929).
Howard, V.	Das Ego Jesu in den synoptischen Evangelien (Marburg, 1975).
Hutton, W.R.	'The Salt Sections', ExpT 58 (1946/7) 166-8.
Iersel, B.M.F. van	'La vocation de Lévi (Mc. II,13-17par.). Tradition et rédaction' in De Jésus aux

Evangiles (ed. I. de la Potterie; Gembloux, 1967), pp. 212-232.

Isaksson, A.   Marriage and Ministry in the New Temple (Lund, 1965).

Jeremias, J.   'Mc 10.13-16 Parr. und die Übung der Kindertaufe in der Urkirche', ZNW 40 (1941) 243-5.

'Γωνία, κτλ', TDNT I, pp. 791-3.

Jesus' Promise to the Nations (SBT 24; ET by S.H. Hooke; London, 1958).

Infant Baptism in the First Four Centuries (ET by D. Cairns; London, 1960).

'Paarweise Sendung im Neuen Testament' in New Testament Essays: Studies in Memory of T.W. Manson (ed. A.J.B. Higgins, Manchester, 1961), pp.136-143.

The Parables of Jesus (ET by S.H. Hooke; London, 1963).

'Das Lösegeld für Viele (Mk. 10,45)' in his Abba: Studien zur neutestamentlichen Theologie und Zeitgeschichte (Göttingen, 1966).

'Die älteste Schicht der Menschensohn-Logien', ZNW 58 (1967) 152-172.

New Testament Theology I (ET by J. Bowden; London, 1971).

Jewett, R.   Paul's Anthropological Terms (Leiden, 1971).

Johnson, E.S.   'Mark 8:22-26. The Blind Man from Bethsaida', NTS 25 (1978/9) 370-383.

'Mark 10:46-52: Blind Bartimaeus', CBQ 40 (1978) 191-204.

Juel, D.   Messiah and Temple (SBL Dissertation Series 31: Missoula, Montana, 1977).

Käsemann, E.   'Sätze Heiligen Rechtes im Neuen Testament', NTS 1 (1954/5) 248-60; ET by W.J. Montague in his New Testament Questions of Today (London, 1969), pp. 66-81.

Keck, L.E.   'Mark 3.7-12 and Mark's Christology', JBL 84 (1965) 341-58.

Kee, A.   'The Question about Fasting', NT 11 (1969) 161-173.

'The Old Coat and the New Wine', NT 12 (1970) 13-21.

Kelber, W.H.   'Mark 14.32-42: Gethsemane - Passion Christology and Discipleship Failure', ZNW 63 (1972) 166-187. The Kingdom in Mark (Philadelphia, 1974).

Kilpatrick, G.D.   'The Gentile Mission in Mark and Mark 13.9-11' in Studies in the Gospels (ed. D.E. Nineham; Oxford, 1955), pp. 145-158.

Kittel, G.   'ἀκολουθέω, κτλ', TDNT I, pp. 210ff.

Klein, G.   'Die Zwölf Apostel (Göttingen, 1961). 'Die Berufung des Petrus', ZNW 58 (1967) 1-44.

Kuby, A.   'Zur Konzeption des Markus-Evangeliums', ZNW 49 (1958) 52-64.

Kuhn, K. G.   'Jesus in Gethsemane', EvTh 12 (1952/3) 260-285.

Künze, M.   Das Naherwartungslogion Markus 9,1 par. (Tübingen, 1977).

Lafontaine, R.and Beernaert, P.M.   'Essai sur la structure du Marc', Recherches de science religieuse 57 (1969) 543-561.

Lambrecht, J.   Die Redaktion der Markus-Apokalypse (AnalBib 28; Rome, 1967). 'The Relatives of Jesus in Mark', NT 16 (1974) 241-258.

Leaney, A.R.C.   'Theophany, Resurrection and History', SE V = TU 103 (1968), pp. 101-113.

Légasse, S.   'Approche de l'Episode préévangélique des Fils de Zébédée (Marc x 35-40 par.)', NTS 20 (1973/4) 161-177.

Lehmann, M.   Synoptische Quellenanalyse und die Frage nach dem historischen Jesus (BZNW 38; Berlin, 1970).

Lescow, T.   'Jesus in Gethsemane', EvTh 26 (1966) 141-159.

Lightfoot, R.H.   History and Interpretation in the Gospels (London, 1935). The Gospel Message of St. Mark (Oxford, 1950).

Lindars, B.   'Matthew, Levi, Lebbaeus and the Value of the Western Text', NTS 4 (1957/8) 220-2. New Testament Apologetic (London, 1961).

Linton, O   'Evidences for a Second-Century Revised Edition of St Mark's Gospel', NTS 14 (1967/8) 321-355.

Lohmeyer, E.   Galiläa und Jerusalem (Göttingen, 1936).

Lohse, E.   Märtyrer und Gottesknecht: Untersuchungen zur urchristlichen Verkündigung vom Sühntod Jesu Christi (2nd edn, Göttingen, 1963).

'υἱὸς Δαυίδ', TDNT VIII, pp. 478-488.

'Χειροποίητος,' TDNT IX, p. 436.

Loisy, A.   Les Evangiles Synoptiques, 2 vols (Ceffonds, 1907-8).

L'Evangile selon Marc (Paris, 1912).

Lorenzen, T.   'Ist der Auferstandene in Galiläa erschienen?', ZNW 64 (1973) 209-221.

Lövestam, E.   Spiritual Wakefulness in the New Testament (Lunds Universitets Arsskrift, N.F. AVD. 1, Bd 55 Nr. 3, 1962-3).

Luz, U.   'Das Geheimnismotiv und die markinische Christologie', ZNW 56 (1965) 9-30.

McCasland, S.V.   'The Way', JBL 77 (1958) 222-230.

McCurley, F.R.   '"And After Six Days" (Mark 9.2): A Semitic Literary Device', JBL 93 (1974) 67-81.

Macdonald, J.(ed.)   Memar Marqah (BZAW 84; Berlin, 1963).

McDonald, J.I.H.   'Receiving and Entering the Kingdom. A Study in Mark 10.15', SE VI = TU 112, pp. 328-332.

McKelvey, R.J.   'Christ the Cornerstone', NTS 8 (1961/2) 352-9.

The New Temple (Oxford, 1969).

McKinnis, R.   'An Analysis of Mark X 32-34', NT 18 (1976) 81-100.

Mánek, J.   'Fishers of Men', NT 2 (1958) 138-141.

Manson, T.W.   The Church's Ministry (London, 1948).

Marxsen, W.   'Redaktionsgeschichtliche Erklärung der sogenannten Parabeltheorie des Markus', ZTK 52 (1955) 255-271.

Masson, C.   'La Transfiguration de Jésus', RTP 14 (1964) 1-14.

Meeks, W.A.   The Prophet King (Suppl. NT XIV; Leiden, 1967).

Menzies, A.   The Earliest Gospel (London, 1901).

Michaelis, W.   'ὁδός, κτλ, TDNT V, pp. 42ff.

Minear, P.S.   'The Needle's Eye', JBL 61 (1942) 157-169.

Commands of Christ (Edinburgh, 1972).

'Audience Criticism and Markan Ecclesiology' in Neues Testament und Geschichte (Oscar Cullmann zum 70. Geburtstag; ed. H. Baltensweiler and Bo Reicke; Zürich and Tübingen, 1972), pp. 79-89.

Mohn, W. 'Gethsemane (Mark 14.32-42)', ZNW 64 (1973) 194-208.

Montefiore, C.G. The Synoptic Gospels (London, 1909).

Morgenthaler, R. Statistik des neutestamentlichen Wortschatzes (Zürich, 1958).

Mosley, A.W. 'Jesus' Audiences in the Gospels of St Mark and St Luke', NTS 10 (1963/4) 139-149.

Moulder, W.J. 'The Old Testament Background and Interpretation of Mark X.45', NTS 24 (1977/8) 120-7.

Moulton, J.H. and Howard, W.F. A Grammar of New Testament Greek, Vol. II (Edinburgh, 1929).

Muddiman, J.B. 'Jesus and Fasting (Mark ii.18-22)' in Jésus aux origines de la christologie (ed. J. Dupont; Gembloux, 1975), p. 271-281.

Müller, U.B. 'Die christologische Absicht des Markusevangeliums und die Verklärungsgeschichte', ZNW 64 (1973) 159-193.

Mussner, F. Der Jakobusbrief (Herders Kommentar; Freiburg, Basel, Wein, 1964).

Neirynck, F. 'Duplicate Expressions in the Gospel of Mark', ETL 48 (1972) 150-209.
'Minor Agreements Matthew-Luke in the Transfiguration Story' in Orientierung an Jesus (Für Josef Schmid; ed. P. Hoffmann; Freiburg, 1973) pp. 253-266.

Nauck, W. 'Salt as a metaphor in Instructions for Discipleship', StTh 6 (1952) 165-178.

New, S. 'The Name, Baptism, and the Laying on of Hands', in F. Jackson and K. Lake, The Beginnings of Christianity. Part I: The Acts of the Apostles (London, 1920-3), V, pp. 121ff.

Niederwimmer, K. Askese und Mysterium (Göttingen, 1975).

Oepke, A. 'παῖς, κτλ', TDNT V. pp. 639-648.

Pallis, A. Notes on St. Mark and St. Matthew (London, 1932).

Perrin, N. Rediscovering the Teaching of Jesus (London, 1967).
What is Redaction Criticism? (London, 1970).
The New Testament: An Introduction: Proclamation and Paraenesis, Myth and History (New York, 1974).
A Modern Pilgrimage in New Testament

Bibliography

	Christology (Philadelphia, 1974).
	The Resurrection Narratives (London, 1977).
Pesch, R.	Naherwartungen: Tradition und Redaktion in Mk 13 (Düsseldorf, 1968).
	'Levi - Matthäus (Mc 2.14/Mt 9.9; 10.3), ein Beitrag zur Lösung eines alten Problems', ZNW 59 (1968) 40-56.
	'Das Messiasbekenntnis des Petrus (Mk. 8.27-30)', BZ 17 (1973) 178-185.
Potterie, I.de la	'Le sens primitif de la multiplication des pains' in Jésus aux origines de la christologie (ed. J. Dupont; Gembloux, 1975), pp. 303-329.
Räisänen, H.	Die Parabeltheorie im Markusevangelium (Helsinki, 1973).
	Das "Messiasgehimnis" im Markusevangelium (Helsinki, 1976).
Rawlinson, A.E.J.	The Gospel according to St. Mark (London, 1942).
Rengstorf, K.H.	'ἀποστέλλω', TDNT I, pp. 398-447.
	'δοῦλος, κτλ', TDNT II, pp. 261ff.
	'μανθάνω, κτλ', TDNT IV, pp. 390ff.
Repo, E.	Der 'Weg' als Selbstbezeichnung des Urchristentums (Helsinki), 1964).
Richardson, A.	The Miracle Stories of the Gospels (London, 1959).
Robbins, V.K.	'The Healing of Blind Bartimaeus (10.46-52) in the Marcan Theology', JBL 92 (1973) 224-243.
	'Last Meal: Preparation, Betrayal and Absence (Mark 14:12-25)' in Kelber, pp. 21-40.
Robinson, J.A.T.	'Elijah, John and Jesus: An Essay in Detection', NTS 4 (1957/8) 263-281 = Twelve New Testament Studies (SBT 34; London, 1962), pp. 28-52.
	'The Parable of the Wicked Husbandmen: A Test of Synoptic Relationships', NTS 21 (1975) 443-461.
Robinson, J.M.	The Problem of History in Mark (SBT 21; London, 1957).
Roetzel, C.J.	Judgement in the Community (Leiden, 1974).
Roloff, J.	Apostolat - Verkündigung - Kirche

(Gütersloh, 1965).
'Anfänge der soteriologischen Deutung des Todes Jesu (Mk.x.45 und Lk. xxii.27)', NTS 19 (1972/3) 38-64.

Sass, G. 'Zur Bedeutung von δοῦλος bei Paulus', ZNW 40 (1941) 24-32.

Schenk, W. 'Tradition und Redaktion in der Epileptiker-Perikope, Mk 9.14-29', ZNW 63 (1972) 76-94.
Der Passionsbericht nach Markus (Berlin, 1974).

Schenke, L. Studien zur Passionsgeschichte des Markus (Wurzburg, 1971).

Schille, G. Die urchristliche Kollegialmission (ATANT 48; Zürich, 1967).

Schlatter, A. Das Evangelium nach Markus (Stuttgart, 1961).

Schlier, H. 'ἔλαιον', TDNT II, pp. 470-3.

Schmahl, G. 'Die Berufung der Zwölf im Markusevangelium', TTZ 81 (1972) 203-213.

Schmithals, W. The Office of Apostle in the Early Church (ET by J.E. Steely, London, 1971).
'Der Markusschluss, die Verklärungsgeschichte und die Aussendung der Zwölf', ZTK 69 (1972) 379-411.

Schnackenburg, R. 'Mk 9,33-50' in Synoptische Studien (Festschrift für A. Wikenhauser; München, 1953), pp. 184-206.
'"Das Evangelium" im Verständnis des ältesten Evangelisten', in Orientierung an Jesus (Für Josef Schmid, ed. P. Hoffmann; Freiburg, 1973), pp. 309-324.
'Apostles Before and During Paul's Time', in Apostolic History and the Gospel (Biblical and Historical Essays presented to F.F. Bruce, ed. W.W. Gasque and R.P. Martin; Exeter, 1970), pp. 287-303.

Schneider, J. 'βαίνω,κτλ', TDNT I, pp. 519-522.

Schramm, T. Der Markus-Stoff bei Lukas (SNTS Monograph Series 14; Cambridge, 1971).

Schroeder, H.H. Eltern und Kinder in der Verkündigung Jesu (Hamburg - Bergstedt, 1972).

Schürmann, H. Quellenkritische Untersuchung des lukanischen Abendmahlsberichtes, III Jesus Abschiedsrede: Lk 22,21-38 (Münster, 1957).

Bibliography

Schwarz, G. "'...ἀπαρνησάσθω ἑαυτὸν ..."? (Markus viii 34 Parr.)', NT 17 (1975) 109-112.

Schweizer, E. 'πνεῦμα, κτλ', TDNT VI, pp. 389-451.
Lordship and Discipleship (SBT 28; London, 1960).
'Anmerkungen zur Theologie des Markus' in Neotestamentica et Patristica (Freundesgabe O. Cullmann; Leiden, 1962), pp. 37ff.

Simsonsen, H. 'Zur Frage der grundlegenden Problematik in form-und redaktionsgeschichtlicher Evangelienforschung', StTh 26 (1972) 1-23.

Smith, C.W.F. 'Fishers of Men', HTR 51 (1959) 187-203.

Smith, M. Clement of Alexandria and a Secret Gospel of Mark (Cambridge, Mass., 1973).

Snoy, T. La rédaction marcienne de la marche sur les eaux (Mc., VI, 45-52)'. ETL 44 (1968) 205-241, 433-481.
'Les miracles dans l'évangile de Marc', Rev. Théol. Louv. 4 (1973) 58-101.
'Marc 6,48 "... et il voulait les dépasser." Proposition pour la solution d'une énigme' in Sabbe, pp. 347-363.

Snyder, G.F. 'The Tobspruch in the New Testament', NTS 23 (1976/7) 117-120.

Stagg, F. 'The Abused Aorist', JBL 91 (1972) 221-231.

Stein, R.H. 'A Short Note on Mark xiv.28 and xvi.7', NTS 20(1973/4) 445-452.
'Is the Transfiguration (Mark 9:2-8) a Misplaced Resurrection-Account?', JBL 95 (1976) 79-86.

Stemberger, G. 'Galilee - Land of Salvation?' in W.D. Davies, The Gospel and the Land, pp. 409-438.

Strecker, G. 'Das Geschichtsverständnis des Matthäus', EvTh 26 (1966) 57ff.
'The Passion and Resurrection Predictions in Mark's Gospel (Mark 8:31, 9:31, 10:32-34)', Int 22 (1968) 421-443 = ZTK 64 (1967) 16-39.
'Literarische Überlegungen zum ἐυαγγέλιον. Begriff im Markusevangelium', in Neues Testament und Geschichte (Oscar Cullmann zum 70. Geburtstag, ed. H. Baltensweiler and Bo Reicke; Zürich and Tübingen, 1972), pp. 91-104.

Talbert, C.H.	Literary Patterns, Theological Themes, and the Genre of Luke-Acts (SBL Monographs 20; Missoula, Mont. 1974).
Taylor, V.	The Passion Narrative of St. Luke (SNTS Monograph Series 19; Cambridge, 1972).
Theissen, G.	Urchristlichen Wundergeschichten, (Gütersloh, 1974).
Thrall, M.	Greek Particles in the New Testament (NT Tools and Studies, III; Leiden, 1962).
Thompson, W.G.	Mattthew's Advice to a Divided Community: Mt. 17.22 - 18.35 (AnalBib 44; Rome, 1970).
Tinsley, E.J.	The Imitation of God in Christ (London, 1960).
Tooley, A.	'The Shepherd and Sheep Image in the Teaching of Jesus', NT 7 (1964) 15-25.
Trevijano, R.	Comienzo del Evangelio: Estudio sobre el Prologo de San Marcos (Burgos, 1971).
Trilling, W.	Christusverkündigung in den synoptischen Evangelien (München, 1969).
Trocmé, E.	'Pour un Jésus public: les évangélistes Marc et Jean aux prises avec l'intimisme de la tradition' in OIKONOMIA (Festschrift für O. Cullmann; ed. F. Christ; Hamburg-Bergstedt, 1967) pp 42-50.
	'L'expulsion des marchands du Temple', NTS 15 (1968/9) 1-22.
Vaganay, A.	'Le schématisme du discours communautaire à la lumière de la critique des sources', RB 60 (1953) 203-244.
Vielhauer, P.	'Gottesreich und Menschensohn in der Verkündigung Jesu' in Festschrift für Günther Dehn (Neukirchen, 1957), pp. 51-79.
Walter, N.	'Zur Analyse von Mc.10.17-31', ZNW 53 (1962) 208-218.
Weeden, T.J.	'The Cross as Power and Weakness (Mark 15:20b-41)' in Kelber, pp. 115-134.
Weihnacht, H.	Die Menschwerdung des Sohnes Gottes im Markusevangelium (Tübingen, 1972).
Weiser, A.	Die Knechtsgleichnisse der synoptischen Evangelien (München, 1971).
Weiss, J.	Das älteste Evangelium (Göttingen, 1903).
Weiss, K.	'Ekklesiologie, Tradition und Geschichte in der Jüngerunterweisung Mark 8,27 - 10,52'

Bibliography

	in Der historische Jesus und der kerygmatische Christus (ed. H. Ristow and K. Matthiae; Berlin, 1961), pp. 414-438.
Wichelhaus, M.	'Am ersten Tage der Woche', NT 11 (1969) 45-68.
Wilhems, E.	'Der fremde Exorzist: Eine Studie über Mark. 9.38ff', StTh 3 (1949) 162-171.
Winter, P.	On the Trial of Jesus (Berlin, 1961).
Wohlenberg, G.	Das Evangelium des Markus (Leipzig, 1910).
Wuellner, W.H.	The Meaning of "Fishers of Men" (Philadelphia, 1967).

Index of Authors

Daube, D.	51,103,104, 161,250	Grundmann, W.	25,46,64,71, 78,90,93,97, 102,145,185, 195
Dautzenberg, G.	51,52,131		
Davies, W.D.	22,97		
Déaut, R. le	131		
Debrunner, A.	See Blass, F.	Haenchen, E.	19,47,50,51, 69,90,92,94, 95,103,105, 115,197
Dehn, G.	71		
Delling, G.	103		
deMause, L.	93		
Dibelius, M.	130	Hahn, F.	17,19,27,52, 65,121,144
Didericksen, B.K.	103,105		
Diels, H.A.	48	Hamilton, N.Q.	241
Dinkler, E.	22,26,27, 48	Hauck, F.	93,118
		Hawkin, D.J.	134
Donahue, J.R.	215,220,221, 222,223,225	Hedinger, U.	46
		Held, H.J.	69,70,72
Dormeyer, D.	158,202	Hengel, M.	33,48,49
Doudna, J.C.	23,65,102, 117,130,178	Hiers, R.H.	223
		Higgins, A.J.B.	52
Dupont, J.	159	Hilgert, E.	223
		Hirsch, E.	115,185
Ebeling, H.J.	22	Holladay, C.H.	48
Egger, W.	49,178,195, 197,198,203, 211,212	Hooker, M.D.	52,53,132
		Horstmann, M.	17,20,22,23, 26,27,44-45, 46,47,52, 53,60,61,64
Eppstein, V.	223		
Evans, C.F.	174		
		Howard, W.F.	97
Feneberg, W.	51	Howard, V.	131, 156
Feuillet, A.	60,131	Hutton, W.R.	97
Fitzmyer, J.A.	17		
Foerster, W.	144	Iersel, B.M.F. van	173, 178
Freyne, S.	185,186	Isaksson, A.	103
Fuller, R.H.	52,144,202, 203	Jeremias, J.	47,97,102, 108,109,131, 132,158,196, 202,224,225
Gärtner, B.	222		
Gaston, L.	220,222,223, 224,225	Jewett, R.	51
		Johnson, E.S.	138,139,143, 144
Gerhardsson, B.	250		
Gnilka, J.	7		
Goguel, M.	116,118	Juel, D.	220,221,222, 223,224
Grant, F.C.	64		
Griffiths, D.R.	97		
Griffiths, J.G.	48	Käsemann, E.	17,50

Index of Authors

INDEX OF BIBLICAL REFERENCES
(Only passages which have been commented on are included)